Airport Economics

This book provides a comprehensive guide to the economics of airports for all managers, regulators and educators within the aviation industry. Written by three renowned experts but made accessible and relevant for all those working within the industry, or aspiring to do so, it is the perfect entry point for learning about the underlying economics of airports as a crucial component of the air transport system. It explains the cost structures of airports and then relates these to how airports determine their charges.

It explains how charges at different airports vary, whether this is due to different types of traffic, different input prices, ways of producing outputs or different levels of efficiency. Most airports are publicly owned or regulated, and there has been a trend towards privatisation. The book explains how airports have been regulated and assesses how well the regulatory structures have performed; it discusses the trend towards light-handed regulation and the reliance on competition where this exists. The book examines the problems of limited capacity at airports and how these are resolved through slots and charging systems, and the long-term solution of investment in airports—why it is controversial, and how it can be achieved effectively. It also considers the environmental impacts of airports and the issues these pose for managers, from the well-known problems of airport noise to the growing recognition of the impacts of air transport on climate change, and the roles airports play in mitigating these consequences.

Written for airport and airline managers, regulators and students, this book will suit Bachelor's and Master's programmes on air transport management.

Peter Forsyth has been at Monash University since 1997, originally as Professor of Economics, and as Adjunct Professor since 2014. Much of his research has been on transport economics and especially on the economics of aviation. He has published widely in both tourism and aviation. In recent years Peter has done considerable research on economic policies to reduce greenhouse gas emissions of aviation. In 2015 he was made a Fellow of the Air Transport Research Society.

Cathal Guiomard was the Commissioner for Aviation Regulation in Ireland between 2006 and 2014. He is currently Assistant Professor in Aviation Management at the Dublin City University (DCU) Business School, Ireland, where he teaches aviation management, aviation economics and regulation. He engages in research on aviation and regulatory issues. He is Chair of the Programme Board of the BSc degree in Aviation Management.

Hans-Martin Niemeier is the Director of the Institute for Transport and Development at Bremen University of Applied Sciences. He is Chairman of the German Aviation Research Society and a member of the Advisory Board of the European Aviation Conference. He chaired the COST Action "Air Transport and Regional Development". From 2014 to May 2019, he was a member of the Performance Review Body of the Single European Sky.

Managing Aviation Operations

Series Editor: Peter J. Bruce
Associate Editor: John M. C. King

The purpose of this series is to provide a comprehensive set of materials dealing with the key components of airline and airport operations. To date, this innovative approach has not been evident among aviation topics and certainly not applied to operational areas of airlines or airports. While more recent works have begun, in brief, to consider the various characteristics of operational areas, the *Managing Aviation Operations* series will expand coverage with far greater breadth and depth of content.

Airlines and airports are devoid of specific topic knowledge in ready-made, easy-to-read, creditable resources. Tapping into industry expertise to drive a range of key niche products will resource the industry in a way not yet seen in this domain. Therefore, the objective is to deliver a collection of specialised, internationally sourced and expertly written books to serve as readily accessible guides and references primarily for professionals within the industry. The focus of the series editors will be to ensure product quality, user readability and appeal, and transparent consistency across the range.

Airline Operations Control
Peter J. Bruce and Chris Mulholland

Aviation Leadership
The Accountable Manager
Mark Pierotti

Strategic Airport Planning
Mike Brown

The Regulation of Air Transport
From Protection to Liberalisation, and Back Again
Barry Humphreys

Airport Economics
Peter Forsyth, Cathal Guiomard and Hans-Martin Niemeier

For more information about this series, please visit: www.routledge.com/Aviation-Fundamentals/book-series/MAO

Airport Economics

Peter Forsyth,
Cathal Guiomard and
Hans-Martin Niemeier

Routledge
Taylor & Francis Group
LONDON AND NEW YORK

Designed cover image: © Getty Images

First published 2023
by Routledge
4 Park Square, Milton Park, Abingdon, Oxon OX14 4RN

and by Routledge
605 Third Avenue, New York, NY 10158

Routledge is an imprint of the Taylor & Francis Group, an informa business

British Library Cataloguing-in-Publication Data
A catalogue record for this book is available from the British Library

Library of Congress Cataloging-in-Publication Data
Names: Forsyth, P. (Peter), author. | Guiomard, Cathal, author. | Niemeier, Hans-Martin, author.
Title: Airport economics / Peter Forsyth, Cathal Guiomard and Hans-Martin Niemeier.
Description: Abingdon, Oxon ; New York, NY : Routledge, 2023. | Series: Managing aviation operations | Includes bibliographical references and index.
Identifiers: LCCN 2022061430 | ISBN 9780367742782 (hardback) | ISBN 9780367742768 (paperback) | ISBN 9781003156901 (ebook)
Subjects: LCSH: Airports—Economic aspects. | Aeronautics, Commercial.
Classification: LCC HE9797 .F677 2023 | DDC 338.4/7387736—dc23/eng/20230505
LC record available at https://lccn.loc.gov/2022061430

ISBN: 978-0-367-74278-2 (hbk)
ISBN: 978-0-367-74276-8 (pbk)
ISBN: 978-1-003-15690-1 (ebk)

DOI: 10.4324/9781003156901

Typeset in Bembo
by Apex CoVantage, LLC

Contents

Figures

Tables

About the authors

Peter Forsyth came to Monash University in 1997, and has been Professor of Economics, and was for some time Chair of the Department of Economics. Much of his research has been on transport economics (especially on the economics of aviation), and on the economics of tourism. He has published widely in these areas, including *Tourism Economics and Policy, Second Edition* (with L Dwyer and W Dwyer, Channel View, 2020). He has been interested in airport economics for several years and has paid particular attention to pricing, capacity allocation and regulation. More recently he has done considerable research on economic policies to reduce emissions of aviation, and published *Aviation and Climate Change: Economic Perspectives on Greenhouse Gas Reduction Polices* (with F Fichert and H-M Niemeier, Routledge, 2020). In 2015 he was made a Fellow of the Air Transport Research Society.

Cathal Guiomard is an Assistant Professor in aviation management at the Business School of Dublin City University (DCU) in Ireland. He chairs the programme board of the DCU BSc in Aviation Management. He lectures on the economics of regulation and aviation management and publishes in the area of aviation regulation. He is a member of the advisory board of the European Aviation Conference. In 2022, he was a member of the Irish government's Task Force on Aviation Recovery. Prior to his academic career, from 2008 to 2014, he led Ireland's Commission for Aviation Regulation, responsible for setting price-caps on the aeronautical charges of Dublin airport and of the Irish Aviation Authority, for licensing Irish airlines and for enforcing the EU passenger rights and EU slots regulations in Ireland.

Hans-Martin Niemeier is a Director of the Institute for Transport and Development at Bremen University of Applied Sciences. He is Chairman of the German Aviation Research Society and member of the Advisory Board of the European Aviation Conference. He led the research projects "German Airport Performance" and "German Aviation Benchmarking" and conducted the studies "Airport benchmarking by economic regulators" and "Market power of Amsterdam airport" for the Netherlands Competition Authority and "Comparative study (benchmarking) of the efficiency of Avinor´s airport operations" for the Norwegian Ministry of Transport and Communication. He chaired the COST Action

"Air Transport and Regional Development". From 2014 to May 2019 he was member of the Performance Review Body of the Single European Sky. He has published on privatisation, regulation and competition of airports, the reform of slot allocation and on airline and airport alliances. In 2021 he was made a Fellow of the Air Transport Research Society.

Preface

Books usually have a history. Our fascination with airports goes back a long time. It started with Peter writing his PhD thesis about London Heathrow in the 1970s. Peter expanded his research work into trade and tourism, but aviation and airports remained a core part of his research interests. Meanwhile in the 1970s, as a high school exchange student, Hans-Martin flew to New York with a stopover in Shannon, Ireland, where aircraft needed to refill their fuel tanks (and where Hans-Martin had his first Irish coffee). Hans-Martin was fascinated by flying, but never expected to spend so much time on airports. For that to happen, his job, at the Ministry of Economic Affairs of the State of Hamburg, necessitated that he start thinking about airports. In 1992, he worked for the Ministry on a plan to reduce the noise for the inner-city Hamburg airport. Privatisation and reforming airport regulation at Hamburg airport were other topics he had to work on. He was pleasantly surprised to find how much economics could contribute to these topics. In 2000 he switched to academia. Peter and Hans-Martin, with David Gillen, Martin Kunz, Jürgen Müller, David Starkie, and Hartmut Wolf, started a series of workshops of the newly founded German Aviation Research Society (GARS). Cathal was one of the first speakers, in 2002, as a result of an invitation from David Starkie. Cathal was an economist working for the Irish airports regulator and was looking for a forum to discuss the regulatory economics of airports. Like Hans-Martin, in his day-to-day work, he felt a need to discuss airport regulatory work with researchers and academics. The GARS workshops led to lively discussions and were very fruitful. One result was the 2004 volume by Peter Forsyth and others, The Economic Regulation of Airports. This has been translated into Chinese and is still the bestseller of the series of books published as a result of the GARS seminars.

The GARS workshops and the Hamburg Aviation Conference, which is the predecessor of the European Aviation Conference, created a network of academics, regulators, industry managers and consultants who were fascinated by aviation and who shared a desire for a forum that would allow serious discussions of airport issues. This group further expanded, which explains why our list of acknowledgements is so long.

Peter and Hans-Martin cooperated on many papers presented at these workshops. Out of this cooperation came the idea of a book on airport economics, but it never really took off because other projects were always more urgent. In 2014, when

Cathal switched back from regulation to academia, we restarted this book. Again, luckily, John King took our ambitions seriously and offered a contract to publish such a book. It is a book by three academics who have sought to provide theoretical analysis and practical advice on airport management and policy. The backbone was always economics. We think that this is a fruitful perspective which offers tools for policy and management.

Acknowledgements

The authors thank the many people who directly and indirectly assisted with the production of the book.

Academic work is in some ways a collective enterprise, and so our teachers and lecturers, co-authors and colleagues over the years have contributed to the project. In particular, the members of the German Aviation Research Society (GARS) network and the participants in the European Aviation Conference (EAC) and its predecessors, discussed airport issues and research with us that was related to the contents of the book.

Among those, we would mention the late Mike Tretheway, also David Starkie, David Gillen, Wolfgang Grimme, Nicole Adler, Achim Czerny, Barry Humphreys, Thomas Immelmann, William Morrison, Andrew Charlton, Brian Pearce, Hendrik Stansch, Michael Stanton-Geddes, Jagoda Egeland, Benny Mantin, the late Hartmut Wolf, Juergen Mueller, Eric Pels, Ofelia Betancourt, Doramas Jorge-Calderon, Sonia Huderek-Glaspa, Sven Maertens, Eric Njoya, Dan Elliot and Dieter Wilken.

The authors especially thank the following colleagues for reading and commenting on one or more draft chapters of the book: Margaret Arblaster, Darryl Biggar, Frank Fichert, Anne Graham, Estelle Malavolti and Gianmaria Martini.

We are grateful for research assistance, and in particular to Shravana Kumar, Arian Raeesi and Oscar Sanabria.

We are also thankful to the editors of this series, John King and Peter Bruce, and are glad to continue our association with Guy Loft at Routledge.

Abbreviations

A4ANZ	Airlines for Australia and New Zealand
A4E	Airlines for Europe
AC	Average Cost
ACCC	Australian Competition and Consumer Commission
ACA	Airport Carbon Accreditation
ACI	Airports Council International
ACI EUROPE	Airports Council International Europe
AdP	Aéroports de Paris
AENA	Aeropuertos Españoles y Navegación Aérea
AFC	Average Fixed Cost
AIP	Airport Improvement Program
ANA	Aeroportos de Portugal
ANSP	Air Navigation Service Providers
APD	Air Passenger Duty
ARI	Aer Rianta International
ATC	Average Total Cost
ATC	Air Traffic Control
ATM	Air Transport Movement
ATRS	Air Transport Research Society
ATU	Airport Throughput Unit
AVC	Average Variable Cost
BA	British Airways
BAA	British Airways Authority (until 1987; after 1987 the name changed to BAA)
BBI	Berlin Brandenburg Airport
BOT	Build, Operate, Transfer
CAA	Civil Aviation Authority
CAEP	Committee on Aviation Environmental Protection
CAPEX	Capital expenditure
CAR	Commission for Aviation Regulation
CBA	Cost–Benefit Analysis
CBD	Central Business District
CC	Competition Commission

CCC Climate Change Commission (UK)
CDG Charles de Gaulle Airport
CGE Computable General Equilibrium
CMA Competition and Markets Authority
CO_2 Carbon Dioxide
CPI Consumer Price Index
DAA Dublin Airport Authority
DEA Data Envelopment Analysis
DLR German Aerospace Center (Deutsches Zentrum für Luft- und Raumfahrt)
DMU Decision-Making Unit
DOT (US) Department of Transportation
DWL Dead-Weight Loss
EASA European Aviation Safety Agency
EBIT Earnings Before Interest and Tax
EBITDA Earnings Before Interest, Tax, Depreciation and Amortisation
EEA European Economic Area
EIA Economic Impact Analysis
EIB European Investment Bank
ERP Equity Risk Premium
ETS Emissions Trading Scheme
EU European Union
EV Electric Vehicle
FAA Federal Aviation Administration
GA General Aviation
GARS German Aviation Research Society
GDP Gross Domestic Product
GHG Greenhouse Gas
IATA International Air Transport Association
ICAO International Civil Aviation Organization
ITF International Transport Forum
KPI Key Performance Indicators
LCC Low-Cost Carrier
LGW London Gatwick Airport
LHR London Heathrow Airport
LRAC Long-Run Average Cost
LTO Landing and Take-Off
MBMs Market-Based Measures
MC Marginal Cost
MEC Marginal External Cost
MES Minimum Efficient Scale
MTOW Maximum Take-Off Weight
NOX Nitrogen Oxide
NPV Net Present Value
OAG Official Airline Guide
OECD Organisation for Economic Co-operation and Development

OFT	Office of Fair Trading
PAX	Passengers
PSO	Public Service Obligation
RAB	Regulatory Asset Base
RFR	Risk-Free Rate
ROR	Rate of Return
RPI	Retail Price Index
SFA	Stochastic Frontier Analysis
SRAC	Short-Run Average Cost
SSNIP	Small but Significant and Non-Transitory Increase of Price
TFP	Total Factor Productivity
TRL	Transportation Research Laboratory
VAT	Value-Added Tax
VFR	Visiting Friends & Relatives
WACC	Weighted Average Cost of Capital
WEB/WEI	Wider Economic Benefits/Wider Economic Impacts
WLU	Work-Load Unit

1 An introduction to airport economics

1.1 Introduction: What is airport economics?

There are now several books about the different aspects of airports—airport management, marketing, finance and the planning and operation of airports. This book is about the economic aspects of airports. It intentionally concentrates on the economic aspects, and only looks at other aspects where needed, for example, looking at the financial aspects when it discusses privatisation, or marketing when the retail side of airports is discussed.

Airport economics is about how to get the best value out of an airport or airport system. How well does it serve the needs of passengers, and increasingly, shippers? How well does it perform in terms of profitability? What are the costs and benefits of the airport's operations for the region it is in? Airports create externalities such as noise and greenhouse gas emissions—how can these undesirable aspects be eliminated or minimised? Airport expansion is difficult, in terms of land and financial requirements, so how can we determine what investments are necessary?

When we talk about "good value", what do we mean? One meaning is that we add up the various benefits from having the airport, compare them to the costs of having the airport, and try to get the greatest net benefit. This approach is often described as maximising welfare. While the sum totals of benefits and costs are important, it is also relevant to recognise the distribution of the benefits and costs. It may be that one way of operating an airport will maximise the net sum in a way which yields benefits that exceed costs, but that the bulk of the benefits accrue to the well-off, while a slightly smaller net benefit might be achieved with a much more equal distribution of the net benefits.

Maximising net benefits is not the only objective we can set for our airports. An alternative would be to maximise profits. Until the 1980s, most airports around the world were owned by central or local governments, and the net benefit objective would have been seen as appropriate. Since then, many airports have been privatised, and many now have profit as their core objective. Airport economics is the study of how airports will work under such various objectives. Profit objectives provide incentives: for the airports to be efficient, but also for the airports to use their market power to increase prices and profits. This creates a need for institutions such as regulators, which have a big role in how airports operate.

DOI: 10.4324/9781003156901-1

As we note in Section 1.2, there has been considerable research on the different parts of airport economics. Some of these areas have attracted research attention for many years, such as land use and access, noise and the environment, cost recovery and investment evaluation. As the airport institutional picture has become more complex, a number of newer issues have come to the fore, including privatisation and regulation, allocation of scarce capacity, competition between airports, and how to handle problems such as greenhouse gas emissions. These issues are introduced in Section 1.2.

What is special about airports? In many respects, airports are utilities like energy and telecommunications services, and like transport hubs such as railway stations. There are several aspects which are not unique to airports, but others which need special attention. Some of these are:

- Airports can be very large, land-intensive urban investments which pose major issues about where they are located. While investment in telecommunications is straightforward, and conventional power stations are not too difficult to site, airports are quite problematic—sometimes governments establish special Commissions to evaluate options.
- Airports are an essential part of the wider transport industry, which includes airlines. Good performance of airports is essential for good performance of airlines and other parts of the transport system.
- Airports can have major impacts on the region in which they are located.
- Expanding airports is very difficult, and this means that making effective use of existing capacity is all the more important.

We are all aware of the national and regional role of airports. But this often hampers the objective of their serving the needs of airlines and passengers. Airports have been seen as status symbols, though less so now than in the past. Award-winning architects design terminals—these can be pleasing to the eye, but are expensive to build and use. Initially, airports were boring utilities, needed to provide connectivity for a city. Over the last couple of decades, airports have been built in obscure places, such as Don Quijote airport (now closed), named after a fictional bumbler, in Cuidad Real in Spain. Clearly, the economics of good evaluation have not always been followed.

In this book we emphasise a number of matters:

- Good public policy, which we interpret as gaining the greatest benefit from an airport.
- The implications of changes in public policy for airports.
- How the airport's goals can best be pursued—whether that goal is maximisation of profits or of the net benefits for the airport's region.
- Economic efficiency in pricing and operations, and tackling market failures such as use of market power, and taking full account of externalities such as emissions and noise.
- The wider economic benefits and costs of aviation.

1.2 Old and new issues

A good way of thinking about the different issues in the economics of airports is to divide them into old and new issues. Over the past forty years or so the issues of interest have changed. The old issues are still of concern, though some of them have receded in urgency, and new issues have emerged.

Old issues

The economics of airports had become a field of study by the beginning of the 1980s. Fortunately, we have at our disposal a comprehensive and authoritative survey of airport economics written by Alan Walters in 1978 (who was a member of the Roskill Committee into the Third London Airport, an evaluation of options for London which reported in the early 1970s). Hence, we have an outline of the key issues in airport economics as it was at the beginning of the 1980s. Some of the key issues were as follows.

Patterns of demand

Several characteristics of demand were of interest, in particular, the distinction between business and leisure travel. Airports exist to serve the airline industry, and this distinction had become established in the airline industry. Estimates of the elasticity of demand for airports, being a derived demand, had been quite low, though they depended on the nature of the traffic (lower elasticities the longer the route flown). Over time, with the deregulation of domestic aviation, and the liberalisation of international routes, the distinction between domestic and international traffic has become less important.

Cost conditions

How costs varied with output was an important issue from the beginning. There was considerable interest in the short run. It was argued that there were substantial indivisibilities, particularly associated with runway use. A single runway could handle a large number of aircraft movements; even today a large airport like London Gatwick only has one runway. The view developed that once the runway had been developed, the cost of using it would be low. Thus, the short-run marginal cost was taken to be low.

The cost of using the runway for different aircraft sizes and types (jet or turboprops) was regarded as fairly similar. One aspect of cost is that longer-distance flights require longer runways. In the 1980s, airports started running out of capacity, and the question of what the long-run costs might look like (and whether airports were natural monopolies) was given more consideration.

Pricing

The cost conditions of airports, with low short-run marginal costs, combined with lumpy capital or investment costs meant that airports had a cost recovery problem.

To achieve maximum efficiency, prices should be set at marginal cost, but this would fail to cover the capital costs of the airport. Economists have proposed a number of ways to achieve cost recovery at minimum loss of efficiency (such as multi-part tariffs) but practice was ahead of theory. Airports had developed systems of weight-based prices, partly because, at an earlier stage, heavier aircraft imposed heavier costs on runways. As it turns out, weight-based prices are a good proxy for Ramsey prices (which are a variant of charging what the market will bear) and are a way of covering costs at minimum efficiency loss.

As some airports were running out of capacity, congestion and delays became evident. In the US, delays were starting to be serious at some major airports, and this was also starting at European airports. In the latter, there were the beginnings of the slot system, which required airlines to have a slot to use the airport. Pricing solutions, including peak/off-peak pricing, were also beginning to be recommended.

Externalities—noise

Airport noise has long been a problem, though the noisiness of the aircraft has been greatly reduced over the years. By the 1980s, it had been measured in a scientific way, and its costs were also being measured. Even at that point, the measured cost was much less than might have been expected from the sharp public reaction to it. Airport noise around urban areas was a major factor in the British Government's decision to build the third London airport at a remote, but costly, site (a plan later abandoned). This situation continues today, whereby airports are rarely built or expanded where noise is thought to be a problem. It might therefore have been expected that noise pricing would be common in airports. As it turns out, there has not been much serious noise pricing, though many airports have noise curfews.

Evaluation and access

By the time Walters (1978) was writing, a number of airports were being assessed using rigorous cost–benefit techniques. The best ways of measuring the costs and benefits of airport expansion and development had been established, notably by the Roskill Committee. A major part of the task was assessing the costs and benefits of airport access, given that such costs (new roads, rail lines and congestion costs imposed by buses and cars) can be a large part of the overall cost. This means that when new airports are proposed, a menu of different sites needs to be evaluated.

New developments and issues

Some of the important policy issues of thirty years ago remain topical, such as location and access, costs and pricing, evaluation, and noise. Today, a host of new issues need to be resolved. These include capacity rationing, privatisation and economic regulation, airport competition, the emergence of the low-cost carrier sector, and the environment.

Excess demand and rationing of capacity

As more airports have run out of capacity, first in the US and then in Europe and Asia, and as it is difficult to increase airport capacity, how can the limited capacity available be used best? The answers given in the US and Europe/Asia are different.

In the US, there is little formal rationing of airport capacity, so extensive delays mount. In most other countries, a system of airport slots has developed. To use a busy airport, an airline needs to have a slot. In most countries, these slots are allocated by "grandfathering", which means that over time, as demand mounts, airlines that already have slots keep them. This creates problems, especially for airlines seeking to enter an airport. Sometimes airlines are able to obtain slots in informal "grey" markets, but in the UK, slot trading is permitted. These slots are valuable, and a daily slot pair for London Heathrow has sold for as much as $75m.

Privatisation and regulation

Prior to 1987, nearly all major airports were owned and run by governments. Smaller airports were often owned by local governments, and there were a few private airports. In 1987, the British government privatised most of its airports, including the London airports. Since then, there has been a general move towards privatisation, with Australia privatising its major airports since 1997, some (predominantly partial) privatisations in Europe (Brussels Frankfurt, Hamburg and Vienna) and privatisation of airports in India, Mexico and, more recently, Japan. The US did not join the move to privatisation, and most major airports in Asia also remain government owned. Thus, there has been a gradual but not precipitate shift in airport ownership.

That change poses a question for regulation. Many airports have market power, which they could use to increase prices, to the detriment of their airline and passenger customers. When airports have been privatised, this is normally accompanied by price regulation. In addition, many airports which remain in government ownership, such as Amsterdam Schiphol, are regulated.

There is now a growing complaint that privatised airports (especially the lightly regulated airports) are misusing their market power and setting excessive prices. This concern is led by the airline industry groups, such as the International Air Transport Association (IATA) and Airlines for Europe (A4E). Competition regulators, such as the Australian Competition and Consumer Commission (ACCC) have also been critical of airport pricing.

Efficiency and benchmarking

The measurement of airport efficiency has become very important. In the past, it was assumed that government ownership would ensure that airports would deliver their services at a low cost. The same assumption was made of all public enterprises. By the 1980s, views were changing. Economists started measuring the productive efficiency of public and private regulated firms and found many to be quite inefficient; airports were no exception. There has been a boom in evaluating the productive efficiency of airports. Such airport benchmarking has become an issue of public, and especially regulatory, policy. Airports are themselves interested in how their efficiency compares to other airports. Productivity measurement of airports has shed light on issues such as whether public or private airports are more efficient, whether competition affects performance, and how the different forms of regulation affect productivity.

Low-cost carriers and secondary airports

At first, major cities had major airports, and smaller towns had small airports, and these mainly served their urban and regional communities. But some large airports acted as hubs for interconnection between long-haul flights—for example, London Heathrow was a connecting point for travellers from New York on their way to Glasgow.

With deregulation of airlines, starting in the US, then Europe, and then spreading further, Low-Cost Carriers (LCCs) sought to fly between airports as economically as possible. They began to use secondary airports which were cheaper; sometimes LCCs were not able to gain slots to use the busier, main airports. Passengers were willing to travel to secondary airports to get a low fare. Airlines like Ryanair were pioneers in setting this trend. As a result, some secondary airports (Charleroi near Brussels, Belgium, Weeze near Düsseldorf, Germany) grew to be moderately large, even though the towns they served were quite small. This raises the question—can airports compete with one another?

Competition and marketing

The traditional view of the airport business was that it was a natural monopoly, which meant that the market was served at lowest cost by a single airport, except for a handful of very large cities with two or more airports. Airports were located too far apart to provide competition for airports in other cities. This view is now challenged. Low-cost carriers, using secondary airports, have increased competition between airports, at least for the large leisure travel sector. In addition, a number of smaller airports (including some converted military bases) have entered the market to compete for a share of the LCC business.

The classic example is that of the UK, which is a geographically small country with a high population density. In many areas of the UK, a passenger might have three or four airports within an hour's drive to choose from. Other countries are less dense and have less intense competition between airports, but competition does exist. This competition puts pressure on airports to make their services more attractive, which they could neglect when they did not have to worry about competition. The result has been a change in airport pricing. Major airports are trying to capture some of the LCC market and have been adjusting their prices to do so. They cannot simply reduce prices, as this would upset their old customers, so they offer discounts to airlines (legacy or LCC) which offer new routes. The main beneficiaries of this price structure are the LCCs.

If an airport has two or three active competitors, does it need to be regulated? In the UK, formal price regulation has been scaled back (e.g., removed at Manchester Airport) where regulators concluded that there was sufficient competition. Further, airports need to market themselves more. It is no longer true that "build it and passengers will come". With no competition, passengers had little or no choice. Now airports must attract airlines and passengers away from an alternative airport. Airports seek to attract new airlines and to develop new routes. Hub airports also realise that airlines have a choice over which airports to use for flight connections.

Increasing non-aeronautical revenues

Non-aeronautical services, such as retail, food and beverage, office space, and car parks were once regarded as a necessary add-on to the main airport service, that of serving flights, but were only a moderate source of revenue. Over time, these services have grown to account for more than half of total revenues. Airports have become "shopping malls with runways". Airports are often sited on valuable land, and they try to make the best use of this by expanding the services they offer. While not a problem, this raises some questions. An important one is the treatment of non-aeronautical revenues at price-regulated airports. Should the profits from non-aeronautical services be used to subsidise aeronautical charges (the single till approach), or should the profits be kept by the airport owner (the dual till)?

Airports, regional development and job creation

The evaluation of airport investments has also been an important facet of airport economics, but how broadly defined are the possible benefits and costs? The traditional (recommended) approach was cost–benefit analysis. More recently, there have been attempts to measure a broader set of benefits and costs. There could be wider economic benefits (or impacts) of aviation, which airports have enabled. One is the greater connectivity to other destinations. Airports are associated with an increased economic output of the region they are located in, and with additional jobs. However, this does not mean that they bring additional jobs to the overall national economy, except in times of recession.

Freight airports

As air transport has grown, freight carried in aircraft has increased too. In terms of tonnage, air freight is still small relative to that of land-based transport modes, but in terms of value, air accounts for 35% of total international traffic, according to IATA. Much of this freight is handled through passenger-serving city airports. However, specialised airports have also developed which concentrate on freight, or which combine passenger services with large, dedicated freight operations. Examples include Cologne, with a large UPS freight facility, and Leipzig Airport, with a DHL facility. These operate as freight hubs for the whole of Europe. In the US, Memphis is the hub for FedEx. Air freight is typically used for high-value items such as computers, and for products where speed of delivery is essential, such as seafood and flowers. The important requirement for a freight airport is that it operates 24 hours a day without a night curfew. This is to allow flights to hub throughout the night. Very important also is to have clearly adequate capacity so that cargo airlines can operate with minimal delays. Freight airports came into their own during the COVID-19 pandemic, with a boom in parcels traffic.

"Green" airports

Noise and local emissions have long been an issue with airports. However, greenhouse gas emissions have now become a large challenge for airports. The greenhouse gas emissions from the operation of aircraft account for the bulk of air transport emissions, at about 2–5% of total global emissions. But with the move to zero emissions by 2050, airports are taking their contributions to emissions seriously. Fortunately, it is easier to reduce emissions at airports than for aircraft in flight. Airports can be built with low emissions materials, such as low-emission concrete, the terminals can be fitted with solar panels, and electric surface vehicles can be used.

The COVID-19 pandemic

The pandemic created a number of unexpected challenges for airports. Overnight, demand for their services evaporated, and busy airports found that they were serving only 5% of normal traffic. Airports faced crises before, notably after 9/11 and the 2008 financial crisis, but the pandemic caused a much larger and sustained reduction in traffic. Airports do not generally have problems financing their operations, but the pandemic forced private airports to seek new funding. This is not a critical problem for airports with market power, since they have good credit lines. However, it is a problem for airports which face strong competition, especially the smaller ones. There is also the problem of how quickly the airports can repair their balance sheets. Airports with some market power can raise their prices, though this does not help the airline industry. Often the decision is made by the regulator, which will determine whether an airport will be permitted to raise prices, and if so, over what time span it can do so. As yet it is not clear whether the pandemic will produce any sustained changes in the way airports are operated.

1.3 An outline of this book

We can divide the book into three parts:

Part 1: Demand, Costs and Pricing;
Part 2: Ownership, Regulation and Efficiency, and
Part 3: Environment and Impacts
Part 1 sets out the basics of airport economics.

In Chapter 2, the demand side of airports is introduced, starting with consideration of the location decision. Long-established airports have occupied a particular location for many years, but when new airports are contemplated, the controversial issue of location needs to be resolved.

In Chapter 3, costs and market structure are discussed. Airports have particular cost characteristics. One is that short-run (variable) costs tend to be low for a large range of outputs until the airport runs out of capacity. Fixed costs can be high, however. Additional traffic can be served only after large new investments are made (e.g., in an additional runway).

In Chapter 4, demand and supply (or costs) are brought together to examine pricing. Small to medium sized airports tend to have plenty of capacity, but may find it difficult to cover their costs. With large airports, the problem is likely to be one of excess demand which leads to congestion. The problem then is how to ration scarce capacity efficiently and effectively.

Part 2 explores airports in a wider context.

In Chapter 5 the ownership issue is introduced. With some airports in public ownership and others in private ownership, what are the owners' objectives for the airport—maximising the overall benefits, less costs of operation, or maximisation of profit, or something else? The chapter then analyses investment, and the expansion of capacity through investment.

In Chapter 6, the implications of privatisation are analysed. As already mentioned, airports can often use market power to raise prices and limit output. These adverse effects can be reduced if the airport is regulated. In other cases, the airport may be faced with competition from nearby airports, and if so, regulation might be superfluous.

In Chapter 7, airport efficiency and quality issues are discussed. It is desirable that airports are cost efficient, and thus there needs to be some effort in measuring efficiency. This is of particular relevance when regulators are determining what prices to allow the airport to charge. It is also desirable that passengers receive airport services at the level of quality they desire; different passenger groups may have different quality preferences. When the airport is regulated, there can be incentives for the airport to downgrade quality, and this effect needs to be resolved.

Part 3 looks at the broader impacts of airport operations.

In Chapter 8, the environmental aspects of airports are discussed. One negative aspect of airport operation, recognised for many years, is that of noise. On the other hand, the impact of the airport on greenhouse gas emissions is something which has only lately been seen as a problem.

In Chapter 9, the economic impacts of airports are reviewed. This is a controversial area about which many strong claims are made. Airports do have a clear role in facilitating the wider economic benefits of aviation, such as connecting cities and regions. Airports do increase the development of the regions they are in. However, there are costs too, airport investments are costly, and need to be evaluated rigorously.

Towards the end of each chapter, we introduce a "controversy"—these are issues which the material contained in that chapter can help to explain.

Space limitations prevent us from exploring some other aspects of airport operations and policy. One of these is the airline–airport relationship, which is discussed in airport management and marketing studies. We say little about taxation, since much of the taxation of air transport takes place at the airline level—for example, the UK Air Passenger Duty. The particular problems of airports in developing countries as well as the role of freight and freight airports are not discussed. The book is global in scope, though the examples and references to policy discussions tend to be from Europe rather than from Asia or the US, again because of space limitations.

Reference

Walters A A (1978) "Airports: An Economic Survey", *Journal of Transport Economics and Policy*, 12, 125–150

Appendix

Welfare Economics or The Economics of Microeconomic Policy: A Brief Outline

Welfare economics is the economic analysis of microeconomic policy. Much of the content of this book consists of exploring ways of achieving the best performance of an industry—in this case, airports. We shall be drawing on an established set of ideas throughout the book, namely, those of welfare economics—these ideas provide us with a practical guide to developing airport policies. This Appendix provides a brief outline of the main concepts of welfare economics (see Boadway and Bruce, 1984; Rees, 1984).

What is the output of an airport?

Before going further, it is necessary to set out what the "output" of an airport is. Airports produce several types of aeronautical output—they handle flights or "movements", they enable passengers to board and alight from aircraft at terminals, they handle air cargo, and they provide parking for aircraft. In addition, they produce a myriad of non-aeronautical services, such as retail, car parking and office space. The core output is providing infrastructure for airlines to land and take-off, and there are several ways to measure these services—passengers handled, flights handled, freight handled or some composite of these, such as "workload units" or WLU. In the figures we are using, we often use a generic term "output" for simplicity, though it should be understood that output measurement is more complex in reality.

Objectives

There are several objectives which can be adopted for a nation's airports. A key one is economic efficiency. Efficiency means that the net benefit for all of those affected from having an airport is maximised. There are other possible objectives which might be pursued—an important one is equity. For example, an airport might be operated not to maximise efficiency, but rather so that some target group, such as regional travellers, get special help. The definition of those affected by having an airport might be broad, taking account of more than just airport owners, airlines and passengers, but encompassing local communities and businesses. A possible objective, especially for privately owned airports, could be one of maximising the profits for the owners. It is also possible that the owners may choose to not maximise the profits coming to them, but rather let the management dominate.

While there are therefore several possible objectives, it is likely that economic efficiency will be a key one, and it is important to know how this can be maximised, even if this is not the only objective. There are several types of efficiency which are relevant for airports—these include allocative efficiency, productive efficiency, and dynamic efficiency. Efficiency also requires the absence of rent seeking.

Allocative efficiency

Allocative efficiency (or Pareto efficiency, named after the economist who first analysed it in detail) is to do with allocative issues. One aspect is the allocation of an airport's services between users; specifically, are all passengers served who are willing to cover the costs the airport incurs to serve them? In a perfect market, this is achieved in the long run when prices are equal to marginal costs. Such a first-best solution is hardly possible for airports to achieve (see later). There are several allocative issues which arise with airports, including how the airport prices its services, how it chooses its investments, and how capacity at the airport is allocated between users. Two issues closely related to allocative efficiency are surplus and marginal cost pricing.

Consumers' and producers' surplus

To maximise overall welfare or benefit, it is helpful to set out what it comprises. Two key sources of benefits or surpluses which come about from the airport being available are the consumers' and the producers' surplus. These are shown in the Appendix Figure. Output is shown on the *x*-axis, and price and cost on the *y*-axis. Suppose demand is shown by D, and marginal cost is shown by MC. Suppose also that the price is P_1. Some consumers are just prepared to pay P_1, but most are prepared to pay something more than this, hence they gain a surplus. Diagrammatically this is shown as the triangular area AP_1E_1. Suppose further that there are no fixed costs, then the area below the price but above the MC, P_1E_1FG, is the profit, or producer's surplus of the airport. In addition, there may be some producers' surplus enjoyed by the suppliers to the firm, such as workers.

Marginal cost pricing

An important rule is the marginal cost pricing rule. Other things equal, maximum efficiency is achieved when the airport sets its prices at marginal (rather than average) cost. The maximum of consumers' and producers' surplus is achieved when the firm sets price, P_2, at marginal cost. This is a social maximum—in this case, the firm could make higher profits, though the total surplus would be less. If the firm sets price at P_1, it increases its profits, but the total surplus is less than if it prices at P_2. The difference between the surplus at P_2 and the maximum possible surplus is E_1E_2F

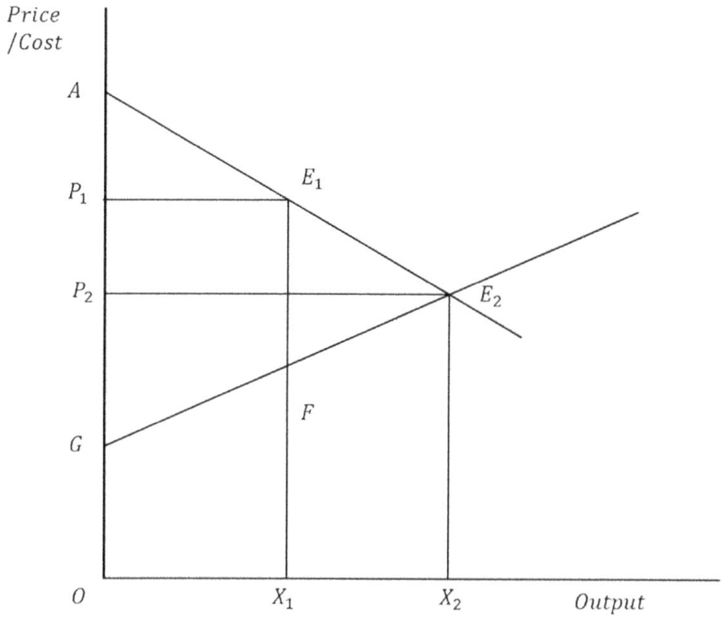

Appendix Figure Consumer's and Producer's Surplus

is often termed the "deadweight loss" (or DWL) from inefficient pricing (such as the price which a monopoly will charge). Sometimes the maximum surplus is achieved at a price which fails to cover total costs—this is often the case with airports, especially those which have ample capacity. In this case, the consumers' surplus is positive, but the producer's surplus is negative.

Productive and cost efficiency

Until the 1980s, there was little attention paid to other types of efficiency. However, from then on there was increasing attention given to productive efficiency, which deals with how efficiently firms are producing their outputs. In other words, are their costs being minimised? Before the 1980s it was tacitly assumed that firms, including airports, normally kept costs at a minimum. Empirical work suggested that this was often far from being the case, and that many firms, especially those which were not operating in competitive markets, were allowing their costs to be high. This has been particularly true of airports, which were often not under much competitive pressure to keep their costs down (see Chapter 7 on airport efficiency). As a result, privatisation (Chapter 5) was often suggested as a means of reducing airport costs, and regulation (Chapter 6) was seen as a way of achieving a good balance between productive and allocative efficiency.

Dynamic efficiency

A rather less common concept is that of dynamic efficiency. This is not a very clearly defined concept, but it refers to efficiency over time. It can deal with how an airport handles its investment plans, and how it develops new processes and products.

Rent seeking

An important concept, for airports, is that of "rent seeking". Rent seeking refers to the investment of resources in efforts to create monopoly. This comes about when profits, or rents, are created but there is uncertainty as to who has the right to enjoy them. As a result, many players spend real resources in order to capture some share of them. An example would be when airport slots are being allocated. If the rules of slot allocation are very clear, in open and transparent markets, rent seeking should not emerge. However, if there is dispute as to who should gain the slots, and airlines resort to litigation, or lobbying of governments, there is likely to be rent seeking, and some of the rents will be wasted. Regulation can also give rise to rent seeking if the parties (airports and airlines) become involved in expensive actions to try to get decisions favourable to themselves.

First-best and second-best

In practical policymaking, it is usually the case that the ideal policy is not attainable, and the best that can be hoped for is a policy with obvious limitations. Think of the pricing policy of an airport with spare capacity. Marginal cost may be very low, and setting price equal to it, the first best option, will lead to the airport incurring losses. If the airport is a private airport, it will not be prepared to stay in business, and if it is a public airport, the (cash-strapped) government will not be willing to cover the losses. However, the airport is still worth having. The airport may be able to cover its costs, though not by pricing at marginal cost. In short, while the first-best policy is not practicable, a second-best policy is. Thus, the concept of the "first-best" and the "second-best" came about as ways of evaluating policy options. Usually, it is worth working out what the first-best policy is, and if that is unattainable then working out what the best second-best policy is.

Market failure and government failure

Much production takes place in market economies. This is because markets work well in general. However, sometimes they fail, and this gives rise to the concept of "market failure". A good example of market failure is the presence of monopolies. There are several problems with monopolies—they set prices too high, and they are thus allocatively inefficient, and the lack of competition enables them to produce at higher than minimum cost, and thus they can be productively inefficient. They can also give rise to rent seeking by parties trying to create a monopoly. To an extent, the deficiencies of monopolies can be addressed by regulation. Many, though not all, airports operate as monopolies.

Another form of market failure is externalities. These come about when the firm does not take into account all of the economic effects of its production as these effects do not work through the price system. Externalities can be positive or negative. The two main forms of negative externalities from airports are noise and emissions (Chapter 8), including greenhouse gas emissions. Wider economic benefits (WEBs), which could include increased connectivity, could be a positive externality of airport operation (Chapter 9). There can be other market failures, such as those stemming from incomplete markets and the existence of public goods.

There can also be government failures. These are less closely defined, but they may be important. It is difficult for well-intentioned governments to set up conditions which lead their enterprises to perform efficiently. As a result, governments often privatise such businesses. Aside from public enterprise issues, there are problems of insufficient information, limited control over the bureaucracy and problems of political processes.

The market economy and efficiency

In a first-best world, a market economy will give rise to economically efficient outcomes. However, the world we live in is a second-best world, with many market and government imperfections. When we are dealing with practical policy questions, we cannot assume a first-best world. However, sometimes it is safe to assume that markets get things tolerably right, and sometimes it is not safe to do this. Resolving which assumption is appropriate requires judgement on the part of the policymaker. If an airport serves airlines whose routes are mainly competitive, it will be safe to assume that end markets are performing well, but if the airport is serving many monopolistic markets, the implications of this may need to be taken into account, for example in setting prices.

Partial and general equilibrium

The economy is a complicated mechanism. In many cases, it is not necessary to take into account all of the myriad markets that an airport interacts with. For example, if the task is to measure how productive a group of airports are, it will probably be sufficient to simply concentrate on the inputs and outputs of the airport production process. This would be a case of partial equilibrium analysis. With other airport issues, partial equilibrium analysis is not sufficient since many markets will be affected in different ways. For example, if there is a proposal to make a major runway extension to an airport, there will be many markets across the economy affected. The airline market itself, alternatives to air travel such as rail, inbound and outbound tourism markets and urban travel markets will all be affected. In addition, there may be impacts on the distribution of income. This then becomes a problem of general equilibrium. This might be handled by looking at all of the markets affected one by one, but ideally, the general equilibrium problem should be analysed using a computable general equilibrium (CGE) model. These have been used in airport evaluations (Chapters 5 and 9).

Interpreting the figures

Many of the diagrams in the following chapters (e.g., Chapter 4) show prices, costs and consumers surplus benefits which accrue to the airlines—but how are passengers affected? Effectively, they pay the cost of the airport's services which the airline pays, plus the cost of all the other inputs which the airlines use, if the airline market is competitive. In the Figure, it is not necessary to show the effect on passengers in addition to the effect on the airlines—a €1 increase on airport charges gives rise to a €1 increase in airline fares. There are exceptions to this—when the airport capacity is constrained, such as by slots, the cost to the airline includes the opportunity cost to it of using its scarce slots. If the price charged to the airline is increased, the airline is forced to absorb all of the increase, and the price to the passenger is unaffected.

Another qualification to this is where the airline industry is not competitive in the markets served by the airport—a situation which is often not the case. The price to the passenger will not be equal to the price to the airline plus the cost of all the other inputs used by the airline. This needs to be borne in mind when interpreting the diagrams, which of necessity, include simplifications.

References

Boadway, R and N Bruce (1984) *Welfare Economics*, Oxford, Blackwell

Rees, R (1984) *Public Enterprise Economics*, 2nd ed., London, Weidenfeld and Nicolson

Part 1

Demand, costs and pricing

2 Location, demand and forecasting

2.1 Introduction

Air transport of persons and freight requires airports as points of interchange with other modes (car, rail and public transport) and as points of interchange within air transport (connecting flights, hubs). In transport geography, airports are treated as central and intermediate locations used to transport persons and freight from the origin to the destination of their journey (Rodrigue, 2020). Airport locations serve the surrounding agglomeration and markets (their hinterland) and should be easily accessible from the regional transport system.

Airports can be classified as inner-city airports, metropolitan airports and remote airports. The geographical pattern of airports reflects choices and the planning of the regions and nations, but these choices are very dependent on the decisions of earlier planners. History matters. We shall reflect on this issue in the first section. In the next section, we discuss ground access. While the accessibility of airports should be part of the location choice, it is very often so only to a minor extent. Managing ground access has therefore become a major problem for airports. The demand for airports is a derived demand. We discuss the demand characteristics and the factors influencing the elasticity of demand in Section 2.3, which lays the foundation for the final section on forecasting demand. Airports are long-term investments and need good traffic forecasts even though these are difficult to produce since the future is risky and uncertain. Surprisingly, this might be not the most relevant reasons while forecasts are very often wrong.

2.2 Where to build?—history matters

Airport planners face conflicting goals when deciding where to build an airport. First, there are technical factors, such as weather conditions, altitude and availability of land. These considerations dominated the initial decisions about airport location, which were also often influenced by military considerations.[1] In terms of accessibility, airport sites closer to the Central Business District (CBD) are preferable for business travel, but these sites lead to higher costs as land is scarce. In addition, there are negative externalities from noise and other emissions, which make such locations unpopular with local residents. Optimising by balancing the marginal benefits

DOI: 10.4324/9781003156901-3

and costs is very difficult, as cost and benefit information is not readily available and would also require considerable foresight over many decades. Airport masterplans and public planning try to balance these trade-offs and the geographical pattern of airports in countries is the outcome of those choices. The majority of airport sites were selected at the beginning of the 20th century in developed countries. These airports have been extended in the 1960s and 1970s. Some small regional airports have been built as greenfield projects, and others were military airfield conversions. Only a few large airports have been built recently, including Denver International (1995) and Austin Bergstrom International (1999) in the US, and in Europe, Athens International (2001), Istanbul New Airport (2019) and Berlin Brandenburg International (2020). According to Rodrigue (2020), there is a clear tendency over the last 100 years for large airports to be built further away from the CBD. This is a plausible tendency given the trends of suburbanisation.

To illustrate the importance of history, we consider cases of airport expansions in Germany, which is a densely populated country (see Box 2.1). This case study is in many respects typical. It shows how difficult it is to find "optimal" locations and also difficult to add new airport capacity in densely populated areas. In principle, airport policy has three options:

1. *Expansion of the existing airports.* This has so far been true in London. In 1970, the Roskill Inquiry proposed a new airport at Cublington, 65 km outside of the centre. The recommendation was not followed. Instead, passenger numbers grew from 15 million in 1968 to more than 115 million at the existing airports. Larger aircraft with higher load factors and increases in the number of slots allowed airports to serve more passengers. This is true of many airports in densely populated countries such as Germany (see Box 2.1).
2. *Replacement of the main airport by a larger airport on a new site.* The most famous (though negative) example is Mirabel airport which was opened in 1974 as a substitute for the city airport of Montreal. This never worked. In the UK, the Airports Commission (2015) evaluated a replacement for Heathrow airport, the Thames Hub Airport, to be located 34 km outside London but rejected it as too costly.
3. *Expanding capacity by adding a second airport at a new site.* This was the policy in Paris where in addition to Paris Orly, the new Charles de Gaulle (CDG) airport opened in 1974. Passenger numbers at Charles de Gaulle grew faster than at Orly. In the mid-1990s CDG overtook Orly and now has more than twice the number of passengers. Similar cases are the airports in the Milan and Rome region. In these cases, the new airport became the main airport over time. In other instances, the new airport absorbed only part of the demand and remained smaller. This is the case in Amsterdam where Schiphol airport remains the main hub for the Netherlands; smaller satellite airports like Lelystad are planned to serve leisure and other niche markets. An interesting example of a second airport is given by Sydney. Sydney's Kingsford Smith Airport (KSA) is located close to the CBD. It is a hub for Qantas. Land is scarce, but it was allowed to build a third runway in 1994. Since the 1970s, plans for a second airport have been discussed

and in 2014 the government decided to build a new airport Western Sydney International Airport at a 44 km distance from the CBD.[2]

The International Transport Forum at the OECD has analysed a number of airport expansions in large urban areas. It recommends the following five principles (Thompson et al., 2014, p. 12):

- use existing capacity efficiently
- evaluate a wide range of options by means of cost–benefit analysis (CBA)
- adopt flexible planning processes to allow for unforeseen changes in the future
- protect the interests of those negatively affected by noise and other emissions
- provide legitimacy and stability in the democratic planning process

The first principle is discussed in Chapter 4. Slots, slot constraints and the structure of airport charges are key issues for the efficient use of airports. The London airports with secondary slot trading, and a per-aircraft movement charge, adhere better to this principle than do the German airports where slot markets are not used and weight-based charges incentivise the use of small aircraft. Capacity-constrained US airports rely on queuing to ration demand, which is the most inefficient way to utilise capacity. The second principle is discussed in detail in Chapter 9. The capacity extensions in Germany do not satisfy this principle either as decisions are not based on CBA. In contrast, the case of a second airport in Sydney (Forsyth, 2014) and for an adding runway for the London area evaluated the impacts on economic welfare. The third principle is discussed in Chapter 8. Thompson et al. (2014, p. 23) argue that "noise nuisance is the key constraint on expansion for most airports". This was certainly true for Düsseldorf which is restricted from using the second runway's capacity. The Düsseldorf case also confirms that communities negatively affected by airport expansion have lost trust in the planning process. The legitimacy of the planning is the fifth principle. In Germany public planning lacks independence, so neighbouring communities do not participate in the planning exercise and instead go to court. The Airports Commission (2015) was more successful at trust-building when it assessed the case for a new runway for London.

Box 2.1 Case study: Choice of location for airports and capacity expansion in Germany

In Germany, the location of airports had usually been decided before the Second World War, very often under undemocratic regimes. In the 1950s airports were rebuilt, and runways were extended to handle turbo-prop aircraft. In the early 1960s, the new generation of jets led to steady growth of air traffic so that many German states and municipalities considered plans to close down existing airports and instead build new larger airports, capable of serving intercontinental flights. Such plans were blocked by the local communities for noise reasons. In the 1970s and 1980s, capacity at German airports was better utilised as, for the first time, capacity became scarce at a number of airports. In 1965, Frankfurt airport had applied for planning approval for a new (western) runway. This process turned into a long-lasting political struggle and led to a widely shared belief that airport extensions were nearly impossible to achieve. This belief was also strengthened by the failure to extend Düsseldorf airport, which had applied in 1969 for permission to build a second parallel runway. Fourteen years later the runway was approved. In 1993, the construction was finished, but the use of the two runways was limited to the capacity of one runway. The conflict is still continuing, and Düsseldorf is one of the most slot-constrained airports in Europe. In Frankfurt, although in the 1980s the regional government promised to seek no further extension, in 1997 it began a mediation process for a fourth runway, which was successful. Parliament unanimously supported the extension under the condition of more strict night curfews. Construction of the fourth runway was finished in 2011, but even today demonstrations against the extension are held regularly.

Hamburg airport was built in 1911 on what was then the outskirts of Hamburg, but has since become an inner-city airport. In the 1960s, plans were made to close it and build a central Northern Germany International Airport. These plans stopped in the 1970s but were revitalised after unification in the 1990s. However, in 1995, this option was finally discarded and a noise budget was set. Since then, Hamburg airport has gained acceptance, but environmental concerns have remained an issue.

While in general, existing airports were extended, for specific reasons this did not happen in Munich and Berlin. At the old inner-city Munich airport, an aircraft crash led to the decision to build a new airport far from the city. Planning started in 1963 and the airport opened in 1992. As traffic grew faster than forecasted, Munich airport planned a third runway in 2005, which was approved in 2011, but stopped in 2012 by a public vote. Since then, all attempts to reverse this decision have failed. In the case of Berlin, the city used to have three airports, Tegel and Tempelhof in the former West Berlin, and Schönefeld in the former East Berlin. Soon after German reunification, planning started for a new hub airport, Berlin Brandenburg International (BBI). In the planning process, two commissions recommended different locations and, in the end, the Federal Ministry, following pressure from special interests of airports, chose Schönefeld, thereby disregarding the mediation process (a special public dispute resolution mechanism). In June 2002, the two Länder of Berlin and Brandenburg decided to move all air traffic to BBI. In August 2004, the plans were approved and the airport was planned to open in 2007. This date was then postponed several times. The initial construction costs were €2.83 billion but have since at least tripled (Müller, 2021). BBI finally opened in 2020 (for an evaluation, see Chapter 9).

Table 2.1 Capacity extensions at the six main German airports

Airport	*Berlin Brandenburg*	*Düsseldorf*	*Hamburg*	*Frankfurt*	*Munich*	*Stuttgart*
Location chosen/ opening	1996/2020	1914/1927	1911	1934/1936	1969/1992	1936/1939
Runway extensions and changes (year and meters)	N.A.	In 1952 up to 2475 m, in 1969 up to 3000 m	From 1935 to 1964, runways to 3,250 m and 3,666 m	North runway in 1959 up to 3,900 m. South runway in 1960 to 3,000 m	N.A.	1951 up to 1,800 m, 1961 to 2,250, in 1996 to 3,345 m
New Runway	Two runways 3600 m and 4000 m	Second parallel runway in 1993	No	Runway west in 1984 Fourth runway in 2011	Third runway voted down in 2012	Promise to build no new way up to 2,043 m
Length planning & construction for capacity extensions	24 years	24 years for second runway	3 years for apron extension	Runway West: 22 years Fourth Runway: 10 years	13 years	NA
Mediation	Yes	No	No	Yes	No	NA
Capacity increase 1992 to 2021	84* to 78 = −7.1%	34 to 47 = 38.2%	42 to 48 = 14.2%	66 to 106 = 60.1%	68 to 90 = 32.3%	24 to 48= 100%

Source: Niemeier (2014) and Airport Coordination Germany

It is a challenge to gain acceptance and democratic support for major airport extensions. Instead of public planning, a "mediation" exercise was practised at two extensions. While it was of limited use in Berlin, it played a major role at Frankfurt. Overall, capacity could not be increased as fast and as much as airport managements initially sought, but that might have also been too early. Peak capacity, measured by the number of slots, has been increased since 1992 by 14–38% with given runways and by up to 100% with runway extensions, but Berlin is an exception. Scarce capacity is rationed by slots without secondary trading (see Chapter 4). The conflicts between the airports and their neighbouring communities in Frankfurt, Düsseldorf and Stuttgart have been more intense than in Hamburg (Niemeier, 2014).

2.3 Airport access

As airports have often been built at "suboptimal" sites, managing ground access can be difficult, as there are different interests and cooperation with the public authorities to be considered (Budd et al., 2011). From the viewpoint of society, ground access should be so managed that the total social travel costs (i.e., costs to all affected) for air passengers and freight are minimised across the hinterland of the airport. These costs include the private costs of the airlines, of the airport (aeronautical and commercial activities), and of surface transport (private car, public transport and rail). Most rail is not high speed and social costs and benefits include the negative externalities of congestion, noise and other emissions, as well as the positive externalities of agglomeration. These costs are influenced in the long run by land use. There are many different markets in the supply chain, of which some are monopolistic, competitive or publicly owned, and managed with different policies and with different forms of organisation (e.g., central versus regional authorities). Externalities are at best partially internalised. Hence, it is rather unlikely that the total travel costs are minimised, but to date that has not been thoroughly studied.

The transport system should connect the airport well to its hinterland. This includes a good connection to the CBD, in particular for business travellers. Most travel to and from an airport is by private car and for freight, by truck. At most airports, the local roads authority is responsible up to the airport threshold, and the airport from that point. The land-side access roads within the airport property are operated by the airport and belong to the airport's assets. While the airport can manage the traffic within its boundaries, outside it relies on the public authorities. Road congestion is the main potential factor in increasing total travel costs. At the margin, some travellers might switch to an alternative airport or to another traffic mode. The airport can only indirectly influence how well road congestion is managed, as the public authorities decide on the capacity of the road network and traffic management. Likewise, the airport has control over parking inside the airport boundaries, but not off site. Without congestion, car parking is also an instrument to gain passengers from overlapping catchment areas of competing airports. Pricing of car parks has, in principle, an effect on total travel costs and on the attractiveness of the airport. If parts of the catchment area are captured and offsite parking is an imperfect substitute, the airport has market power and can price these services above competitive levels and earn profits.[3] The large share of commercial revenues derived from highly profitable car parking suggests many airports have and use such market power (see Chapters 3 and 6).

Public transport is an alternative to the private car and can take many forms including commuter trains and metro, bus and taxi services, and ride-hailing options. These modes also have lower environmental costs per traveller than the private car. Good public transport thus increases the attractiveness of the airport and reduces the carbon footprint. Interestingly, some airports have themselves had to pay the cost of railway branch lines while, for others, the municipal authority has paid for extension or shared the cost with the airport. A recent example of airport provision of transport is the people mover at Bologna airport connecting to Bologna main train station. It was fully financed as a separate entity by the airport, which has been part-private since 2015.

Larger airports such as Amsterdam, Brussels, Frankfurt and Charles de Gaulle are directly connected to the train and high-speed network. This increases the catchment area, reduces the total travel costs from some regions and has a positive effect on passenger numbers. Furthermore, by creating an overlap of airport catchment areas, it can reduce the market power of airports (see Chapter 6).

Land use policy can create agglomeration effects and thus be an instrument of regional policy, in which the airport is central. City planning and regional marketing can provide areas for aviation-related economic activity. Schiphol's airport city is a well-known example which locates business services beside the airport's terminals. Firms locate here for better access to the airport, which acts as a multimodal hub. Such agglomerations improve information and labour skills. Firms get locked in to gain cost advantages. These effects are often called catalytic effects in Economic Impact Studies, but are poorly analysed even when they are not combined with dubious multiplier effects (see Chapter 9). The Schiphol model has been influential in other countries and has contributed to what Appold and Kasarda (2011) called "Aerotropolis".

Land use policy can also increase or reduce noise. Airports often complain that too many houses are built near the airport, and afterwards these new neighbours complain about noise. On the other hand, as land is scarce, the airport competes with housing, businesses and green field parks. Noise reductions make areas attractive. Noise caps for airports, combined with city planning, can integrate these conflicting interests and minimise noise conflicts. In practice, of course, this is difficult to do.

Airport surface access has not been the subject of much research. Button (2017) summarises the state of the art well:

> we have some idea of the relevant control variables that need to be considered in looking at surface access markets, but generally little idea of the scale of the interaction between it and airline markets. At the very least, the latter requires

knowledge of the reciprocal cross-price elasticities of demand between landside and airside which currently is largely missing.

More studied are the direct price elasticities of demand, a topic to which we turn next.

2.4 Demand characteristics and networks: the basics

Demand for airport aeronautical services is a derived demand, as is the demand for air transport. According to the theory of derived demand, a profit-maximising airline will demand an input from the airport up to the point that the marginal expense of that input is equal to the marginal revenue from using that input. This theory assumes that the airline and the airport are price takers. As we argued earlier, such intense competition is unrealistic, but it can serve as a benchmark for policy, because such supply chains maximise economic welfare. It also provides a suitable framework to discuss the empirical evidence on the demand for airport services. One can separate demand into demand for movements (commercial and general aviation) and demand for passengers and freight. In turn, passenger demand can be split up into distinct business, leisure and visiting friends and relatives (VFR) demands.

In general, the demand function for a good or a service relates to its own price, the price of substitutes, income and a number of other factors. The effect on demand is measured by the elasticity, which is the proportionate change in demand for a one percent change in one of the other variables (own price, price of substitutes or income). We apply this to airports—following the classic study on airports by Walters (1978)[4]—in two stages. We firstly present the findings on elasticities of demand for air transport (airline services) and secondly, we analyse the demand by airlines for airport services.

Walters reviewed passenger demand for air transport, especially with respect to the price elasticities of airfares. He argued that as the elasticities did not reflect the waiting and access times, they underestimated the true elasticities. The full elasticity was difficult to estimate precisely but his "conjecture is that the total (value of time plus fare) elasticity of demand is around 1.5 to 2.0, varying with the length of haul and the composition of traffic" (Walters, p. 130).

Walters wrote before the liberalisation of air transport. This liberalisation prompted further research into elasticities, which has been reviewed by Gillen et al. (2003) and Gillen (2017). Their analysis shows that the leisure segment is price elastic, and business travel is inelastic (see Table 2.2). Both relationships depend on the journey length. They also emphasise that the estimates do not measure underlying elasticity after removing the influence of factors such as flight frequency and service quality.

Table 2.2 shows that business travellers are less price sensitive than leisure passengers for both international long-haul and for short-haul traffic. On the other hand, there is no real difference in price sensitivity between domestic long-haul business or leisure travel. In a subsequent review of elasticities studies, Kincaid and Tretheway (2007)[5] point to another important issue. They argue that, in broad terms, the studies find an air travel price elasticity of around 1.3 but this is an overestimate because the research holds constant all of the routes, carriers, destinations and modes. In the

Table 2.2 Elasticities of air transport demand

Travel segment	*Median own airfare elasticities*
Long-haul international business	−0.265
Long-haul international Leisure	−0.933
Long-haul domestic business	−1.15
Long-haul domestic leisure	−1.12
Short/medium haul business	−0.73
Short/medium haul leisure	−1.52

Source: Gillen et al. (2003)

case of energy prices, which tripled between 2003 and 2008, the higher costs would have been passed on by all airlines and all transport modes. Allowing for the increase in the cost of energy changes the elasticity value from elastic to inelastic (−0.6).

Oum et al. (1992) report a price elasticity for freight in the range of −0.8 to −1.6. The value for the cross-price elasticity of passenger air transport is between 0.08 and 0.51. One of the main influences on the growth of air transport is income. Gillen et al. (2003) report an income elasticity of 1.39 (median) which is similar to that of Kincaid and Tretheway (2007), who found that a 1% increase in income would lead to a rise in air transport of between 1% and 2%. Textbook economics takes preferences as unchanging, but more advanced economics treats them as endogenous. An example from Scandinavia is "flight shaming" which may have reduced air travel, but it is too early to tell how long-lasting these effects are. So far, no elasticities of changes in taste have been reported.

Secondly, Walters (1978) analysed demand by airlines for airport services. He begins with the demand for commercial aircraft movements and concludes that "most of the expected increase in passenger demand may be absorbed by a rise in passengers per aircraft" (p. 132). In the 1970s and 1980s this was largely a result of the first generation of jet aircraft. Later on, liberalisation led to higher load factors due to revenue management by airlines. In the other direction, airlines tried to offer higher frequency with smaller aircraft. Getting these changes right is far from trivial in forecasting and we shall discuss later cases where forecasts for airport extensions were completely wrong.

Walters then discusses the effects of airport charges and responses of airlines. Here he observes

> in airport discussions the landing fee is often treated in a paradoxical fashion. On the one hand, it is often alleged that variations in the landing fee will have little or no effect on the demand for runway capacity, since the landing fee is but a small fraction—perhaps 2% or at most 7%—of the total costs of the trip. On the other hand, one hears, often in the same speech and sometimes in the same sentence, that, if landing fees are increased too much at Heathrow, London will lose much valuable traffic to Paris.
>
> (Walters, p. 132)

This observation has not lost its relevance. A 10% increase in airport charges leads, with an elasticity of 2 and a cost share of 7%, to a 0.14% reduction in passengers. Today, the share of costs might have a wider range between full services and low-cost airlines, but this hardly changes the result that the price elasticity of airport charges is essentially quite low. What can change the picture is the substitution effect, that is, if an individual airport increases airport charges, airlines may switch to other airports and passengers switch to other transport modes or to other tourist destinations. Here it is difficult to generalise. Perth airport (like many in Australia) has no good substitute and no competition from high-speed trains. The substitution effect can be almost completely ignored and hence the reaction of demand is strongly inelastic. The airports of Manchester and Stansted face a chain of substitutes from neighbouring airports such as Leeds, Midland and Luton. Here the substitution effect is relevant and can turn an inelastic reaction into an elastic one. The elasticity can even make it unprofitable for the airport to raise prices substantially. In this case, the airport would lack market power and not need regulation, which is why both Manchester and Stansted are no longer formally price regulated (see Chapter 6).

In analysing the demand for airport services, it is also important to distinguish between outbound and inbound traffic. Demand for outbound traffic is generated from the airport's catchment area. For business travel, Hamburg airport and Amsterdam airports have high outbound traffic, but Rhodes does not. High incomes also generate substantial outbound leisure travel from Hamburg and Amsterdam, but again not in Rhodes. VFR traffic in Hamburg is only minor, is moderate in Amsterdam, tiny in Rhodes, but large in Boston. Hamburg is not a hub airport and only about 2% of its traffic are transfer passengers, Rhodes is likewise purely a spoke, but Amsterdam airport is the hub of KLM and one of the largest hub airports in Europe.

2.5 Demand forecasting

Even without the exceptional shocks of the 2008–2010 Great Financial Crisis (GFC) and the 2020–2022 COVID-19 pandemic, aviation traffic forecasting is very challenging. "The central fact is that forecasts of airport activities are almost certainly wrong. Again and again, the reality of what actually happens at an airport at some future time differs significantly from what forecasters anticipated" writes Richard de Neufville (2017), an expert in airport planning. This raises the question of why so many forecasts have been wrong, and whether or not we should give up long-term forecasting. To seek answers, we firstly discuss the distinction between risk and uncertainty. Secondly, we analyse the logical structure of a forecast to better understand what it means to say that a forecast is wrong. We also explain the standard approach to forecasting air transport. Thirdly, we present a few cases where we discuss the reasons why those particular forecasts were wrong. We finish with the issues of airport location and access, and how to include this in forecasts.

1. *Risk and Uncertainty*. Clearly, forecasting for a period of 30 or even 10 years is a challenge, but so is forecasting some events which are near. It is more difficult to forecast the exchange rate in a few days or months than it is to forecast the

average temperature next summer. This is because some variables are more stable over time and others less so. Rothschild (1969) has criticised the habit of assuming that the distant future is always more difficult to forecast than the near future. So, it is relevant for airports to make the distinction between the ideas of risk and of uncertainty, described in the writings of Frank Knight and John Maynard Keynes. Risk describes future events to which we can assign a subjective probability of their occurrence to allow the use of net present value models. However, there is also uncertainty: events of which we do not have the knowledge even to attach any probability to them. To paraphrase Keynes, an investor in a new runway or a new greenfield airport does not know, over the next 20 years, whether there will be a war nor whether zero real interest rates will prevail.[6] Aircraft are usually used for decades, but will the engineering designs for 1200-seat aircraft be in use in the next 30 years? Milton Friedman (1976), who rejected Keynes's distinction between risk and uncertainty, would claim that investors have a subjective valuation of such mega aircraft and other factors over the investment horizon. John Kay (2016) has recently criticised Friedman: "If you had described your smartphone to Mr. Friedman in 1976 he would not have understood what you were talking about, far less been able to speculate intelligently on the probability that it would be invented or bought". Uncertainty, not just risk, remains a factor for long-term forecasting at airports. So, does uncertainty explain the errors in many airport forecasts are wrong? To answer that question, we must better understand what it means that a forecast is correct or incorrect.

2. *The Logical Structure of Forecasts and the standard approach to demand forecasting.* De Neufville (2017) asks the reader to test his claim that all forecasts are wrong by comparing the passenger forecasts with the realised ones. This is too simple. The forecaster makes forecasts for passengers and flights, let us say 15 years ahead. Consider the example of Hamburg airport. In 1995, about 13 million passengers were expected for 2010. But that year, the Icelandic volcano Eyjafjallajökul erupted, with cancellations of about 100,000 flights in Europe. Nobody foresaw such an eruption in 1995 when three traffic forecasts had been prepared for Hamburg airport (Table 2.3). The airport management used the BFUB/Fischer consultancy to forecast passengers and commercial movements. The local government used the consultancy MKmetric. In addition, there was a passenger demand forecast by the German Aerospace Centre (DLR) for all German airports (Niemeier, 2004).

One could argue that in terms of passenger numbers all these forecasts were right, or roughly right, but this neglects that the forecasts were based on certain assumptions. These included the absence of volcanic ash to allow the normal operation of air traffic control. Such external shocks are excluded by the *ceteris paribus* or other-things-equal assumption. Other assumptions included: the level of GDP in origin and destination markets, trade levels, and the degree of liberalisation and competition in the aviation market.

Given these factors, the forecasters apply the elasticities previously discussed to forecast derived demand (passenger and movement numbers). To evaluate the forecasts, we need to consider if the other-things-equal assumptions were realised: if the

Table 2.3 Forecasts for Hamburg Airport

Forecasts	*2010 passengers (millions)*	*% difference from outturn (12.9 million)*	*2010 commercial movements (thousands)*	*% difference from outturn (139 thousand movements)*
BFUB/Fischer	13.9	+6.8%	195	+ 40.6%
MKmetric	13–13.3	+0.2 to 2.6%	155–172	+11.7 to 24%
DLR	13.4	+3.4%	NA	NA

Source: Niemeier (2004)

inputs from other forecasts (GDP, etc.) were realised, and if elasticities and specification of the demand function also held. In the case of Hamburg airport, strong urbanisation and the rise of low-cost carriers were not foreseen. Without these factors, which each raised traffic, the forecasts would have overestimated demand. The GFC of 2008/2009 makes things even more complicated, as it is similar to a volcanic eruption. Macro economists are not good in forecasting such crises. Forecasts for airports usually assume a certain growth rate of GDP and do not pretend to forecast the business cycle. So, it could be that GDP was at a lower level than the forecasts assumed. This discussion shows that evaluating forecasts is not as easy as some authors might think and also not sufficiently discussed by air transport economists.[7]

For commercial movements or flights, the over-forecasting is very substantial. The number of commercial movements is important for the design of the runway and the apron. In the case of Hamburg airport, the forecasts were used to seek planning approval for an apron extension. The number of parking positions required depends mainly on the number and size of the aircraft. BFUB/Fischer extrapolated a trend of commercial movements independently from the passenger forecasts, which was completely unlikely. Average passengers per commercial movement were assumed to rise from 68 in 1995 to 71 in 2010. The alternative forecast of MKmetric derived the number of commercial movements from passenger demand. Given the supply of aircraft, which is largely known from the manufacturers, the model calculated profitable load factors for each destination and aggregated this for the number of commercial movements. MKmetric forecast 77–86 passengers per commercial movement for 2010. It warned that 155,000 movements would be a very optimistic number, with 172,000 movements an extreme case. At the time of the forecast, it was expected that liberalisation and competition would cause airlines to continue to increase load factors and to order larger aircraft. This proved true and by 2019 commercial movements had only reached 140,000 with 17.3 million passengers. The mistake was to assume that higher passenger numbers would mean higher movement numbers although Walters had already warned against this assumption.

3. *Wrong forecasts for German airport masterplans.* The case of Hamburg airport can be generalised to other German airports, as Thießen (2016) showed. That study examined the accuracy of the forecasts that German airports submitted to public inquiries into capacity extensions. In Figures 2.1 and 2.2, forecast growth

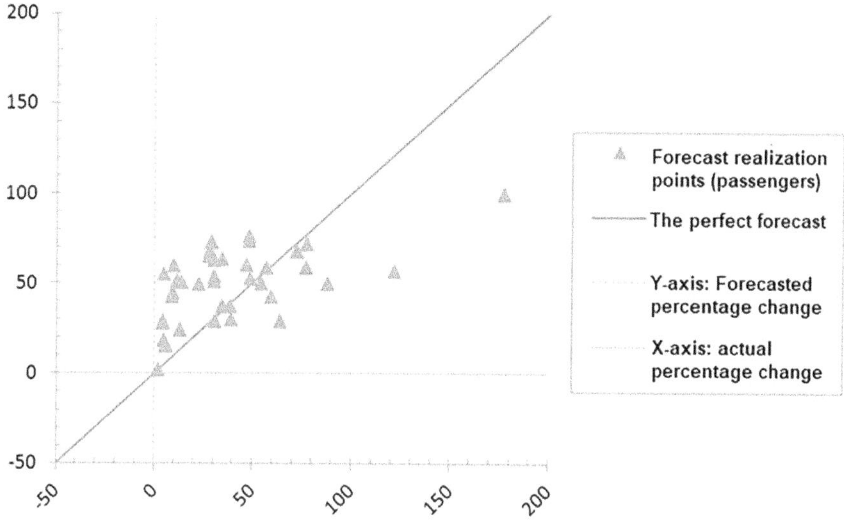

Figure 2.1 Evaluation of Forecasts of Passengers

Source: Thießen (2016)

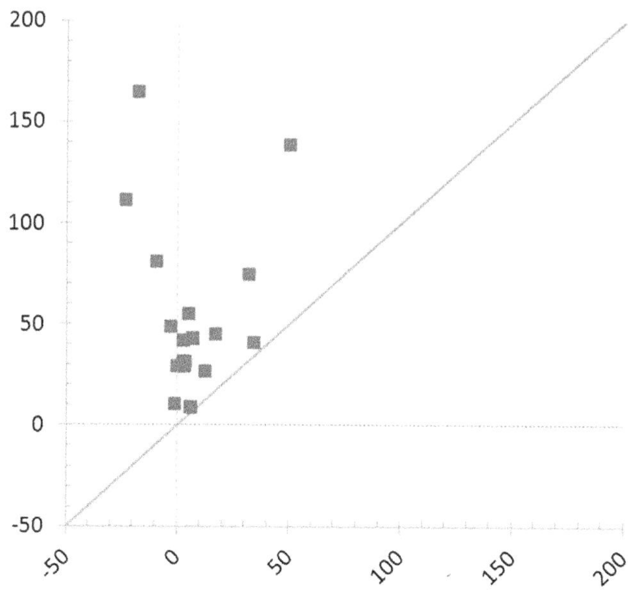

Figure 2.2 Evaluation of Forecasts of Total Movements

Source: Thießen (2016)

is reported on the vertical axis and the outturn growth on the horizontal axis. Accurate forecasts would lie on the 45-degree line and good forecasts would be clustered around that line (Rothschild, 1969). However, the results indicate a systematic bias: some two-thirds of passenger forecasts are too optimistic. This bias is even greater for aircraft movements. Not a single forecast underestimated the number of movements, all were overestimates, and some predicted growth at airports where movements declined.

For other European countries, there is no comparable study of the quality of forecasts, but there is evidence of substantial overcapacity. Maertens (2010) found excessive investment in runways for intercontinental flights at 80 of 115 secondary European airports. "White elephant" airports are found in Germany and elsewhere. Kassel Calden, a newly built airport between Hannover and Frankfurt, reached only 64,926 passengers in 2015, which was 20% of the expected worst-case forecast. For Don Quijote airport in Spain, 2.5 m passengers were foreseen for 2011 but it was used by only 100,000 passengers. In April 2012 the airport was closed, and more than one billion Euros were lost (Niemeier, 2016).

Systematic errors in forecasts are not explained by the uncertain future. They are the results of the political economy of such "mega projects". According to Flyvbjerg et al. (2003), forecasts for a large number of transport projects (not just airports) have been too high. This was not due to a lack of knowledge of the drivers of transport. The investors and proponents of these project commissioned overly optimistic forecasts that indicated the project's expected benefits would exceed its costs. Afterwards, the forecasts and the benefits fall short, but the costs were higher than expected. The failure of mega projects is explained by the lack of accountability in the public and private sectors. Flyvbjerg et al. argue that forecasts should be made by independent organisations subject to peer review.

Box 2.2 Controversies in Airport Economics: Will business travel return after the COVID crisis or will Zoom prevent this?

During the pandemic, everybody switched to online methods, such as Zoom, to communicate. Experts argue that a benefit of COVID has been this breakthrough in communication technology. Managers who used to fly to meet clients have used Zoom or similar services to discuss business. This has worked surprisingly well. Instead of flying to meetings in London or Singapore, managers are now thinking twice if this could not also be done online and, in less time, and at less expense for accommodation and for flights. Zoom seems to be the better alternative for internal meetings, but also for many external meetings in which personal contact is not essential. Business travellers are often key to making airline operations profitable. The network carriers target higher-paying business passengers with Frequent Flyer Programs to bind them to their airline. Low-Cost Carriers also try to take some share of this market. Business travellers are important for airports also. They fill airport lounges rented by the airlines. Airports have created conference centres and built hotels to cater to business traffic. Parking and other commercial revenues are strongly influenced by this group of travellers as well.

If Zoom is a good substitute for business travel, this segment of passengers will not return to pre-COVID levels, at least for a number of years. Forecasts for demand for airport capacity will need to be adjusted downwards, as will plans for extra capacity and quality of service would be different. Keith Mason (2020) of Cranfield University argued along these lines and produced some well-researched supporting analysis; but Marc Gaudry (2020), a leading transport economist and modeller of travel behaviour, reached the opposite conclusion. While for Mason, Zoom is a substitute for flying, for Gaudry Zoom is a complement for flying. He argues that while telecommunication has long been considered as a substitute for transport, the data show that transport in general has continued to grow over the last 100 years. He argues further that Zoom is not so different from existing forms of telecommunication and that we should not repeat the same forecasting mistake. No doubt people will use Zoom intensively, but this may also make them more inclined to meet and to see business partners. Researchers have used the internet to cooperate intensively and are working more closely together than when they had to rely on postal service, but this has just led academics to make more trips and fly to more conferences. So, is Mason or Gaudry right? We do not know yet, but the problem can be studied with the instruments of demand analysis.

2.6 Location, access and how to model this in forecasting

In forecasting air transport, and also airport demand, there has been a tendency to do this separately from other transport modes. The reason was that air transport, in particular long-haul travel, was not subject to any competition from other modes and that incorporating other modes would increase complexity without any gain. This then led to regression models that used only a few explanatory variables, such as GDP and Gross Regional Product, trade levels, and airfares for the different market segments such as business, leisure and VFR. With competition from high-speed trains and from other airports, this led to some further adjustments, but the basic framework remained the same. In the earlier discussion of the importance of location and access (section 2.3), Button argued that such models leave out a large number of factors which have a bearing on air transport demand for an airport. Mandel (2014), of MKmetric, has criticised this approach as forecasting air transport demand from airport to airport, while the correct approach should be between origin and destination of the travellers. For example, the business traveller making a return trip from a suburb of Heidelberg (near Frankfurt) to Brussels city centre has many options: car or public transport to the airport followed by the flight to Brussels and then taxi or metro or public transport to the destination; versus high-speed train; versus private car. and will base their decision on generalised transport costs. The many competing modes are not captured in models which focus only on the flights between the airports. Incorporating these options into the model would seem to be superior and offer more insights for airport managers, planners and politicians seeking to develop their airport and their region.

2.7 Conclusions

In many cases, the location of airports was chosen a hundred years ago. Airports can attract other businesses, thereby creating regional external economies. In many regions, airports compete with other land uses, and noise and other emissions lead to conflicts with neighbours. Adding capacity in metropolitan areas is therefore difficult. The planning process needs to be open and fair. It should be guided by techniques such as cost–benefit analysis, as was true for Sydney and London, but very often this is not the case. Managing well airport access with public and private transport is difficult. Parts of the supply chain are monopolistic, and congestion and environmental externalities are hard to internalise. It seems unlikely that the social marginal generalised transport costs are minimised.

Demand for air transport is derived from demand. Overall, demand for the services of airlines is income elastic and price inelastic, but this differs among market segments and also depends on the availability of good substitutes (e.g., high-speed rail). Airlines and passengers demand services from the airport. This derived demand is highly inelastic unless good substitutes (e.g., nearby airports) are available.

Long-term forecasts are often criticised for "always being wrong" but this overlooks the basis on which they are made. Forecasts are based on reasonable assumptions. These might not eventuate and turn accurate into a false forecast. The reverse may also happen. Uncertainty and risk play a major role in forecasting and limit our knowledge, but these cannot explain why airport traffic forecasts are over-optimistic to a large degree. Such forecasts reflect the tendency of the supporters of a project to overstate the benefits, which contributes to overcapacity at many airports and to "white elephant" airports. The quality of forecasts has not been studied thoroughly. One problem might be that forecasters model demand as if passengers travel from airport to airport. Models capturing the choices of passengers between different transport modes, from the origin to the destination, is likely to be superior, in particular if access costs are an important part of the generalised transport costs.

Notes

1 The locations of all current Irish airports were chosen around 1910 by the predecessor organisation to the Royal Air Force.
2 An interesting option is to split the traffic in national and international. In Tokyo the existing airport Haneda is for domestic flights while the new airport Narita is for international traffic. In Osaka Itami is for domestic and Kansai for international traffic.

3 Car rental concessions are similar to car parking. They are also an instrument to influence total travel costs and are part of the commercial revenues, but they play a rather negligible role in influencing road congestion.
4 For a review of the determinants of air travel demand in studies, see Wang and Gao (2021).
5 The most recent survey of air travel elasticities is the Master's thesis by Kucherenko and Dybvik (2019) which finds very similar values as Gillen et al. (2003) and Kincaid and Tretheway (2007).
6

> By "uncertain" knowledge, let me explain, I do not mean merely to distinguish what is known for certain from what is only probable. The game of roulette is not subject, in this sense, to uncertainty . . . The sense in which I am using the term is that in which the prospect of a European war is uncertain, or the price of copper and the rate of interest twenty years hence, or the obsolescence of a new invention, or the position of private wealth owners in the social system in 1970 . . .. About these matters there is no scientific basis on which to form any calculable probability whatever. We simply do not know.
>
> "(Keynes, 1937, p. 213)

7 Exceptions are the OECD/ITF Roundtable "Forecasting Airport Demand" (OECD, 2016), the review of UK Airports Commission Forecasts by the International Transport Forum (OECD, 2015), and "Forecasting Air Transport" Joint Workshop organed by Airbus, DLR and G.A.R.S. Cologne (Thießen, 2016). In addition, forecasts are evaluated in price-cap regulation (Dublin Airport, 2006) as the forecast is an important factor setting the cap. There are incentives to deliberately over- or under-forecast traffic. In price-regulated airports, where forecast airport traffic increases the denominator of the price-caps and ceteris paribus, reduce the allowed charge, airports have a motive to understate future traffic (and airlines vice versa). But, when airports are planning a large increment of investment, they have the opposite incentive—to forecast large future increases in traffic, to justify the investment and to give the impression that future customers will be available to pay for that extra capacity.

References

Airports Commission (2015) *Airports Commission Final Report*, London, Airports Commission, July

Appold, S J and J D Kasarda (2011) "Seeding Growth at Airports and Airport Cities: Insights from the Two-Sided Market Literature", *Research in Transportation Business and Management*, 1, 91–100

Budd, T, S Ison, and T Ryley (2011) "Air Surface Access Management: Issues and Policy", *Journal of Airport Management*, 6, 80–97

Button, K (2017) "The Other Side of an Airport's Two-Sided Market: Issues in Planning and Pricing Airport Surface Access", *European Journal of Transport and Infrastructure Research*, 17, 442–456

De Neufville, R (2017) "Airport Systems Planning and Design", in L Budd and S Ison (eds), *Air Transport Management*, London, Routledge, 62–93

Dublin Airport (2006) "Dublin Airport Passenger & Aircraft Movement Demand Forecast Report", Ref DAPF06/01, available at www.aviationreg.ie/_fileupload/Image/PR_AC2_PUB5_DAA_TRAFFIC.pdf

Flyvbjerg, B, N Bruzelius and W Rothengatter (2003) *Megaprojects and Risks—An Anatomy of Ambition*, Cambridge, Cambridge University Press

Forsyth, P (2014) "Air Capacity for Sydney", in *Expanding Airport Capacity in Large Urban Areas*, Roundtable Report 153, Paris, International Transport Forum, OECD Publishing, 61–83

Friedman, M (1976) *Price Theory*, Chicago, Aldine

Gaudry, M (2020) "A Letter to the Scientific Advisory Board of the European Aviation Conference Prompted by Communications-Based Adjustments to COVID-19 Conditions", November, available at www.researchgate.net/publication/344465082_Covid-19_and_the_long-term_implications_for_the_business_travel_market_Has_Zoom_and_Teams_killed_business_travel

Gillen, D W (2017) "Aviation Economics and Forecasting", in L Budd and S Ison (eds), *Air Transport Management*, London, Routledge, 23–40

Gillen, D W, W G Morrison and C Stewart (2003) *Air Travel Demand Elasticities: Concepts, Issues and Measurement*, Ottawa, Department of Finance, Government of Canada

Kay, J (2016) "The Enduring Certainty of Radical Uncertainty", *Financial Times*, April 5–July 19, available at www.ft.com/content/ec5520c4-fb23-11e5-8f41-df5bda8beb40

Keynes, J M (1937) "The Ex Ante Theory of the Rate of Interest", *Economic Journal*, 47, 663–669

Kincaid, I and M Tretheway (2007) *Estimating Air Travel Demand Elasticities*, Vancouver, InterVISTAS

Kucherenko, A and J S Dybvik (2019) *Price Elasticity of Demand in Air Passenger Transport Markets: A Meta-Analysis*, Master thesis, LOG950 Logistics, Molde, University of Molde

Maertens, S (2010) "Drivers of Long Haul Flight Supply at Secondary Airports in Europe", *Journal of Air Transport Management*, 16, 239–243

Mandel, B (2014) "Contemporary Airport Demand Forecasting: Choice Models and Air Transport Forecasting", in *International Transport Forum Discussion Paper*, Paris, OECD

Mason, K (2020) "Covid-19 and the Long-Term Implications for the Business Travel Market: Has Zoom and Teams Killed Business Travel?", available at www.researchgate.net/publication/344465082_Covid-19_and_the_long-term_implications_for_the_business_travel_market_Has_Zoom_and_Teams_killed_business_travel

Müller, J (2021) "A Case Study of the Politics of Airport Construction: The New Berlin Airport", in A Graham, N Adler, H-M Niemeier, O Betancor, A Antunes, V Bilotkach, E Calderón and G Martini (eds), *Air Transport and Regional Development Policies*, London, Routledge, 240–267

Niemeier, H-M (2004) "Capacity Utilisation, Investment and Regulatory Reform of German Airports", in P Forsyth, D Gillen, A Knorr, W Mayer, H-M Niemeier and D Starkie (eds), *The Economic Regulation of Airports*, Aldershot, Ashgate, 163–189

Niemeier, H-M (2014) "Expanding Airport Capacity under Constraints in Large Urban Areas: The German Experience", in *Expanding Airport Capacity in Large Urban Areas*, Roundtable Report 153, Paris, International Transport Forum, OECD Publishing, 107–141

Niemeier, H-M (2016) *Aviation 30 Year's Ahead—an Economist's View*, Sejong, KOTI 30th Anniversary International Seminar, Sejong National Research Complex Auditorium, August 24

OECD (2015) *Forecasting Airport Demand, Review of UK Airports Commission Forecasts and Scenarios*, ITF Roundtable Reports, Paris, OECD Publishing

OECD (2016) *Airport Demand Forecasting for Long-Term Planning*, ITF Roundtable Reports, Paris, OECD Publishing

Oum, T, W G Waters and J Yong (1992) "Concepts of Price Elasticities of Transport Demand and Recent Empirical Estimates", *Journal Transport Economics Policy*, 26, 139–154

Rodrigue, J P (2020) *The Geography of Transport Systems*, 5th ed., London, Routledge

Rothschild, K (1969) *Wirtschaftsprognosen: Methoden und Probleme*, Heidelberg, Springer

Thießen, F (2016) "Forecasts of German Airports Development—Lessons Learned from Two Most Active Forecasters", presentation given at Forecasting Air Transport, Joint Workshop organed by Airbus, DLR and G.A.R.S. Cologne, October 5–7, available at www.garson line.de

Thompson, D, S Perkins and K Van Dender (2014) "Executive Summary", in *Expanding Airport Capacity in Large Urban Areas*, Roundtable Report 153, Paris, International Transport Forum, OECD, 7–44

Walters, A A (1978) "Airports-An Economic Survey", *Journal of Transport Economics and Policy*, 12, 125–150

Wang, S and Y Gao (2021) "A Literature Review and Citation Analyses of Air Travel Demand Studies Published Between 2010 and 2020", *Journal of Air Transport Management*, 97, 102135

3 Costs and market structure

3.1 Introduction

The cost and market structure nature of the airport industry is a controversial one among industry and policymakers, and among economists. The airline body IATA (2009, p. 9) argues that "Airports and ANSPs do possess market power and natural monopoly characteristics" while ACI-Europe, a representative body for airports, states that

> airports used to be considered as something akin to natural monopolies. But airports must now compete with each other for passengers and airlines which have significantly more choice than in the past. . . . The result is a more competitive and dynamic airport market.
>
> (Copenhagen Economics, 2012)

If airports are natural monopolies, competition between them will not be feasible, but if they are not, competition is feasible. Economists have a well-developed theory of natural monopoly which has been widely accepted, but the empirical results are controversial.

Before dealing with this controversial topic, we turn to less controversial issues. We firstly provide a broad description of the main cost elements of an airport. Thereafter we consider the short run and discuss the high fixed and low marginal cost nature of airports that have excess supply. We also treat the case of excess demand which give rise to delay and congestion costs. Then we look at the long run and explain the concept of natural monopoly, discuss various aspects of this theory, in particular economies of scale, scope and density, the difference between fixed and sunk costs and the lumpiness of airport investments, the growing importance of commercial revenues at airports with implications for airport costs, and the role of barriers to entry and exit. Thereafter we summarise the results.

3.2 The cost elements of an airport

Like other businesses, airports use capital, land and labour to produce output and have to pay for these production factors. These expenditures are more or less well

DOI: 10.4324/9781003156901-4

documented in the yearly accounts of airports. But these bookkeeping costs are only part of the economic costs of an airport. Bookkeeping costs are explicit costs and are historical. Economic costs are forward looking and decision orientated. They are based on the opportunity cost principle—that is, they measure the costs of a good by the alternative uses that are forgone by producing this good. They consist of explicit and implicit costs of airport activities, including the cost of delays and congestion which we shall cover later, as well as the external costs, such as noise and other environmental emissions, which will be discussed in Chapter 8.

Accounting reports show that airports invest a lot of capital in runways and terminals. These costs also include the cost of the land, but in a number of cases the land has been given free or at a low, subsidised price. Runways have to fulfil certain safety and operational criteria. Their configuration depends on the markets that airlines want to serve. Aircraft such as the Airbus 320 or the Boeing 737 need runway lengths of between 1800 and 2500 metres. Long-haul aircraft need at least 2700 metres of runway length. According to Maertens (2009), the costs of a new runway or an extension of an existing runway in Germany ranged from €267 to €10,000 per square metre for projects at the beginning of the century. The large cost differential is explained by the difference in the cost of land, including its preparation. Such costs can be extremely high, such as for the planned new runway of Heathrow airport which crosses a motorway. The costs of terminals also differ substantially. Starkie (2010) has given evidence that small regional airports in the UK have terminals which are modularised in case of growing passenger numbers, but can also be closed and used for alternatives if traffic falls sharply. The other extreme is represented by a large terminal such as Terminal 5 at London Heathrow which cost about £4.3bn. in 2008. The configuration of terminals depends also on the future traffic they are designed for. Aircraft, in particular the A380, need a different terminal layout than normal wide bodies. While in small regional UK airports, baggage can be handled by hand, Terminal 5 has a fully automated baggage handling system. Terminals may also be designed to suit different airlines. A full-service carrier requires higher quality lounges and minimum connecting times compared to a low-cost carrier. A few airports have differentiated their terminals and offer low-cost terminals to gain a competitive advantage. These terminals can be much cheaper than the others.

Accounting reports also reveal that airports spend a lot on wages. A substantial part of the labour costs is for safety and security. Another important factor is ground handling. In Austria, Germany and Italy, airports offer these services themselves while in other countries ground handling is outsourced and provided by airlines or third-party handlers. Ground handling is relative labour intensive, but it is a business with low margins and low wages. The treatment of ground handling explains to a large degree the substantial difference between airports in the share of labour in total costs. In Amsterdam Schiphol wages are 17%, and in London Heathrow 21%, much lower shares than at Frankfurt and Vienna, both at 47%. There are different degrees of outsourcing among European airports, but also among airports in different world regions. US and Canada have outsourced many more activities than their European counterparts. Accounting reports also show a large share of other expenses. This category partly reflects outsourcing, but even Frankfurt airport with relatively little outsourcing has a share of 37% for other services. These costs include water and energy, among others.

There is no standard for reporting airport costs, so that comparisons across airports involve substantial efforts. An early comparison was done by the Polytechnic of Central London in the 1980s. It reported costs of Western European airports consisting of labour (42%), capital (22%) and other costs (operational services, maintenance, and the costs of outsourcing; 38%) (Doganis, 1992). Doganis also pointed out the substantial difference with US airports, with shares for labour of 22%, for capital of 44% and other costs of 34%. This is due to the heavy involvement of airlines in airport management, with contracts for terminals and other activities which in Europe are done by the airports themselves (for the US, see Chapter 5). Even today the US has generally a lower share of labour costs, which is largely due to the fact that the public US airport system has not changed through privatisation and regulation as it has in Europe or elsewhere. In Europe, the cost structure changed through liberalisation of ground handling and through outsourcing. On average, the share of labour has decreased from 42% in 1990 to 33% in 2015, while the shares of capital and others have increased from 18% to 22% and from 41% to 45% (Graham, 2018).

From the perspective of economics, these accounting costs offer valuable information, but do not show how airports will efficiently adjust their outputs to an increase or decrease in demand. To understand this, we analyse airport costs in the short and the long run. In the short run at least one of the factors cannot be adjusted but is fixed. Over time, the adjustment becomes easier and in the long run all factors are variable. The distinction between short and long run is a theoretical distinction—short and long are not referring to a particular period of time such as one or five years.

Before discussing how costs vary, it is helpful to distinguish some aspects of cost, which may be relevant in the short run and the long run (Baumol, 1987; Silvestre, 1987). These are:

- *Economies and diseconomies of scale.* A firm experiences economies of scale when it can double production without doubling its costs, so that unit costs are lower as the firm gets larger. Diseconomies of scale are the reverse and occur when costs rise proportionately faster than production.
- *Indivisibilities.* An indivisibility is an input that can only be provided in fixed units. The obvious airport example is the runway. An airport can have a single runway, or two runways, but not 1.5 runways. As a result, costs are discontinuous; unit costs probably fall as output is increased and the fixed costs of building the runway are spread over a larger output, but once capacity is reached, costs rise sharply as an additional runway is needed.
- *Specialisation.* The size of the market determines the division of labour. Larger firms allow for more specialisation and also for more outsourcing.
- *Economies of scope.* Economies of scope are reaped if the firm saves costs by producing two or more products jointly, rather than separately. This is also the case of cost complementarities which reduce the marginal cost of one good if more

of the other good is produced. A good example is the hub and spoke networks of airlines, which are driven less by scale, but more by scope economies.

- *Economies of density* occur when, for example, the traffic at an airport increases and larger aircraft, which have lower unit costs, can be used to provide a service.
- *Scarcity of factors.* With increasing size, it might become increasingly more expensive to get the necessary inputs for large firms. The classic example is land, which is more expensive in populated areas.
- *Sunk costs.* These are costs which, having been expended, cannot be recouped. A good example is the cost of building a runway. If the airport is not used, the cost of building it cannot be recovered.

3.3 Cost in the short run

In the short run, some productive factors used at an airport cannot be adjusted; terminals and runways take a considerable time to build. Additional labour can be employed but infrastructure cannot be increased in the short run. Hence, runways and terminals are taken as fixed (see Figure 3.1). Furthermore, when runways and terminals are increased, this is possible only in large increments. Runways are "indivisible". One runway can serve 170,000–215,000 aircraft movements. It is not possible to produce an additional output of say 20,000 movements with 0.1 runway. The same holds for terminals, though to a lesser degree (see later). Airports have high fixed costs relative to other industries. The cost of producing one more unit of output, the marginal cost, is rather low if the airport has spare runway and terminal capacity. An additional movement causes some wear and tear to the runway, which needs to be guided by air traffic control at the airport and served by ground handling

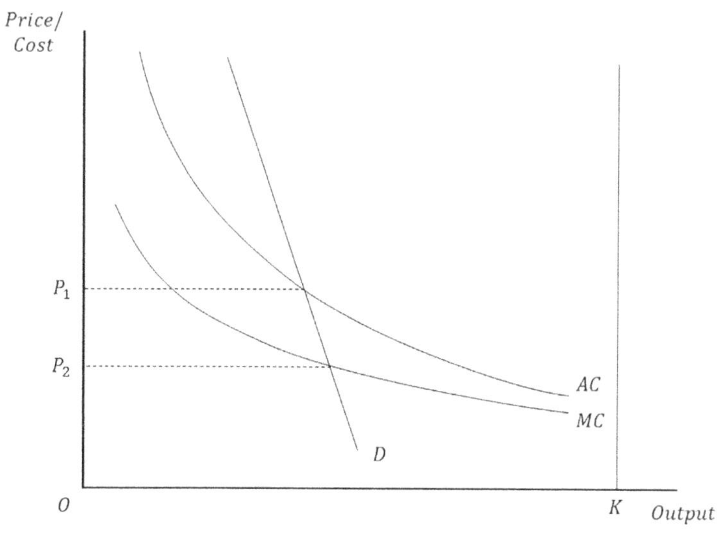

Figure 3.1 Short-run Average and Marginal Cost for an airport with abundant supply

and other services. The marginal costs for small and large aircraft are in general similar. The costs of landing an Airbus 350 do not differ much from an Airbus 320. The long-run capital costs required to serve some larger aircraft are high, as they need an upgrade of the runway and terminal, but once these investments have been made the marginal costs are similar to those of a narrow-body aircraft.

The typical way to represent short-run costs in most industries is by means of a U-shaped curve. The high fixed costs, low marginal cost nature of airports, combined with a sharp indivisibility as runway capacity is reached, make airports' costs different (see Figure 3.1). Suppose marginal cost is low and constant, but average cost though falling is above marginal cost even at capacity, K. This has some important implications. As the marginal cost is well below the average costs, setting a price at marginal costs does not cover total costs and leads to a deficit unless the deficit is covered elsewhere—for example by the taxpayer. If the objective is to maximise the overall net benefits from having the airport, and also cover costs, airport can do this by differentiating prices, for example by charging more to price inelastic airlines (see Chapter 4). In practice, this can be done through weight-related prices.

Airports' fixed costs become obvious when output falls to such a low level that the airport has to close. The variable factors and costs can be reduced. In a well-functioning economy, workers leave the airport and find jobs in other businesses. But runway and terminal costs cannot be reduced. If the runway and the terminals cannot be used for an alternative purpose, then these fixed costs are sunk and lost forever. Runways and terminals represent "relationship specific" investments that have value only in a specific relationship, namely with airlines. If airlines find it unprofitable to use an airport, then the capital invested in an airport is sunk. Airlines and airports have many things in common. Both have high fixed costs. The difference between airports and airlines is that aircraft are "capital with wings"—that is, they are fixed costs, but in case a route becomes unprofitable these fixed costs are not sunk because the aircraft can be redeployed on other routes. This is not the case with a runway or a terminal. Of course, this picture is somewhat simplified. Airlines which built up hubs have also relation-specific investments, and their hub investment would be sunk if the airport closed. Likewise, some airport land could be used for other economic purposes. But these exceptions do not invalidate the broad point, that the capital costs of airports are sunk but those of airlines are not.

Now let us turn from the shutdown case to the opposite, when demand to use the airport is growing. If demand curve shifts outward, the airport can increase its output. To make matters manageable, we shall concentrate on marginal and variable costs only (fixed costs are added later). There is an important additional aspect, namely delay and congestion costs. As the airport has less spare capacity, delay costs faced by airlines and passengers mount up. Costs will be high at the peak, when capacity is at a premium, and low when capacity is ample.

In Figure 3.2, we have added the marginal delay costs to the marginal operational or monetary costs so that the marginal costs are now increasing. In Chapter 4, we discuss how best to ration demand via charges or slots when capacity is scarce.

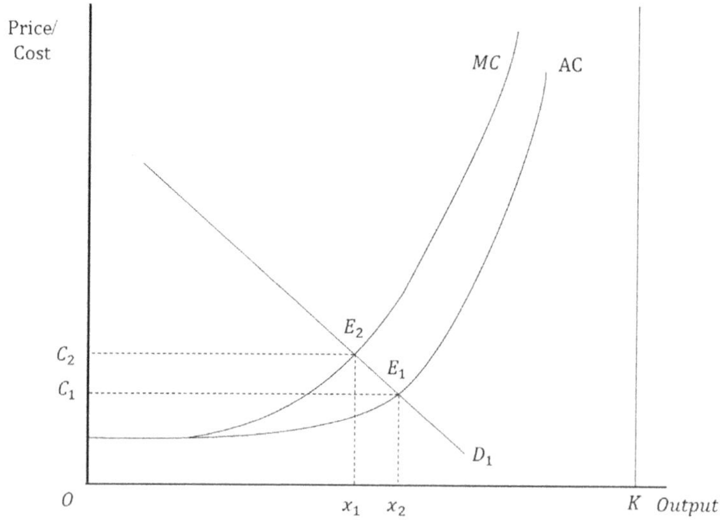

Figure 3.2 Short-run Average and Marginal Cost for an airport with excess demand

This model can be extended. Capacity does not have to be completely fixed. It might be possible to add capacity by enlarging the apron or allowing off-ramps. Terminal capacity can be extended through modularisation. This might lead to higher marginal and average costs. The costs for commercial activities are partly related to the terminal costs.

There are only a few empirical studies of the short-run costs of airports (Table 3.1). All of these studies concentrate on the operational or monetary costs of the airports, and they do not estimate the delay or congestion costs, which mainly fall on the airlines and their passengers rather than airports. Ülku et al. (2017) analyse 41 Norwegian and 26 French airports for the period 2002–2010. These are small airports of between 5,000 passengers and 7 million passengers per annum. Average operational costs fall rapidly as traffic increases, in particular, for airports with fewer than half a million passengers. Pels et al. (2010) analyse 36 airports in Europe, Asia, Australia, US and South Africa for the period from 1993 to 2000. The airport size ranges from 4 m to 56 m passengers per year. These studies exclude costs for ground handling and commercial activities such as car parking. Pels et al show that average operational costs decrease with an elasticity of 0.5 over the whole output range—in other words, costs fall by 0.5% for each 1% increase in traffic. The number of passengers is the most important cost driver.

Falling short-run total average costs are also found by Voltes-Dorta and Pagliari (2012) for 194 worldwide airports, and by McCarthy (2014) for 50 US airports. Marginal costs are below average costs (see also Hankimov and Mueller, 2014; Nunez-Sanchez et al., 2020), as long as there is sufficient capacity. If demand reaches capacity of the runway or the terminal, delay and congestion costs become important.

The empirical studies are summarised in Table 3.1. They cover monetary costs.

Table 3.1 Short-run costs of airports

Study	*Period*	*Sample of Airports*	*Inputs*	*Output*	*Method*	*Results*
Hakimov and Mueller (2014)	1998–2007	9 German airports	Staff costs, Other operating costs, capacity of runway	PAX, movements, freight	Short-run cost function	Marginal costs are below average costs
Pels et al. (2010)	1993–2000	36 airports in Europe, Asia, Australia, US and South Africa	Operational costs Assets as fixed factor	PAX, Movements	Short-run cost function	Average operational costs are decreasing with an elasticity of 0.5
McCarthy (2014)	1996–2008	50 US airports	Labour, outsourced maintenance, and repair and airport operations. Runways as fixed input	Movements	Variable Cost Function	1% increase in departures increases short-run operating costs by 0.27%. Large hubs have 25% higher average than medium hubs, but 20% lower marginal costs.
Nunez-Sanchez et al. (2020)	2009–2014	25 AENA airports	Labour, other operating costs, and terminals surface fixed input	PAX, sum of maximum take-off weight	Variable Cost Function	Passenger cost elasticity of 0.257, marginal costs below average costs
Ülkü et al. (2017)	2002 and 2010	85 European regional airports	Labour, other operating costs, and runway length as fixed input.	PAX, Freight	Regression analysis	Average operational costs are decreasing
Voltes-Dorta and Pagliari (2012)	2007–2009	194 worldwide airports	Labour, materials, terminal surface. Runways as fixed inputs	PAX commercial revenues, cargo, movements	variable cost function	Falling short-run average costs

Source: Articles as indicated

3.4 Costs in the long run and natural monopoly

In the long run, all factors are variable and have sufficient time to adjust. At some point, the capacity of the airport can be extended, and/or a new airport can enter the market. In competitive markets the firms are small and there are no barriers to entry. But in airports, where important assets are indivisible, growth might not mean a set of competing airports but instead lead to a natural monopoly with barriers to entry.

Theory of natural monopoly

Natural monopoly is defined as a situation in which a single (large) supplier would have lower average costs than would a number of (smaller) suppliers. Thus, a single supplier is more cost-efficient. Moreover, if such a market initially has many suppliers, the largest one could undercut the prices of the remainder (while still earning profits) and put them out of business. Such an industry cost structure will tend towards monopoly (hence the term "natural" monopoly). As a monopoly, the large firm will possess market power—the ability to set prices higher than cost. Graphically, such as in Figure 3.3, natural monopoly occurs when the demand curve intersects long-run average costs on a declining part of the LRAC curve. However, natural monopoly may apply even without falling LRAC which, on its own, would lead to an underestimate of the range of a natural monopoly.

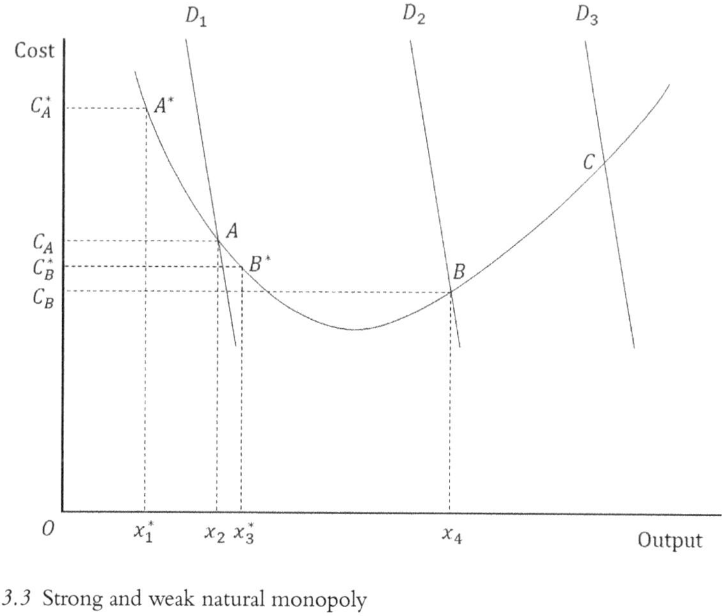

Figure 3.3 Strong and weak natural monopoly

In fact, economies of scale are a sufficient, but not a necessary, condition for natural monopoly. If there are economies of scale over the full output range, then the cost function is subadditive. This means the output can be produced with lower costs by one firm than by two or more. Two firms of equal size would produce the output with cost of point A*. Hence the production technology creates a natural monopoly. But the conditions for a natural monopoly are also fulfilled if the economies are exhausted and diseconomies set it. This is called a weak natural monopoly. In Figure 3.3, point A would be a strong natural monopoly and point B a weak one, while from point C onwards more competitors can be sustained. At point B LRAC is increasing, but two firms of equal size have higher costs of B*.

Airports are multi-product firms—they produce aeronautical services, but also retail, hotel and other services. So far, we have analysed the case of an airport producing a single output. In the multi-output case, it is also possible that all products are produced without economies of scale, but economies of scope reduce average costs and make the cost function subadditive.

Empirical evidence for natural monopoly of airports

The empirical evidence on the shape of the LRAC curve has led to different interpretations (see Table 3.2). The early studies of Doganis and Thompson (1973) and Doganis et al. (1995) suggested that economies of scale run out at a level of 3–5 million passengers. These studies became very influential and led to a consensus that the minimum efficient scale (MES) was in the range of 3–5 million. Tolofari et al. (1990), who suggested an MES of 20 million passengers, were rather neglected. The consensus was questioned with the studies of Pels (2000) and Main et al. (2003), and then with a series of studies by Martin and Voltes-Dorta (2008, 2011), which showed that economies of scale were not exhausted even at 80 million passengers. An MES of this magnitude would certainly imply that most airports are strong natural monopolies.

Before reaching this conclusion, we have to consider the study by Bottasso and Conti (2012). Bottasso and Conti criticise the approach of Martin and Voltes-Dorta, arguing that their method implicitly assumes that the airports can easily adjust their capacity to meet demand. Given the lumpiness of investment, this seems too strong an assumption. Bottasso and Conti argue that airports usually have spare capacity and falling short-run average costs. They suggest using a different method, and to derive from the short-run cost function estimates of the long-run average costs. They have done so for a sample of 24 UK airports for 1994–2005. According to their study, long-run average costs decline up to a scale of 6m passengers, but diseconomies of scale set in after 14 million passengers. The study reminds us to treat empirical results cautiously. Bottasso and Conti (2012), Bottasso et al. (2019) have so far not extended their research to cover non-UK airports, and this, among other aspects,[1] makes it difficult to generalise their results.

Table 3.2 Long-run average costs of airports

Study	*Period*	*Sample of Airports*	*Inputs*	*Output*	*Method*	*Results*
Doganis and Thompson (1973)	1969–70	18 UK airports	Total, capital, maintenance, labour, administrative and operating cost	WLU	Parametric	L-shape cost curve with decreasing average costs up to 3 million.
Tolofari et al. (1990)	1979–1987	7 BAA airports	Labour, Equipment, residual factors, Capital	WLU	Parametric	Economies of Scale until 20.3 million WLU
Doganis et al. (1995)	1993	25 airports thereof 12 European	Labour Capital	WLU	Parametric	L-shape cost curve with decreasing average costs up to 5 million
Salazar de la Cruz (1999)	1993–1995	16 Spanish airports		Passenger	Non-Parametric	Decreasing average costs up to 3.5 million passengers, increasing from 12.5 million
Pels (2000)	1997	35 European airports		Air traffic movements (ATM) and Air Passenger Movements (APM)	Non-Parametric	Average airport of 12.5 Mio. Pax & 150 000 APM operates under constant returns to scale for ATM & increasing returns for PAX
Main et al. (2003)	1988–2001	27 UK airports		WLU and passengers	Parametric	Sharp decreasing costs up to 4 Mill PAX & 5 Mill WLU. Weak decreasing costs up to 80 Mill Pax.
Main et al. (2003)	1998–2001	44 airports of TRL data set		WLU	Parametric	L-shape cost curve with decreasing average costs up to 90 million WLU
Vogel (2005)	1990 to 1999	47 European airports		Passenger	Non-Parametric	Increasing economies of scale of up to 4 million terminal passengers
Jeong (2005)	2003	94 US airports	Labour and other expenditures	WLU and pax	Parametric	Economies of Scale present until 2.5 million pax or 3 million WLU

(Continued)

Table 3.2 (Continued)

Study	*Period*	*Sample of Airports*	*Inputs*	*Output*	*Method*	*Results*
Martin and Voltes-Dorta (2008)	1991–2005	41 International Airports	Capital, labour and materials	WLU, ATM and commercial revenues	Parametric	Economies of scale are not exhausted at any level of output yet reached (83 Mio. PAX)
Martin and Voltes-Dorta (2011)	1992–2008	161 International Airports	Labour, material, capital costs, terminal floor area, warehouse area, runway length, number of gates check-in desks& full-time	Domestic and international PAX, Commercial ATM, Commercial Revenue, Tons of cargo	Parametric	Economies of scale are not exhausted below 90 Mill. PAX. Economies of scope between domestic& international traffic and aviation and non-aviation business activities
Martín et al. (2011)	1991–1997	36 Spanish airports	capital, Labour and materials	WLU, ATM and commercial revenues	Parametric	MES of 25,6 WLUs
Bottasso and Conti (2012)	1994–2005	24 UK airports	Labour, other opex, capital as quasi-fixed input	ATM, pax, cargo, commercial revenue	Parametric	Scale economies up to 6 Mill pax, diseconomies of scale after 14 Mill pax
McCarthy (2014)	1996–2008	50 US airports	Labour, outsourced services, runways as quasi-fixed input	ATM and WLU	Parametric	Mean airport with increasing scale economies at 11 Mio WLU and 129000 ATM
Botasso et al. (2019)	1994–2008	24 UK airports	capital, labour and materials	ATM, pax, cargo, commercial revenue	Parametric	MES at 5 million pax, no scope economies except between national and international pax

Source: Articles as indicated

In interpreting these research findings, we suggest a number of reasons why the MES has shifted over time. Firstly, output is much higher today. Early studies (Doganis and Thompson, 1973; Doganis, 1992) did not have airports of 50–80 million passengers to include in their sample. Secondly, the size of aircraft and higher load factors also mean that the MES increases.[2] Figure 3.4 illustrates this effect for the airports of Glasgow, Heathrow and Gatwick. The average passenger load at the three airports has quadrupled since the early studies, turning a 3–5 million threshold into 12–15 million. The MES estimate would be substantially greater if Dubai airport was included, since it is an airport at which the A380 accounts for a large share of movements, and aircraft below the size of a Boeing 777 are regarded as relatively small.

Larger airport size reflects rising demand for airports which increases economies of density and scope. Early studies probably also had more airports with spare capacity. These airports have since expanded—moving down the short-run average cost curve—and now record lower average costs. The later studies reflect the new data and lead to a higher estimate for the MES.

A number of issues remain to be fully investigated:

- The definition of output in many studies is a problem for two reasons. Firstly, the most common output measure is the workload unit (WLU). This combines passengers and cargo into one number. The mix, however, is arbitrary, since the production processes for each service differ substantially. Secondly, the output of commercial (non-aeronautical) activities is very often disregarded; Bottasso and Conti (2012) is an exception. By focusing on only a part of the airport business (aeronautical services), many studies neglect the multi-output character of airports.
- The sources of economies of scale are insufficiently analysed or understood. Do they stem from the runways or from the terminals? Baggage systems for ground handling might be a good example of product-specific costs which lead to falling average costs, but how important are they? Studies do not have to say much about the sources of scale economies (Kamp et al., 2007).
- Studies of other industries have identified factors like labour costs relative to firm size, as well as bureaucracy and incentives, as sources of scale diseconomies. For example, it seems plausible that wages are higher at Hamburg airport than at the smaller Hannover airport, even allowing for differences in productivity. Furthermore, in other industries, larger firms find it increasingly difficult to set incentives and monitor workers and managers. However, these effects have not been studied for airports so that we do not know much about the diseconomies of scale.
- The cost and scarcity of land is difficult to capture in empirical work and there is evidence that land is not properly priced. Government subsidies or the provision of public land to the airport free or below the market price, lowers measured capital costs and leads to underestimation of scale economies. Other airports are constrained in regard to land. Forsyth et al. (2019) noted that Sydney Airport can increase output but at high cost. Melbourne airport, on the other hand, has spare land and more can easily be purchased. Parallels in Europe are easy to find: there is evidence that Heathrow airport, like Sydney, faces diseconomies in expanding whereas Charles De Gaulle airport is similar to Melbourne.

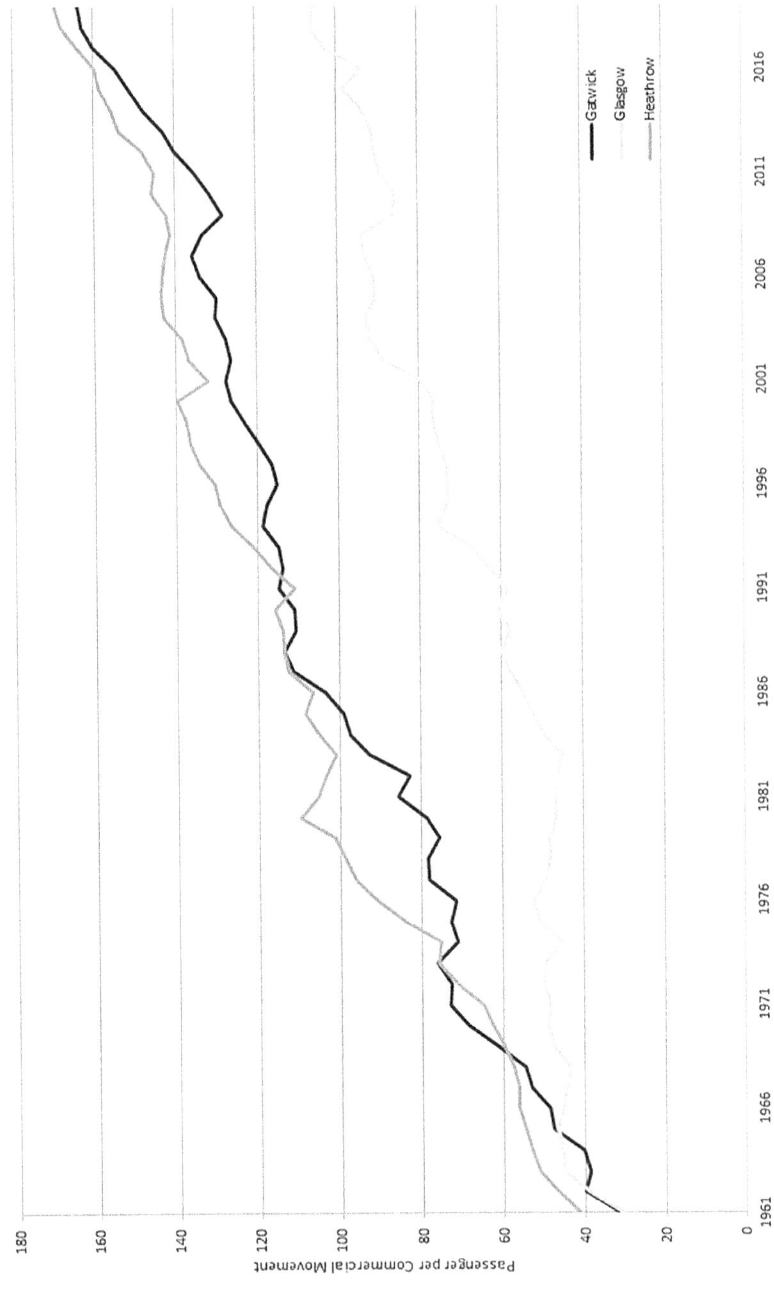

Figure 3.4 Development of Average Passenger Load

Sources: CAA, UK

- Costs measured in these studies are only the private costs of airports, not costs borne by airlines (longer aircraft taxiing times) or passengers (more walking for passenger to reach the departure gates). Other omitted costs are noise and GHG emissions and delays, which can be very large. Under natural monopoly, some of these external costs might be important but others (e.g., noise) might not be.
- Economies of scope, and the multi-product nature of airports. The studies cited analyse airports as if they produced only commercial flights and freight. Combining these as WLUs, airports are treated as producers of a single service. Scope economies are little analysed (Lechmann and Niemeier, 2013) except by Chow and Fung (2009), Martín and Voltes-Dorta (2008, 2011) and Martín et al. (2011). Chow and Fung (2009) consider Chinese airports and look at the possibility of scope economies between air passenger movements and air cargo movements. They concluded that economies of scope exist and have a significant effect on the airports' technical efficiency. Martin and Voltes-Dorta (2011) and Martín et al. (2011) also found scope economies between domestic and international services, and between aeronautical and nonaeronautical activities. To our knowledge, these are the only studies of scope economies. We consider this issue further in Section 3.6 as it relates to airport non-aeronautical activities.

3.5 The nature of airport investment costs: fixed and sunk costs and invisibilities

Starkie (2010) argues that it should not be assumed that airports face high fixed cost. He notes that even a beach might serve as a runway, and a simple tent or container as a passenger "terminal". In both these cases, the investment is not specific to a user, so the investment is not sunk. But these are exceptions, even at small regional airports. Runways have to meet ICAO standards and terminal quality standards for airlines and passengers. Public and private investors seek to avoid sunk costs by converting former military airfield into a commercial airport. While the runway is already built, the location may be far from densely populated areas. In order to compete against existing airports, an investor has to commit to a long-term relation-specific investment to realise the airport's full potential if airlines and others are doing the same (Biggar, 2012; Wolf, 2003). This is also true for major investments at existing airports (see Table 3.3). In particular, a network carrier has high sunk investments at its hubs. Airport capital costs can be partly moderated if airport planning is flexible (Burghouwt, 2007). In the end, it remains a risky long-term investment which, like other public utilities, needs trust. Gomez-Ibanez (2003, p. 3) comments: "The expensive, durable and immobile investments help make all parties—the company, its customers, and the government—vulnerable to opportunism and desirous of stability and commitment".

The specific character of airport investment has implications for competition and market entry. Let us suppose there is an incumbent airport and an investor considering entering the market. For the potential new entrant, the investment costs are not sunk prior to the investment, but they are sunk after the decision is made. The incumbent airport has already sunk its investment cost and could reduce charges to

Table 3.3 Costs of new runways

Airport & country	*Completion date*	*Runway length in km*	*Costs in current US $ m*	*Cost in current US $ per sqm*
Beijing, China	2008	3.8	5,187	1,365
Brisbane, Australia	2020	3.3	1,199	363
Tokyo Haneda, Japan	2010	2.5	7,800	3,120
Incheon, South Korea	2001	3.75	3,864	1,030
Incheon, South Korea	2008	3.75	3,458	922
Incheon, South Korea	2017	4.0	4,524	1,131
O'Hare, USA	2020	3.43	1,384	403
Seattle, USA	2008	2.59	1,463	564
Sunshine Coast, Australia	2020	2.45	364	148

Source: Websites of airports

the low level of short-run marginal cost, which does cover operational average cost but not total average costs. At such a low level of airport charges, the investment of the new entrant is unprofitable and, knowing that the incumbent can react in such a way, most likely it will not risk such an investment. The sunk cost characteristic makes the monopoly incontestable.

Adding capacity does not always involve indivisibilities. A shorter runway which could be extended later would capacity in two steps instead of one. Building terminals in tranches allows the airport to add capacity over time, lessening indivisibilities. Land has to be owned, or at least reserved, for the expanding airport. Even if managed well and efficiently, some indivisibility remains. While large and medium sized airports are usually profitable even if regulated, small and very small airports struggle with profitability. The EU Commission estimated that airports need 5 million passengers to break even, but this was only a rough estimate, not taking into consideration the substantial inefficiencies of airports in Europe.

EU airports appear to have wasted resources building runways for intercontinental traffic. According to Maertens (2009, 2010), such investments were unprofitable for about 75% of the 115 secondary airports with a runway length of more than 2700 metres. Almost 50% of the 115 airports had no regular long-distance flights at all in 2007. There is plenty of anecdotal evidence of this problem, and the incentives of traditional cost-based regulation are in line with these observations. Both factors would substantially raise the threshold to cover total costs. The European Court of Auditors concluded, in 2014, based on a sample of 20 airports, that airport infrastructure financed by the EU had produced poor value for money, and was not successful at attracting traffic with airports oversized (ECA, 2014).

The break-even point for operational costs has been estimated more rigorously (Adler et al., 2013). For the period 2002–2009, the level of traffic needed to break even was estimated to have doubled to 460,000 passengers due to rising security costs, but efficient airports could break even at 166,000 passengers because of their lower costs. The inefficiencies are partly due to airports not making enough use of multitasking, that is, giving staff different responsibilities at different times to reflect the flow of work. For example, a single employee might be available to the firefighting service when needed but carry out other work at other times. High operating costs might reflect technical inefficiencies, but given falling average operational costs, a lack of demand to exploit scale efficiencies.

The costs of additional airport infrastructure, especially runways (Table 3.3) and terminals (Table 3.4), are very large. But unlike an airport's wage bill or energy costs, the capital costs of airport investments are not financed immediately from airport revenues. Instead, the projects are financed from borrowings which are repaid over the expected useful life of the asset, which is generally decades. Each year, a fraction of the investment cost is repaid from airport revenues. These capital costs are composed of a depreciation charge and payments to those who provided the finance (shareholders and bondholders). These payments represent the "cost of capital" or the cost of funds to the airport. The annual capital cost of an airport's asset base therefore reflects conditions in financial markets and especially interest rates. For capital-intensive airports, capital costs are large relative to operating costs. For example, at London Heathrow airport, capital costs (including depreciation) were forecast in 2022 to amount over the following five years to £8 bn., compared to £6 bn. of operating costs (CAA, 2022). Airports' cost of capital is discussed further in Chapter 6.

Table 3.4 Costs for new terminals

Airport and country	*Completion date*	*Size in m²*	*Costs in current US $ m*	*Cost in current US $ per m²*
Adelaide, Australia	2005	75,000	279	3,724
Ankara, Turkey	2006	182,000	355	1,950
Madrid, Spain	2005	470,000	11,760	25,021
Beijing, China	2008	1,300,000	5,187	3,990
Cairo, Egypt	2008	200,200	599	2,989
Dubai, UAE	2008	522,122	5,985	11,462
Ljubljana, Slovenia	2021	10,000	27	2,723
Heathrow, UK	2008	984,252	7,049	7,161
New Orleans, USA	2019	90,000	700	7,441
Toronto, Canada	2004	464,000	4,104	8,844

Source: Websites of airports

Note: While runways produce aeronautical services, terminals provide both aeronautical (e.g., check-in and baggage handling) and non-aeronautical services.

Box 3.1 Controversies in Airport Economics: Why should we keep open airports that should not have been built in the first place?

The COVID crisis has hit the aviation industry hard including small regional airports which, even before the crisis, had problems covering their costs. Many of these airports are in public ownership and, as public bodies, have to balance their budgets. Discussions have started about whether these loss-making airports should be closed. In addition, climate change is of major concern and leads to demands that airports not be subsidised. Conclusion: close down loss-making airports!

In these discussions, it is important to apply the concept of sunk costs correctly. The capital invested in an airport is sunk once it is built. If the benefits, in the form of reduced travel times, exceed the investment and operational costs, including the externality costs, then an airport should be built as it increases economic welfare (On CBA, see Chapters 5 and 9). However, many airports have been built where the benefits do not outweigh the costs. "White elephant" airports are extreme cases, but there are many small airports which have a negative cost–benefit ratio. These airports should not have been built in the first place—but should they now be closed because they do not cover their costs? This could be another mistake; the capital is sunk and unrecoverable. A CBA made today would disregard these costs and investigate whether the benefits henceforward outweigh the operating costs. Operating an airport efficiently may not be that costly. Depreciation does not arise. There may be noise and emission costs to calculate, and these may indeed be high, but with the construction costs no longer relevant, a few daily flights might be sufficient to produce a positive cost–benefit balance. This would justify keeping the airport open although it ought never to have been built.

3.6 The increasing importance of commercial revenues

Over recent decades, non-aeronautical services have become a much more important part of an airport's product mix, sometimes over 50% of the total (though perhaps moderated in recent years; Graham, 2018). Airports now provide a range of services, some only distantly related to their core business, including ground handling, retail, car parking and provision of office and other space. The moves towards privatisation and commercialisation provided a stimulus to retail; airports are sometimes described as "shopping malls with runways". The costs of these shopping malls are reflected in the costs of major terminals (Table 3.4) These developments are largely driven by demand complementarities for aeronautical and commercial services. Here we analyse the cost side, which has been less well studied.

This trend may have increased the economies of scope at airports, which would occur if an input was used to produce an aeronautical service that is also available to produce a non-aeronautical service. Processing passengers through a terminal is a cost of "aeronautical services". But the terminal also provides space that can be rented for commercial services at little or no additional cost to the airport. Providing check-in and baggage handling in a terminal close to retail is more cheaply done together than producing these services separately. Even if the shopping area is separate and located between two terminal buildings, economies of scope exist, insofar as the buildings are shared. Martin and Voltes-Dorta have recognised and quantified these effects. They argue that for airports with over 40 million passengers, a level at which other studies found no economies of scale, economies are still realised at an elasticity of 1.46 because of "the joint production of aviation and commercial outputs" (Martin and Voltes-Dorta, 2011, p. 124).[3]

3.7 Costs, market structure and barriers to entry and exit

Economies of scale and scope affect the market structure of airports. If airports have strong or weak monopoly, in the long run, only one airport would serve the relevant local market. If economies are exhausted at low levels relative to demand, more airports can be sustained in the market. In this case, airports can reach the MES and have no cost disadvantage competing in the market. An oligopoly with few airports, or even a perfect competitive market, could emerge in the local market, at least in theory. Applying the theory, we need to be aware that airports have been built in the past as public utilities, but also to serve the military. As we argued in Chapter 2, history matters for airport location. What has emerged are regional markets with only one airport (e.g., Stuttgart) or a few airports (London). On a national level, these regional markets of airports overlap.

Barriers to entry may be classified as structural, strategic or legal. If the airport has a natural monopoly, the barriers are structural, and entry is not possible. If the incumbent airport chooses to deter entry through pricing and other measures, the barriers are strategic as they depend on the strategy of the airport. If the state has given the airport special rights, these are legal barriers. Structural barriers have been discussed earlier, so that we can turn to the evidence of airports trying to deter entry. One barrier might be predatory pricing, but as far as we know few if any airports have been accused of predatory pricing; an exception could be BAA's pricing of Stansted airport below marginal costs to compete against Luton airport (Starkie, 2004).

A more likely barrier is a monopoly granted by the state. The state can grant an existing airport a monopoly by not permitting other airports to be built and operated in close vicinity. In the case of a natural monopoly, this might be efficient. Granting monopoly rights can be a legitimate policy (see, e.g., patent rights), but it need not be. If demand is strong enough, two or even more airports can be sustained. In such a case granting monopoly rights to one airport might lead to inefficiencies and prevent effective competition. In 1985, Starkie and Thompson (1985) recommended breaking up the BAA monopoly in the London region, but it took more than 20 years for policy to follow this recommendation. Malina (2010) also argues that some regional public authorities in Germany have created market power through joint ownership of airport. So far, no separation has occurred and indeed under the privatisation processes, investors try to monopolise markets and prevent entry. In the case of the new Berlin airport, the public owners shut down three existing airports, refused to give the operational rights to a small regional airport in the wider metropolitan area and instead, erected one large monopoly airport. Other multi-airport cities like Paris, Rome and Milan are operated by one owner.

The construction of new airports, as well as the conversion of military airports into commercial airports, is subject to planning and environmental restrictions. As with monopoly rights, planning and environmental restrictions could be welfare-enhancing or welfare-reducing. The decision to allow the entry of a new airport should be based on a cost–benefit analysis due to the environmental and safety externalities of a new airport. In reality, restrictions might reflect not so much environmental concerns but rather the intention to shelter the incumbent airports.

According to Müller-Rostin et al. (2010) and Niemeier et al. (2022), the European airport industry is characterised by very low rates of entry and exit compared to other industries. In Europe, only 37 airport entries and 44 exits occurred between 1995 and 2019. Most were of publicly owned companies or municipal administrations and decisions therefore follow political, rather than economic rationales. Surprisingly, entry did not occur in markets with excess demand, but in markets with excess supply. Most new entrants were military airfields converted into civil aviation airports, indicating that the investors tried to reduce the risks of investing in long-term relation-specific investments.

3.8 Conclusions

Airports have, in both the short and long run, distinctive cost functions which are different from the usual U-shaped average and marginal cost functions of firms in competitive markets. In the short run, the marginal cost of operating an airport with ample capacity is very low and well below the average costs. Studies show that for a large range of output levels, the marginal costs stay below the average costs. If demand at peak times, and later at all times, leaves no excess capacity, delays occur. They are relatively costly and raise short-run marginal costs.

In the long run, airports could either become a competitive industry or a natural monopoly. This is an empirical question and also a controversial policy question. We show that the standard view that economies of scale stop at a level of 3–5 million passengers are not supported by more recent research. The standard view was based on an unduly narrow concept of natural monopoly and focused too much on economies of scale, ignoring the multi-product nature of airports. Economies of scope and cost complementarity have been studied less, but larger airports are driven by these economies as Martín and Voltes-Dorta (2011) showed. This leads us to the view that, in many local markets, airports are natural monopolies or weak natural monopolies. Such a view is also consistent with the patterns of market entry and exit of airports. For example, entry of airports in Europe has so far not occurred in areas with excess demand. This would have been more likely to happen if the MES was as low as 3–5 million passengers. Typically, in Europe, new entrants used former military airfields. Most of these entries have failed. There are no private investors who are willing to take the risk of building a brand-new airport in regions with excess demand. This conclusion does not contradict the observation that in many regions airports compete because of overlapping catchment areas. Airport locations are often determined by history and city location and at least in some European regions, such as Manchester and London, are so close that competition can work.

Notes

1 Bottasso and Conti (2017) do not discuss the study by Pels et al. (2010) of falling operational costs. They also do not critically discuss the special nature of the UK airports, where the large airports of Heathrow and Gatwick are land constrained, so that diseconomies are to be expected. In other less densely populated countries, this constraint might not be relevant. Furthermore, they do not discuss the Martin and Voltes argument that airports of 40 million Pax and more realise scale economies through economies of scope between commercial and aeronautical activities (see Section 3.6).

2 The MES is defined in numbers of passengers. This measure is very sensitive to factors which do not have much effect on costs. For example, assume that 3 million Pax could be served by 50,000 movements with an average aircraft size of 50 PAX. If aircraft size increases to 180 the 50,000 movements bring in 9 million passengers at similar costs.

3 But Botasso et al. (2019) argue that there are no scope economies and UK airport managers have overinvested in commercial activities.

References

Adler, N, T Ulku and E Yazhemsky (2013) "Small Regional Airport Sustainability: Lessons from Benchmarking", *Journal of Air Transport Management*, 33, 22–31

Baumol, W J (1987) "Indivisibilities", in *The New Palgrave: A Dictionary of Economics*, London, The Macmillan Press Ltd.

Biggar, D R (2012) "Why Regulate Airports? A Re-Examination of the Rationale for Airport Regulation", *Journal of Transport Economics and Policy*, 46, 367–380

Bottasso, A and M Conti (2012) "The Cost Structure of the UK Airport Industry", *Journal of Transport Economics and Policy*, 46, 313–332

Bottasso, A and M Conti (2017) "The Cost Structure of the Airport Industry: Methodological Issues and Empirical Evidence", in J D Bitzan and J H Peoples (eds), *The Economics of Airport Operations: Advances in Airline Economics*, vol. 6, Bingley, Emerald Publishing Ltd., 181–212

Bottasso, A, M Conti and D Vannoni (2019) "Scale and (Quasi) Scope Economies in Airport Technology: An Application to UK Airports", *Transportation Research Part A*, 125, 150–164

Burghouwt, G (2007) *Airline Network Development in Europe and Its Implications for Airport Planning*, Aldershot, Ashgate

CAA (2022) "Economic Regulation of Heathrow Airport: H7 Final Proposals—Summary", CAP2365A, available at https://publicapps.caa.co.uk/docs/33/CAP2365A%20H7%20Summary.pdf

Chow, C K W and M K Y Fung (2009) "Efficiencies and Scope Economies of Chinese Airports in Moving Passengers and Cargo", *Journal of Air Transport Management*, 15, 324–329

Copenhagen Economics (2012) *Airport Competition in Europe*, A report for ACI Europe, Copenhagen, Copenhagen Economics

Doganis, R (1992) *The Airport Business*, London, Routledge Chapman & Hall

Doganis, R, A Lobbenberg and A Graham (1995) *The Economic Performance of European Airports*, Research Report 3, London, Department of Air Transport, Colleague of Aeronautics, University of Westminster

Doganis, R and G F Thompson (1973) *The Economics of British Airports*, Report of an Investigation Sponsored by the Social Science Research Council, London, Social Science Research Council

European Court of Auditors (2014) *EU-Funded Airport Infrastructures: Poor Value for Money*, Luxembourg, Publications Office of the European Union

Forsyth, P, S Kok Fong, H-M Niemeier and T Ülkü (2019) *Is Total Factor Productivity at Major Airports Falling?* 23rd ATRS World Conference, Amsterdam, The Netherlands, July 2–5

Gomez-Ibanez, I (2003) *Regulating Infrastructure*, Cambridge, Harvard University Press

Graham, A (2018) *Managing Airports: An International Perspective*, 5th ed., Abingdon, Routledge

Hakimov, R and J Mueller (2014) "Marginal Costs Estimation and Market Power of German Airports", *Research in Transportation Economics*, 45, 42–48

IATA (2009) *Economic Regulation*, IATA Economics Briefing No. 6, Geneva, IATA

Jeong, J H (2005) *An Investigation of Operating Costs of Airports: Focus on the Effects of Output Scale*, Master's thesis, Vancouver, University of British Columbia

Kamp, V, H-M Niemeier and J Müller (2007) "What Can Be Learned from Benchmarking Studies? Examining the Apparent Poor Performance of German Airports", *Journal of Airport Management*, 1, 294–308

Lechmann, M and H-M Niemeier (2013) "Economies of Scale and Scope of Airports –a Critical Survey", *Journal of Air Transport Studies*, 4, 1–25

Maertens, S (2009) *Das Potential europäischer Sekundärflughäfen im Interkontinentalverkehr*, Göttingen, Vandenhoeck & Ruprecht

Maertens, S (2010) "Drivers of Long Haul Flight Supply at Secondary Airports in Europe", *Journal of Air Transport Management*, 16, 239–243

Main, B, B Lever and J Crook (2003) *Central Scotland Airport Study*, Hume Occasional Papers, 62, Edinburgh, Edinburgh University Press

Martín, J C, C Román and A Voltes-Dorta (2011) "Scale Economies and Marginal Costs in Spanish Airports", *Transportation Research Part E*, 47, 238–248

Martín, J C and A Voltes-Dorta (2008) "International Airports: Economies of Scale and Marginal Costs", *Journal of the Transportation Research Forum*, 47, 1–22

Martín, J C and A Voltes-Dorta (2011) "The Econometric Estimation of Airports' Cost Function", *Transportation Research Part B*, 45, 112–127

McCarthy, P (2014) "Airport Costs and Production Technology: A Translog Cost Function Analysis", *Journal of Transport Economics and Policy*, 48, 427–447

Malina, R (2010) "Competition in the German Airport Market—An Empirical Investigation", in Forsyth, P, D Gillen, J Müller and H-M Niemeier (eds), *Competition in European Airports*, Ashgate, Aldershot, 239–260

Müller-Rostin, C, H Ehmer, H-M Niemeier and J Müller (2010) "Market Entry and Market Exit in the European Airport Market", in P Forsyth, D Gillen, J Müller and H-M Niemeier (eds), *Competition in European Airports*, Ashgate, Aldershot, 27–46

Niemeier, H-M, S Kumar and T Ülkü (2022) *The Effect of Entry and Exit on Airport Competition in Europe*, ITEA Annual Conference, Rome, June 17

Nunez-Sanchez, R, S Hidalgo-Gallego and V Martínez-San Roman (2020) "Airport Charges and Marginal for Spanish Airports Before the Process of Partial Privatisation", *Transport Policy*, 99, 240–250

Pels, E (2000) *Airport Economics and Policy Efficiency, Competition and Interaction with Airlines*, Tinbergen Research Series 222, Amsterdam, Tinbergen Research

Pels, E, D Van Vuren, C Ng and P Rietveld (2010) "An Empirical Analysis of Airport Operational Costs", in Forsyth, P, D Gillen, J Müller and H-M Niemeier (eds), *Competition in European Airports*, Aldershot, Ashgate, 103–118

Salazar de la Cruz, F (1999) "A DEA Approach to the Airport Production Function", *International Journal of Transport Economics*, 36, 255–270

Silvestre, J (1987) "Economies and Diseconomies", in *The New Palgrave: A Dictionary of Economics*, London, The Macmillan Press Ltd.

Starkie, D (2004) "Testing the Regulatory Model: The Expansion of Stansted Airport", *Fiscal Studies*, 25, 389–413

Starkie, D (2010) "The Airport Industry in A Competitive Environment: A United Kingdom Perspective", in P Forsyth, D Gillen, J Müller and H-M Niemeier (eds), *Airport Competition: The European Experience*, Aldershot, Ashgate, 291–309.

Starkie, D and D Thompson (1985) *Privatising London's Airports*, Report 16, London, Institute for Fiscal Studies

Tolofari, S N, J Ashford and R E Caves (1990) *The Cost of Air Service Fragmentation*, Loughborough, Loughborough University

Ülku, T, V Jeleskovic and J Müller (2017) "How Scale and Institutional Setting Explain the Costs of Small Airports: An Application of Spatial Regression Analysis", *Zeitschrift für Verkehrswissenschaften*, 88, 39–65

Vogel, H-A (2005) *Privatisation and Financial Performance of European Airports*, 4th Conference on Applied Infrastructure Research, Berlin, October 8, available at http://wip.tuberlin.de/workshop

Voltes-Dorta, A and R Pagliari (2012) "The Impact of Recession on Airports' Cost Efficiency", *Transport Policy*, 24, 211–222

Wolf, H (2003) *Privatisierung im Flughafensektor: Eine ordnungspolitische Analyse*, Berlin, Springer

4 Pricing and capacity allocation

4.1 Introduction

The task facing an airport in the short run is to ensure that the available capacity is allocated efficiently. Pricing is crucial because it determines how well the airport delivers its services. This chapter presents a brief outline of the way airport services have been priced and capacity allocated in the past, recognising that, after a long period of little change, several new developments have been taking place over the past decade or so. We begin in Section 4.2 with a simple analysis of the basics of airport pricing; this is a model that is quite good at explaining the rationale of pricing at airports with ample capacity (which is most of them).

In Section 4.3 we turn to the more challenging charging issues for airports with scarce capacity. Medium to large airports tend to encounter problems of lack of capacity, leading to congestion and delays. How an airport prices its services can affect this, but airports have also relied on non-price mechanisms to ration demand. In particular, airports in most countries have used a system of airport "slots" to manage excess demand. We outline the basics of the slot system and discuss its advantages and disadvantages. A slot system alters the ways an airport operates, not always in expected ways. One of the main issues with slots concerns how they can be allocated: by auctions, trading or administrative means.

Finally, in Section 4.4, we look at the other side of the airport's operations, namely the non-aeronautical side. This covers the diverse services which airports provide, including retail, car parking, hotels and many other services. It is difficult to be systematic about pricing for these services, but one issue which underlies several of them is whether their pricing reflects the locational advantages which an airport possesses, or whether the airport is taking advantage of market power.

4.2 Pricing airports: the basics

We start by looking at the structure of the charges that airports implement. We can think about these charges in three ways. The first is the actual charging structures at airports. Secondly, at least to some degree, this structure will be different from the ideal or optimal structure, which is the one that is the most efficient. The efficient

DOI: 10.4324/9781003156901-5

charge might be chosen by an airport in the public sector, if its objective is to make the best use of the airport. A third possibility is the structure which maximises profits, which a private owner of the airport might well seek to achieve if allowed by regulators. Therefore, the actual structure and level of charges reflects both the ownership of the airport and the regulation that it is subjected to. Airport economic regulation is discussed in Chapter 6. The pricing and capacity allocation issue is considered here in a static sense; longer-run and dynamic issues are dealt with in Chapters 5 and 6.

Actual charging structures—What do airports do?

The broad principles of airport charging have remained the same for many decades and are based on the maximum take-off weight of the aircraft (MTOW) (De Neufville and Odoni, 2003). Different airports have slightly different structures, but around the world, the approach of weight-based charging has been present until the past decade or so. Sometimes airports charge less for domestic or short-distance flights, or more for international flights (which require more passenger processing).

An alternative to weight-based charges is to base them on the number of passengers carried by the aircraft. Weight-based and passenger-based charges are clearly similar, though not the same. A recent move towards passenger-based charging comes partly as a response to the expansion of LCCs, which have higher load factors than legacy carriers. Legacy carriers will pay less than an LCC operating the same weight of aircraft under passenger-based charging because they have fewer passengers. A passenger-based charge, and an MTOW charge for cargo aircraft, is perhaps a simpler system and this may be the reason why a number of airports have changed from weight-based charging.

Airports also set many further but lower charges to cover other aeronautical services: aircraft parking charges, security charges, charges for the use of ground power systems, fuel throughput charges, Air Traffic Control charges and noise charges. There are now pressures for airports to charge different amounts for aircraft which use fossil and sustainable aviation fuel or SAFs. There has also been a move for airports to unbundle their charges, and only charge the airline for what it actually uses.

There was a time when it was possible to determine what services an aircraft would be charged for by consulting the airport's charges schedule. This is becoming less true, as airports move towards discounting charges (InterVISTAS/ACI, 2022). Discounting has been used to attract airlines to the airport, or to open new routes. An airline may pay lower rates, for say, five years, if it offers a new service. The airport faces a balancing act since established customers will object if they see their competitors being offered lower charges. Related to this is a trend towards airports concluding (confidential) contracts (say, for five years) with airlines for airport services. Evidence from comparing published rates to estimated aggregate payments by airlines suggests that the discounts can be quite substantial.

How should airports set their prices?

Suppose that an airport is seeking to maximise the benefits of its services for the community. What pricing policy should it have? Suppose first that it has adequate capacity to serve all users, and later, it starts to run out of capacity and not every flight can be served when desired. Cost conditions are as described in Chapter 3; the simplest case is where the airport has some fixed costs to keep operations running, along with some variable costs, and that the variable costs are not very large—once the airport is operating, it does not cost much for it to take additional flights (this is a simplifying assumption).

When economists first looked at pricing for public enterprises, such as airports, they determined that the ideal or optimal price, which would maximise the net benefits of the airport, would be prices equal to marginal cost (see the discussion in the Appendix). This means that prices would be very low if capacity is adequate and the additional cost of handling a flight is low. The problem is that the airport will make a loss that will have to be covered in some way. This has been recognised as a problem in public economics for many years, and there have been several solutions suggested.

One solution is two-part pricing, in which there is a charge for access to the service, and a charge for use (Brown and Sibley, 1986). An example is electricity pricing, which involves a periodic fixed charge and a price for the quantity of electricity consumed. This approach has not been used at airports. An alternative is some form of "Ramsey pricing" (Brown and Sibley, 1986). This is named after Frank Ramsey, who, in 1927 suggested a practical way to cover a firm's costs with a minimum loss of output. This was to set prices according to the inverse of the elasticity of demand. Where the demand elasticity is low, set a high price—this will not have much effect on output. Where elasticity is high, set a low price, which has the effect of lessening the reduction in output. It is often queried how practical this rule is and whether it can be applied at airports.

In fact, the principle can be easily applied in airports. The Ramsey rule provides a rationale for weight-based or passenger-based pricing. Flights which are operated by small aircraft will have relatively few passengers and thus limited willingness to pay, while flights operated by large (longer distance) aircraft are likely to have high willingness to pay. Weight is a proxy for elasticity. The airport can cover its costs with least loss of output if it adopts weight-based pricing. This is not a perfect example of Ramsey pricing since the elasticity of airport demand depends on other factors, such as the nature of the traffic and the competitiveness of the routes served by the airport (Morrison, 1982). But the approach is a practical one, as well as an example of practice being ahead of theory. Similar pricing applied to railway charges as early as the 19th century.

The effects of Ramsey pricing are shown in Figure 4.1 (the Appendix discusses how to interpret the Figures). To simplify, suppose the average variable cost (AVC) is also the marginal cost (MC). There are fixed costs including land payments to the government, and average fixed costs are shown as AFC. Suppose that demand is given by D_1. In this case, it is feasible for the airport to set a uniform charge sufficient to cover its average total costs (ATC), but this charge would be high and well

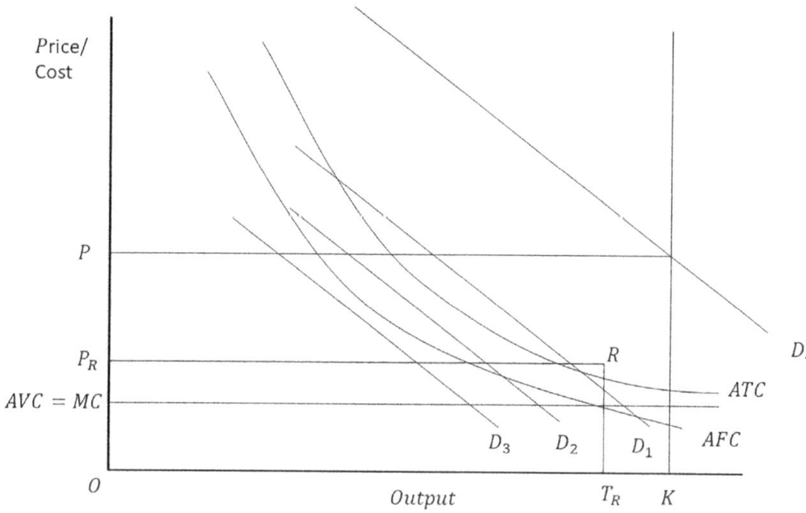

Figure 4.1 Pricing of Airports with abundant supply and with excess demand

above MC. As the most efficient price is MC, the high charges to cover costs would discourage the use of the airport leaving a lot of its capacity unused. If the airport imposes weight-based prices, it would be possible for it to cover its costs at an *average* price, PR, which lies above the demand curve D_3, and represents a price/output combination of R. This covers costs and enables a larger output of T, consistent with all users paying a price above marginal cost. In short, Ramsey pricing is a good "second-best" option. However, when the airport has inadequate capacity, the pricing problem is quite different.

Airport pricing with scarce capacity

Many larger airports have a shortage of capacity. There are examples in Europe, such as London Heathrow Airport and Amsterdam Schiphol, and in Asia, especially in Japan and increasingly in China, and in North America, such as New York La Guardia and Los Angeles. The pricing problem facing these types of airports is shown in Figure 4.1 (Rees, 1984). This is a simple representation, which abstracts from congestion and delays (which are added later). This figure shows a fixed capacity of K, and if demand is D_4, capacity is insufficient to cater to all of the flights that would like to use the airport. Thus, there is a rationing problem. The simplest solution is for the airport to set a rationing price P. This will be the ideal or efficient price, and it rations the available capacity to the airlines that are prepared to pay the highest price for it (the price the market will bear).

The average fixed cost of the airport is AFC, average variable cost is AVC, and average total cost is ATC. At price P the airport covers its costs and in fact is profitable. If so, there is no reason for Ramsey prices. Capacity is scarce, so the best price structure is to charge all users the same price. At this stage, theory and practice part company, since few airports, no matter how busy, set weight-based or passenger-based prices to ration demand. Capacity is allocated by other mechanisms, such as airport slots.

If demand exceeds available capacity, there may be a case for expansion, such as by building an additional runway. Airport capacity tends to be very lumpy[1] and can be expensive or cheap, depending on the location of the airport. Additional capacity changes the pricing problem. Soon after the new runway is built, the airport will have ample capacity again, but at higher fixed and sunk costs. The airport may need to use Ramsey or weight-based/passenger-based pricing to cover its costs. At this stage, the finance director and the economist will be pushing for different strategies. The finance director will want to keep prices high to cover its costs, while the economist will be pointing to the extra capacity of the airport and seeking to use it as much as possible. If the airport continues to grow, the most efficient strategy is to have low prices when the airport has ample capacity and to make up the temporary losses when the airport is once again facing a capacity shortage, when it is easier and efficient for the airport to raise its charges. Unfortunately, most finance directors and airport regulators do not see it this way and try to insist on the airport covering its costs year by year, regardless of the capacity situation.

Small marginal airports

Most airports are small and have ample capacity. Their problem is often one of viability if the airport is unable its total costs regardless of the level of charges. Using Figure 4.1, suppose that the demand curve for an airport is D_2—then there is no price at which the airport can cover its costs. It might be possible to set *average* prices high enough to cover costs using Ramsey pricing, and the airport would be able to survive without subsidy.

Another aspect of the viability question concerns sunk costs. What do the fixed costs of the airport consist of? It might be that they are costs which need to be paid every year to enable operation, such as council rates, government land rent and unavoidable, renewable contracts for maintenance. These costs are fixed in as much as they do not vary with the output of the airport. But other costs are sunk, for example, the costs of building the runway. Suppose that the fixed costs are all sunk. If demand is D_2, the airport would not be able to cover total costs, but it still might be able to cover variable costs and generate revenue sufficient to make a contribution to fixed costs. If demand is D_3 the airport will not be able to cover even all of its variable costs but it might be able to do so using Ramsey pricing.

It is also possible that the airport cannot cover its costs even with Ramsey prices (perhaps only one type of aircraft uses the airport, a typical situation for small airports). Is there a case for subsidy to ensure that a community is served by air transport? This could be true as there are benefits from the airport (and some costs are already sunk). To determine this requires a cost–benefit analysis (see Chapters 5 and 9). In this context, the consumer's surplus (see Appendix) is very relevant. Consumer's surplus benefits might well outweigh the costs of having the airport, providing a case for ensuring its survival.

Peak pricing

The situation depicted in Figure 4.1 is a simple one, and one way to move towards reality is to allow for peaks and troughs in the demand for airport services (Rees, 1984). There are some airports which are busy all day, like London Heathrow. However, the more common situation is where the airport is busy during a morning and evening peak, but not at other times. In Figure 4.1, assume that the demand at the peak is D_4 and the off-peak D_3. In the peak, capacity is scarce and must be rationed, but in the off-peak, capacity is ample. It may be that the profits in the peak are sufficient to cover the airport's fixed costs, and there is no need to use devices such as Ramsey pricing. The best price for the off-peak is one which just covers MC, so that the ample capacity is used fully and, to a degree, airlines switch flights to the off peak, if possible.

Peak pricing solutions are often advocated by economists as an efficient way of resolving capacity allocation problems and are used in other industries, such as hotels, electricity and telecommunications, not to mention airlines. In practice, airports have not used peak-off peak pricing differentials very much (but see Little and McCleod, 1972; Forsyth et al., 2021). There are several reasons for this and perhaps the strongest is that most airports with a peak problem also use slots to ration demand in busy periods, and the way that slots work is that they are equivalent to a form of peak pricing, meaning that the airport does not need to have a formal peak-off peak pricing structure. Airlines tend to oppose peak pricing (though they use it extensively themselves).

Pricing terminal use

Much of the analysis of airport pricing centres on runway pricing, rather than terminal pricing. Terminals can be very large capital investments, and they can be heavily used, leading to congestion and delays. This means that the same sorts of problems can be experienced at terminals as with runways. A difference is that while the marginal costs of runway use can be low, the marginal cost of terminal use can be quite significant. Within the terminal, there may be several labour-intensive processes (though many are being replaced by new technologies). In addition, many of the processes being done in a terminal are not done by the airport itself, but rather by the airlines or third parties. Normally, terminals are not priced independently, though, in setting the airport price structures, airports will take into account the implications for terminal services (e.g., to lessen terminal congestion). The move towards passenger-based pricing reflects this.

4.3 Busy airports with congestion: allowing for delays

Introducing delays

Anyone who travels to busy airports is familiar with delays as a fact of travel. With busy airports, it is not simply a matter of setting prices to allocate scarce capacity, but also to manage delays.

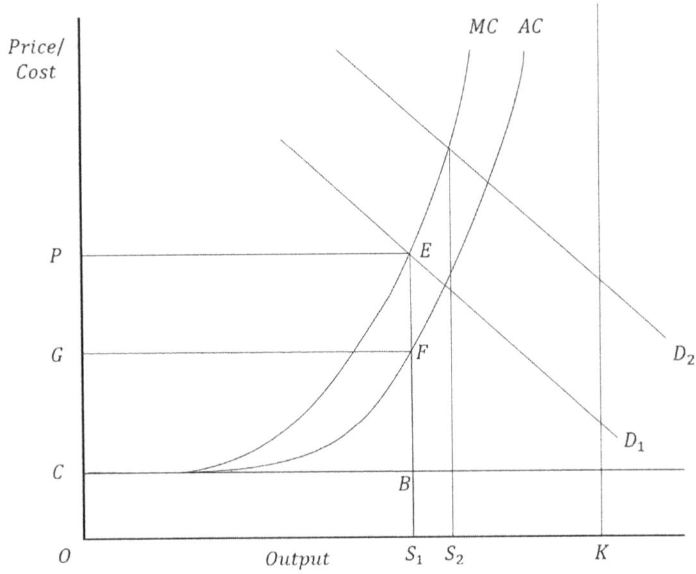

Figure 4.2 Airports subject to Delay Costs

In Figure 4.2, the airport is still shown as having a fixed capacity (say, 40 flights per hour). There are some variable costs of operating the airport if it is lightly used; these are shown by c. Airport congestion problem is like highway congestion. At first, when little used, delays are minimal. As usage increases, the average delay begins to mount. When the road reaches capacity, average delays can be very large (Walters, 1961).

In principle, the same is applied at airports.[2] As more flights try to use the airport, delays become very large, unless the airport manages its capacity in some way. Figure 4.2 shows two types of cost: one is the normal financial cost, and the second is the cost of delay. As the airport gets busier, delays mount, and close to maximum theoretical capacity, financial and delay costs will be very high. (In the transport economics literature, the combination of these costs is often called the "generalised cost".)

In Figure 4.2, two cost curves are shown, the average cost (AC) and marginal cost (MC). The AC curve includes both the overall financial and time cost that passengers and airlines face. The marginal cost curve lies above the average cost. Under congestion, an additional flight faces the same financial costs as all other flights, but it also makes things worse in terms of delay for other flights. Figure 4.2 is completed by a demand curve D_1. The airport can handle demand, but only at higher average and marginal cost. The price which will maximise the net benefits of the airport is P, which leads to S_1 flights being handled, which is less than the theoretical capacity of the airport. It would be possible to have more flights, but only at the expense of more delays, and a price P leads to the best combination of the use of capacity and avoidance of delays.

As with the simpler case of Figure 4.1, the ideal or optimal price can be shown. To maximise the overall benefits of running the airport, price should be set at marginal cost. Depending on how high the fixed costs are (for simplicity, not shown), this price may lead the airport with a substantial profit. While not eliminating delays, this price limits them. The case for marginal cost pricing of airports to reduce delays is much the same as the case for road pricing, as practised for many years in Singapore and now in central London. But it is rare for airport delays to be priced explicitly (and road pricing has been very slow to be adopted). There are some practical problems with marginal cost pricing, but these can be overcome. The main such problem is to identify the optimum E. While the financial costs of the airport are easy for the airport to determine, the delay costs, which depend on how the passengers and airlines value their time, are not. Estimates can be made of the value of time, and thus where the MC curve lies. Pricing at marginal cost is not an exact science, but is possible to make a ballpark estimate, and this is all that is needed to develop a tolerably efficient pricing policy.

It is also possible for airports to be priced at average cost. This is essentially what happens with most airports in the US. Average cost pricing means that flights bear the average delays of all flights, and the airport sets a price equal to the average financial costs of operation. It is an easy pricing policy to implement, but it has one big drawback, namely delays can be very large. It is not surprising that economists have advocated moving to some form of marginal cost pricing to lessen the delays (Morrison and Winston, 2008).

The situation in the US with airport delays can be much worse than Figure 4.2 suggests. In this figure, it is assumed that the airport has enough capacity to satisfy demand. But what if demand is much larger? The system adapts by simply allowing queues to develop, and if the flight due at 5 pm is caught in a queue, it may only get served at 5.30 or 6.30. In short, Figure 4.2 does not allow for flights to be banked up, something which can result in even larger delays. While marginal cost pricing of airports does encounter some difficulties, these are small compared to the waste which large unnecessary delays create.

Using slots to ration scarce capacity

The capacity at the busiest airports around the world is not allocated by either pricing or delays but by slots. This system operates in Europe, Asia and elsewhere and the Americas other than the US (exceptions are Reagan National in Washington and LaGuardia in New York). The basics of the slot system are simple (Gillen, 2008). Slots at preferred airports at preferred times can be very valuable. Airlines do not "own" the slots per se, but apart from some ambiguities, they tend to retain them over the years (see the Box at the end of this chapter).

The slot system developed in an ad hoc fashion, and now it is very much an established practice in air transport. Since slots are valuable, there is an allocation problem. The main way in which they are allocated is through "grandfathering", which means that if an airline is lucky enough to have a slot, it keeps it (subject to a "use it or lose it" rule). There are some situations in which an airline can lose a slot, if for example, it does not use it for an extended period; hence some airlines "babysit" slots for their partners, that is, operate flights to retain the slot. (This became a contentious issue in 2020, when airlines cancelled most of their flights because of a precipitous drop in demand.) The system is administered by local administrative committees in conjunction with the airlines and the airports. IATA holds twice-yearly slot conferences to enable airlines to swap and trade their slots.

The basics of the slot system are shown in Figure 4.2. The airport operates with the same cost curves as before, and same capacity limit. The main difference is that the airport declares a limit on the number of slots it will make available (say, 40 flights per hour for a single runway airport). It can choose however many slots it likes, but it will normally choose something less than the theoretical maximum capacity of the airport. It could seek to choose the optimum level of slots, which would be S_1. This would be equivalent to setting a price equal to the marginal cost. Of course, the airport will face the same problem it faced when estimating the marginal cost curve when setting a price equal to marginal cost (namely, estimating the cost of the delays to the passengers and airline). In practice, the airport will not try to explicitly calculate the marginal cost but will rather try to choose a slot limit which sets a balance between keeping delays down and making more slots available for the airlines. The slot system will thus determine the output of the airport and delays it faces, but not the price at which it sells its services. How it sets its slot allocation process then becomes important, and this determines how valuable the slots are.

A likely price at which an airport might sell its own services is its average monetary cost (often approximately equal to average cost—see Chapter 6). Airlines and passengers face two costs, as before, the cash or financial price of the airport, C, along with the average delay cost. Suppose that the number of slots is set such that the output of the airport is optimised, as though the airport had set a price equal to marginal cost. In fact, a price set to average cost, and a limit on slots of S_1, will not clear the market. Slots will be more valuable than the price the airport charges, and the slot price will be bid up. The market will clear at a price of P—this is what would happen if slots were traded openly. In Figure 4.2, if the slot limit, S_1, is set optimally, the price that the slots will be traded at is S_1E (= P), and this is made up of an amount S_1B (C) which is the amount the airport charges, BF which is the average amount of delay costs faced by the airlines and their passengers, and FE which is the difference between the average and marginal delay cost. FE is the "slot rent" or profit the airlines gain from possession of a slot; a slot is a valuable right, which enables the airline to earn profits. The profits are termed slot rents (like the rent from a valuable piece of land). Slot rents can be very substantial—a pair of slots at London Heathrow airport, one of the world's busiest, has sold for US$75m. There are several implications of these airport slots being so valuable, leading to airlines seeking to protect their slots, and other airlines seeking to obtain them.

Clearly, an important issue is how slot limits are derived. Very often it is government regulators who will decide on how many slots an airport may operate with. Under EU slot rules, the regulator should consult with a coordination committee at a given airport in regard to slot limits. One possibility is that the government regulator will seek to set the slot limits so that overall benefits from the airport are maximised (Forsyth and Niemeier, 2008a). The airport would probably like to have a high output, depending on its pricing freedom. For airlines, it is more problematic, since individually, they would like to have more slots (and a chance of gaining additional ones), but collectively, it is in their interest to have fewer of them (as they will be more valuable then). So, setting of slot limits is controversial. Adler and Yazhemsky (2018) have analysed the major slot constrained 17 European from 2005 to 2013 and concluded that the slot limit is too tight and the overall benefits could be substantially increased.[3]

The ideal slot limit also depends on demand conditions at the airport. It makes sense for a very busy airport to have a higher slot limit than a less busy airport, though this is at the expense of greater delay. Suppose (in Figure 4.2) that the demand for the airport grows from D_1 to D_2. To maximise overall benefits, the airport should have an initial slot limit of S_1 and later it should be raised to S_2. There will be greater delays as the airport grows, but there will also be greater traffic handled. If the airport price remains equal to average costs, there will also be higher slot rents in the second situation.

How slots are allocated

If slots are valuable, how are they allocated? There are three main answers to this question. The most widespread way of allocating slots is through an administrative procedure, such as grandfathering. Another way is through secondary trading, an approach which is only really practised in the UK. A third way which has occasionally been tried in the US is auctioning.

Slot auctions have some attractive properties. An auction means that the slot goes to the user prepared to pay most for it, so that there is minimal chance that the slot ends up with a user which does not particularly value it. The revenue from the auction will go to the airport or the government. There are problems with auctions, as auctions of telecommunications bandwidth have shown. For example—high and variable prices, and the "winner's curse" where the highest bidder pays too much (for a critique of slot auctions, see IATA, 2017).

The administered slot allocation system grew like Topsy. Before the 1960s, airports had adequate capacity, and airlines were able to get slots when they needed them. By the end of the 1960s, some airports such as London Heathrow and some US airports were having problems in catering for all the flights which wanted to use them. A small number of large US airports set up slot systems, though most US airports opted for a first-come-first-served queuing system, which operates to this day. Over time, more and more airports encountered capacity problems, and they set also slot limits. The system became institutionalised, and rules were developed. These included rules on how airlines could keep slots even if their demand for them changed. In particular, "use-it-or-lose-it" rules are usually in place. Slot rights are not a physical asset like aircraft and IT systems are, and airlines rarely include them in balance sheets (though they may if they were purchased from other airlines).[4]

The term "legacy airlines" is an apt term for the airlines which have been operating for much of the post-war period. These are the airlines which have a very substantial legacy of the slots at busy, highly demanded airports. Although initially these were not particularly valuable, with growing congestion, slots became more and more valuable. It is not surprising that most of the slots at the busy airports are vested in the legacy airlines such as British Airways, Lufthansa, Air France-KLM, JAL and US airlines, and smaller legacy airlines. From time to time there is some changeover in slot holdings, as airlines exit markets. Otherwise, slots are tightly held, and it is difficult for other airlines to gain slots. This leads to a situation where it is difficult for new airlines to obtain slots and operate services. It has been a particular problem for LCCs in gaining access to markets, though they have made a virtue out of necessity by going to (sometimes distant) secondary airports. However, when slots become available (perhaps when the airport adds capacity in the form of a new runway), the LCCs seem to be quite willing to use them (as Ryanair has done when slots at Frankfurt airport became available). For a discussion of the problems with administered slots, see NERA, 2004.

A problem of the administered slot allocation system is that it is bureaucratic and inflexible. Using modern optimisation techniques, Ribeiro et al. (2018) have shown in a number of case studies that slots can be better matched and capacity better utilised. Another problem with the current slot system is that the property rights in slots are only vaguely defined. Airlines can keep their slots as long as they abide by the slot rules ("use-it-or-lose-it") though these rules are incomplete. The vague ownership of slots gives rise to problems—see the Box at the end of this chapter. Another inefficiency is slot hoarding. An airline may have some slots for which it does not have a current use. Rather than offering the slots to the market, it will hoard them, intending to use them at some stage in the future. Airlines also "babysit" slots, as discussed.

A third way in which slots are allocated is through secondary trading. This means that airlines purchase slots from other airlines. The UK is the only country which formally endorses slot trading. When an airline decides to sell some slots, perhaps as a result of it wishing to operate fewer flights in a slot-constrained airport, other airlines bid for the slots. There is no formal auction, and often the trading is done confidentially (though clearly the seller and buyer are known, though not necessarily the price). When the US-Europe Open Skies agreement was concluded in 2007, several US airlines sought to purchase slots at London Heathrow. Heathrow is the UK airport in most demand, and it is no surprise that most of the trades have been at this airport and that the highest prices have been recorded at it. Several countries do not permit secondary trading. The EU has been ambivalent and has moved towards permitting slot trades should countries wish to allow it, moving away from its previous outright opposition.

Slots are sometimes exchanged in de facto trades. This happens between alliance partners and subsidiaries of airlines. An airline gives up some slots at one airport and receives other slots. Another de facto means of trading slots is where an airline buys another airline to gain access to its slots, as happened when Lufthansa bought BMI British Midland.

The positive feature of slot secondary trading is that it is possible for the airlines which can make the best use of the slot to gain it and use it, though the slot market is far from perfect. Whatever the initial means of allocation, auctions, grandfathering or trading, there can be a problem of slot dominance at specific airports—thus, for example, Lufthansa has the lion's share of slots at Frankfurt. Some have suggested that trading can facilitate an airline achieving slot dominance, with implications for dominance in the airline markets which are served by the airport. Slot dominance can also be present in airports with grandfathered slots, though the main objection to grandfathering is that there is too little, not too much, exchange of slots.

Slots and peak pricing

Slot markets create a form of peak pricing so that there may be little need for peak pricing (peak pricing may still be needed to ration scarce terminal capacity). Suppose that an airport is slot rationed, and that there are two periods, a peak and an off-peak period. The working of slots is shown in Figure 4.3 (using the simpler Figure without delays). The average variable cost is shown as C. There is a fixed amount of runway capacity, shown by K. Suppose that the airport is busy in both periods, and all of the available capacity is used in these periods. The all-up price for using the airport runways, including the airport charges and the slot rent will be P_1 in the peak period, and P_2 in the off-peak period. If there is secondary trading for slots, the value of the slot will be higher in the peak period than in the off-peak. The runways of many airports are full part of the day, but only part of the day. This is the case when

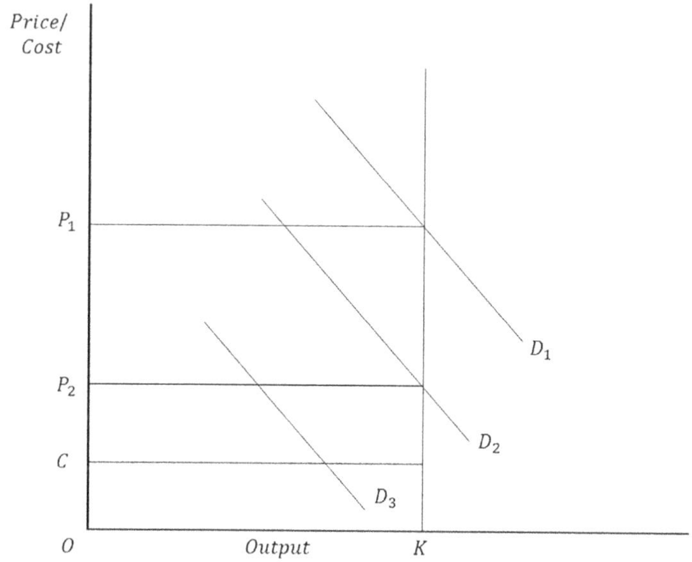

Figure 4.3 Peak/Off-Peak Pricing

demand is D_3 in the off-peak. If this is the case, slots will not have a rationing role in the off-peak, and the slot rent of an off-peak slot will be zero.

Weight-based charges, terminal allocation and pricing

The rationale for weight-based charges was to enable an airport with ample capacity to cover its costs at a minimum loss of traffic. If an airport faces excess demand, and has to ration traffic, then it should not have a problem in covering its costs and the rationale for weight-based charging disappears. If most flights impose the same cost on the airport, the most efficient charging approach would be to charge them all the same. This would avoid the curious situation of a very busy airport with a charging schedule that encourages the use of capacity by small aircraft at the expense of large aircraft (Forsyth and Niemeier, 2008b). This does happen at many crowded large airports which have not revised their charging schedule to reflect excess, not inadequate, demand. In an increasing number of cases, airports have at least recognised the problem and instituted minimum charges, which serve to discourage the very small aircraft from using their capacity at busy times (Forsyth et al., 2021).

Thus far, we have considered only runways. In fact, terminals as well as runways involve large fixed investments and both can face excess demand, or be empty for periods of the day. There is a terminal capacity rationing problem just as much as there is a runway problem. The capacity of the terminal is primarily set by the number of passengers it can handle. An airport may have ample runway capacity but scarce terminal capacity. In some cases, the declared capacity of an airport for slot allocation purposes may be to limit the use of the terminal, rather than the runway.

It is also possible that an airport has a peak problem for both the runways and terminals. The peaks may be at different times. For example, the runway peak would occur when there are many smaller, short-haul flights using the airport, and the terminal peak when large intercontinental flights are using the airport. The airport will have two distinct rationing problems to solve. One simple approach would be to rely on (runway) slots to ration the capacity of the runway, and peak per-passenger prices to ration the use of the terminal(s). London Heathrow airport, which has both a runway and terminal problem, uses slots to ration the runway use and a measure of peak pricing to ration terminal capacity.

Slots or prices—Which are better?

Slots are used in most of the world, and prices are very rarely used. The US queuing system is very inefficient. The other two approaches are potentially quite efficient. Economists typically recommend prices over quantitative solutions such as slots, though this preference is not always well grounded. Under specific circumstances, quantitative solutions can be more efficient than prices. If there is no demand uncertainty, prices and slots will yield the same results. This is shown in Figure 4.2—with demand D_1 and an (optimal) slot limit at S_1, the efficient price is the same as the price which would be achieved if the equivalent number of slots are traded.

But the world in which we live is one of uncertainty. The efficiency of the price and quantity solutions depends on how elastic are the demand and supply functions and how these functions vary under uncertainty. This issue was examined in detail by Weitzman (1974), and it has been applied to airport slots in 2008 by Czerny. If demand is uncertain, it may be difficult to set prices which are efficient and do not lead to high delay costs. It will be easy to set a slot limit which is tolerably efficient. In reality, the choice which most airports have made is to use slots.

We can sum up by noting some key features of the choice:

- Slots can act as a form of peak/off-peak pricing, ensuring fairly efficient use of the airport, especially if combined with per movements charges;
- Slots can be allocated efficiently—but they may not be, given that they are rarely traded;
- Airlines gain from slots, which avoid the need for high airport prices. But then they have the incentive to oppose needed increases in capacity;
- Airports like the use of prices, but typically are prevented from setting market clearing prices by regulators;
- Regulators like the use of slots, which provide them with a means of solving the scarce capacity problem while not imposing high prices which are opposed by airlines and possibly their passengers; but
- Passengers do not gain from the lower airport prices as they need to pay market-clearing ticket prices, embodying slot rents (thus claims by regulators that they are protecting passengers from high prices are hollow).

There is some use of prices to manage congestion, for example, to discourage small aircraft from using the airport at peak times. There is the possibility of using both prices and slots more generally, though so far there has been no case for doing this. Slots seem to be here to stay—the most promising reform will be to improve the efficiency of the allocation of slots, most likely by encouraging the trading of slots.

Some implications of slots

As we have emphasised, both prices and slots have a role in the allocation of airport capacity. The two work quite differently and have different implications for the ways airports, their airlines and their passengers are affected. We consider three aspects of difference.

Regulation and slots

Many airports which are slot limited are also price regulated (see Chapter 6). These are airports which are medium to large, are busy at least during the peak, and are considered to have some market power. To limit the use of this market power, governments often impose price regulations. The ostensible reason for this regulation is to protect airlines, and in particular, passenger interests from high airport charges set by airports with market power.

It is worth checking who is the beneficiary of this regulation. If an airport is slot controlled, and it is facing excess demand, the charges which the airport levies have no bearing on the ticket prices which the passenger pays. As Figure 4.3 indicates, the price to the passenger is set by the intersection of the fixed supply and demand. During the peak, the price is P_1. If the regulator insists on the airport setting a lower price than this, say, at C, all of the benefit of this difference goes to the airlines in the form of slot rents. When the UK CAA sets the price which London Heathrow is allowed to charge, it is essentially carving up the profits of the scarcity between the airport and the airlines. British Airways is the major user of Heathrow airport, and the slot rents which it receives from this airport would constitute a significant proportion of its profits. Passengers are unaffected by what charges are set by the CAA. If the CAA allows Heathrow to charge an additional £10m, the airlines need to pay this amount. However, ticket prices will not rise since they are already at the level the market will bear.

Airline taxes and slots

Airline taxes are becoming more common. There are ticket taxes, such as the UK Air Passenger Duty (APD) and similar charges in other European states; in some jurisdictions, there are airline fuel taxes. In addition, there are policies such as the EU and UK Emissions Trading Schemes (ETSs), which work like taxes. If an airport is effectively slot limited, it will be the airline which pays the tax, not the ostensible payer, the passengers. The airline is wedged between the airport's charges, and the market-clearing ticket price passengers pay (see also Chapter 8.3). If the government increases the tax, the airline pays through a reduction in its slot rents. So, it is not surprising that airlines, and especially those which have much of their business operating from slot limited airports, are very much against airline ticket taxes.

Slots also have implications for taxes intended to reduce greenhouse gas emissions. Where airlines are operating from non-slot limited airports, aviation taxes raise ticket prices and reduce emissions, depending on the elasticities of demand. If the airlines are operating from slot-limited airports, the taxes will have no effect on airline output or emissions. This result is of particular relevance for Europe, which has many slot-limited airports, and which also has many ticket taxes, some fuel taxes, and widespread air transport emissions trading schemes (ETSs).

Slots and investment decisions

As long as the slot limits are set correctly, and the slots are allocated well, slots are an efficient means of allocating airport capacity when it is scarce. They are a good way of solving the short-run capacity problem. However, how well will slots work in the long run? Will they give airports an incentive to invest in the right amount of additional capacity?

The answer is: possibly not (Forsyth, 2008, 2014; Gillen and Starkie, 2016). Slots are a limit on the amount of capacity which can be used, and as a result, airlines, and possibly the airport itself, can gain profits from having limited capacity. Suppose

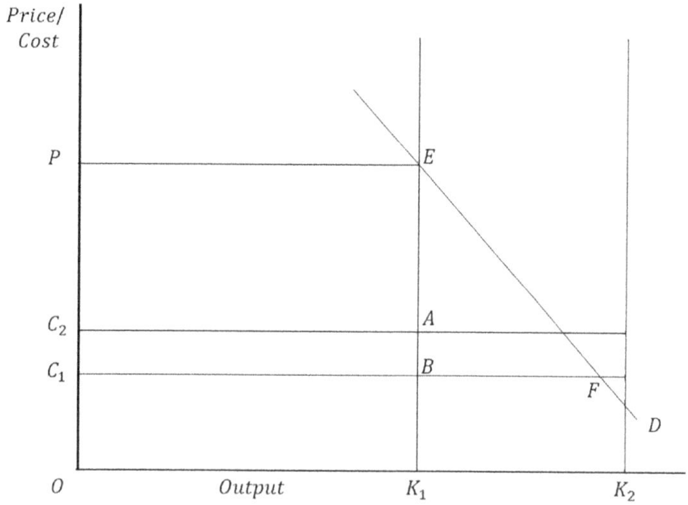

Figure 4.4 Slots and the Incentive for the Airport and Airlines to Invest

that an airport has one runway and that it is intensively used. Slots are in place, and the airlines derive a slot rent from the scarce slot capacity. It is also possible that the airport shares the slot rent, depending on the way it is regulated. If the airport is permitted to cover its costs, plus a little more, the situation of limited runway capacity will be profitable for both the airlines and airport. This is shown in Figure 4.4.

At such an airport, there will be a problem of expanding capacity. A new runway, which increases the capacity from K_1 to K_2, will provide sufficient capacity to cater to all demands. There will be a (net) consumer's surplus gain of EBF if the regulator sets a price of C_1. Suppose that the cost of the runway is less than this consumer's surplus gain, so that the benefits of the runway exceed the costs. To maximise benefits from the airport, the investment should go ahead.

The problem is that the airlines, and airport, do not see it this way. The new runway will eliminate the airline's slot rents so airlines will oppose the investment. If the airport is privately owned, and it is able to enjoy profits without the investment (for example if the regulator has set a price of C_2, above average variable costs of C_1), it will have no incentive to build the (necessary) new runway. Airlines and especially legacy airlines and the airport will all oppose the investment. Only if the airport is regulated at a price of C_1, minimising its profits, will the airport be indifferent to expansion.

There are examples of this unwillingness to invest in new capacity (especially in Europe). As a result, governments sometimes have to pressure airports to make capacity increases. London Heathrow has been very busy for a long time. The UK government evaluated options for a third runway and concluded that it was worthwhile. As soon as it announced its decision that a new runway should be built, British Airways (which had for years bemoaned the lack of capacity) announced that it would oppose it. No doubt it had realised that it would suffer a sharp reduction in slot rents. The airport is still keen to build the new runway (possibly the regulator has been effective in keeping its share of slot rents low, and it sees expansion is being profitable).

The upshot of this is that airlines, and possibly the airport, gain from capacity being inadequate. As a result, some government intervention is needed to ensure that investment in runways is adequate. This is a drawback of relying on slots to allocate runway capacity.

Small aircraft and regional ringfences

Small aircraft, such as those used for regional services, may have difficulty in accessing busy, slot-constrained airports. This will be evident if there is secondary trading of the slots, but these difficulties will also be present when slots are allocated administratively and in "grey" markets. The prices which the slots command, be they formally or implicitly traded, will be high relative to the revenues of the flights, and thus regional flights will be effectively kept out. If alternative airports are available this is not a problem, but often alternatives will not be present. Regional flights serving feeder traffic may be prepared to pay high prices for slots, but regional services to connect communities to capital cities, for business or for medical reasons, may not be prepared to pay high prices. Governments may wish to ensure that these community-oriented flights to have access to the airport. A way to do this is to have a "regional ringfence". For example, if an airport can handle 40 flights in an hour, 8 out of the total 40 could be reserved for regional flights. It could be that only off-peak slots are reserved in this way. Examples of regional ringfences exist in New York's LaGuardia airport, and Sydney airport (Harris, 2021)

What happens when airlines are not competitive?

Matters can be more complex. Airports do not produce final goods—they provide inputs to the airline industry. What goes on in the airline industry—whether airlines are competitive or monopolies—affects how the benefits of airports can be measured. Most analyses of airport pricing assume that airlines are competitive, which they often approximately are. However, some of the routes which an airport serves can be oligopolistic or monopolistic. If this is so, the analysis of airport pricing becomes more complex, since the airlines have some market power vis-à-vis the airport—there is a bilateral monopoly. This needs to be taken into account when setting prices for the airport (see Zhang and Czerny, 2012).

There are at least two aspects which are relevant. Firstly, it is desirable to take into account the more complex market structure when setting prices (or slots) for an airport. For example, if airlines are monopolistic, the effect on what passengers pay will be different from what happens when they are competitive. The benefits and costs of options will be different. This needs to be factored into policy advice. Secondly, it would be possible, in principle, to work out what prices are optimum, bearing in mind possible responses by the airlines. In practice, this would be difficult, since it involves correcting for two sources of market failure, in both the airport and airline markets. Normally, if there is a market failure problem with airlines, it would be better to address this directly (e.g., using a subsidy to airlines), and not to rely on airport pricing or regulation to fix both the airport and airline market failures—something which would be complex and difficult in practice (Niemeier, 2021).

4.4 The pricing of non-aeronautical services

Thus far, we have concentrated on the pricing and allocation of capacity of aeronautical services, including runway services, terminal services and related services. A major part of an airport's operations and income involves the provision of non-aeronautical services. These are very diverse and include car parking, retail, restaurants, offices, aircraft maintenance, goods handling and hotels. Many of these are related to the primary purpose of the airport. However, in recent years, airports have diversified into further activities which have little to do with the primary purpose of the airport, such as gambling, growing hay, and installing wave pools. Until about ten years ago, there was a steady rise in the proportion of airport revenues from non-aeronautical sources, though there has been somewhat of a falling off in recent years.

Space prevents discussion of all of the diverse aspects of the pricing of non-aeronautical services. Rather, it suffices to identify some broad aspects. Typically, an airport will not directly own and operate many of the non-aeronautical services such as shops, offices and restaurants—rather the terminal and other space are leased out to other businesses. The airport will not directly choose the prices which these businesses charge to the public, but indirectly airport operators will affect these non-aeronautical prices through their lease terms and charges. In other words, the airport will indirectly determine the retail prices. Airports do own and operate some facilities, such as car parking, though they may contract out operation to specialist operators. Again, it is the airport which will ultimately determine the prices which the public have to pay.

The pricing of non-aeronautical services can be controversial. Airports have a justified reputation for very high prices; when the Australian Productivity Commission undertakes one of its regular reviews of airport regulation and pricing, the high car parking charges always get considerable attention (Productivity Commission, 2019). The price charged for a cup of coffee will often be a multiple of the price charged in the city, and the price of car parking will be similar to the price charged in the CBD (or more). There are exceptions; some airports make a virtue of charging low prices for parking, especially if they are airports distant from the city and are trying to attract LCC traffic. Some airports which are publicly owned, especially in the US, charge low prices as a matter of policy (but also often do not provide adequate capacity). The pricing of non-aeronautical services is an issue which regulators face, and this is discussed in Chapter 6. This issue has become entwined with the idea that airports could be two-sided markets, with implications for the regulation of aeronautical services as well.

What makes it possible for airports to charge high prices for their services, and enjoy high profits as a result (Forsyth, 2004)? In some situations, high prices do not give rise to high profits, since the costs of supplying the services at distant locations can be high. This would be the case where an airport is based on an island or distant from the city it is serving. However, two main determinants of airport prices are competition and land availability (see also Chapter 2).

Airports are often at the edge of the urban area, some distance from the CBD, and the only access may be highways with few stops. In this situation, there may be limited opportunity for competitors in such services such as hotels, car parking and car hire. In this situation, the airport may have, and use, its market power to charge high prices. In other cases, the opportunities for off-airport services are good, as with the case of airports which are located at the fringe of a city with available land suitable for hotels and car parking. In this case, there can be strong competition for the airport's own services. The airport's car parks will be in competition with off-airport car parks, and the airport will have little ability to charge much higher prices than these. Sometimes, when planning access for airports, governments intentionally restrict the opportunities for off-airport competition to give the airport market power—thus, they unnecessarily restrict access to the road to the airport. This said, airports which do have market power may or may not use it.

Land availability is a critical determinant of pricing of non-aeronautical services. Airports are often, but not always, quite land constrained. There are many services that are all fighting for space. In this situation, airport land, and terminal space, are at a premium. In this situation, there is a locational rent for the scarce land and space. These will go to the highest bidder, in the same way that inner city parking space goes to the highest bidder, and parking spaces are expensive. In this case, the high prices for parking, hotels and coffee are a result of land scarcity, and not necessarily of market power. The presence of locational rents is not an indicator of inefficiency.

But there are other airports that are rather different. These are airports that have plenty of land around the terminals. Within the terminals, there is no lack of space. If this is the case, location is not at a premium, and locational rents are not a cause of high prices. If the price of a cup of coffee or car parking is high, locational rents are not the reason. It is more likely that these airports are making use of their market power. If the cost of a coffee is high in a nearly empty Taj Mahal of a terminal, use of market power is likely to be the cause. This is an issue of inefficiency, which distorts the choices users make. For example, the cost of providing parking may be low, but the high prices are inducing users to use other ways of accessing the airport.

Box 4.1 Controversies in Airport Economics: Who owns the slot rents (and does it matter?)

The way in which slots are allocated, and "owned" by the customers, the airlines, has provoked puzzlement in observers familiar with other industries. Alfred Kahn, the architect of US airline deregulation, noted that slot arrangements give rise to a number of odd, and at some times, undesirable, results (Kahn, 1999).

One distinct problem is that it is not clear just who "owns" the slots. Airlines have a sort of "squatters' rights" to the slots which they have gained in the slot "lucky dip" (though there is no illegality associated with the slots). But the ownership rights are vague, and this gives rise to problems as became clear during the COVID-19 crisis period. "Ghost" flights are operated by airlines to preserve their access to the slots. They are a clear example of rent seeking since they involve the waste of real resources in order to protect airlines' access to the slots. Another problem is the airlines keeping slots which they do not use (witness Wizz Air's attempts to get access to slots which were not being used by other airlines at London Gatwick). If the airlines (or any other parties, such as the airports) had clear ownership of the slots there would not need to be any ghost flights, or use-it-or-lose-it rules, and airlines could sell their slots when they wanted to and buy slots when they want them. The COVID-19 crisis has highlighted the weaknesses of current arrangements regarding slots. Of course, it may be the case that airlines are happy with the current arrangements which grant them very valuable, if loosely defined, rights. Better-defined rights might provoke questioning of who should get the slots—better to not suggest the question which you do not want to be answered.

Another slot problem concerns who should own them. As Kahn points out, it is normal for the owner of the infrastructure to raise its price when demand pushes up against capacity, and when capacity is ample after expansion, it would lower prices and seek to maximise the use of the now ample capacity. With airports, it is the other way around. The airport does not gain when demand pushes against capacity, since the slots and rents go to the airlines. When capacity is expanded, the airport is faced with a cost recovery problem and needs to increase its prices. Fortunately, with airports, this does not have major allocative costs, since the slots allocate the capacity when it is scarce, and when capacity is ample, Ramsey prices or pricing at what the market will bear can be used to ensure that the available capacity will be used effectively. Fortunately, in the airport case, having a situation where the slots are "owned" by the airlines and not the airport will not be too inefficient. It does not matter too much who gains the rights to the slots as long as the property rights to them are clearly defined (which currently is not the case).

4.5 Conclusions

This chapter documented the main ways that airports charge for the aeronautical and the other services they provide. The allocation of airport capacity—a critical task that airports face—was also analysed. Traditional approaches to these issues were presented, as well as more recent developments. We distinguish *actual* from efficient or optimal charges, that is, charges that are designed to utilise airport capacity to the full.

Airport pricing deals with how airports allocate their capacity. Pricing depends on whether an airport has sufficient capacity and, if it does not, on whether it charges more at times of high demand or instead uses non-price mechanisms (slots or delays) to ration demand. Airports with ample capacity have conventionally set charges with reference to aircraft weight and have favoured uniform charges rather than charging more at peak times and less at off-peak times. Generally speaking, airports with ample capacity are good at allocation.

Airports with scarce capacity must ration demand in some fashion to avoid congestion and delay. Prices (airport charges) can influence this, but airports have also relied extensively on non-price mechanisms. Most countries use a system of airport slots to manage excess demand. A slot system alters the ways an airport operates, not always in expected ways. In summary, the track records of airports facing excess demand are mixed. Airports where no rationing prices or slots are used often face extensive delays. Slots provide an effective means of rationing capacity, though they do have some undesirable features (several of which can be corrected). Furthermore, slots create some questionable incentives in the long run.

Finally, the chapter briefly discussed charge-setting for airport's non-aeronautical services. Often, the prices of non-aeronautical services are high; this could be due to land constraints or to the airport taking advantage of market power.

Notes

1 Aircraft separation rules as determined by aviation safety authorities will also have a significant impact on runway capacity.

2 If there are many airlines at an airport the model of road congestion can be applied. But what if there is only one airline? In this case, the costs of delay will fall on this airline and not on others. The airline self-internalises the delay. This is relevant for the US where hub carriers dominate capacity-constrained hubs and slots are not used to ration demand (see Brueckner, 2002).

3 In addition, government regulators often have other goals. For example, regulators are often under pressure about airport noise, and one way in which they respond is by lowering the throughput of the airport. With Amsterdam Schiphol airport the number of slots available has been decided in order to limit noise (see Chapter 9).

4 The slot rights at Heathrow, if combined with the value of the frequent flyer programme, would be significantly greater than all other assets combined in determining the value of British Airways

References

Adler, N and E Yazhemsky (2018) "The Value of a Marginal Change in Capacity at Congested Airports", *Transportation Research Part A: Policy and Practice*, 114, 154–167

Brown, S and D Sibley (1986) *The Theory of Public Utility Pricing*, Cambridge, Cambridge University Press

Brueckner, J K (2002) "Airport Congestion When Carriers Have Market Power", *American Economic Review*, 92, 1357–1375

Czerny, A (2008) "Managing Congested Airports Under Uncertainty", in A Czerny, P Forsyth, D Gillen and H-M Niemeier (eds), *Airport Slots: International Experiences and Options for Reform*, Aldershot, Ashgate, 111–126

De Neufville, R and A Odoni (2003) *Airport Systems Planning, Design and Management*, New York, McGraw-Hill

Forsyth, P (2004) "Airport Rents: Locational and Monopoly Rents at Airports: Creating Them and Shifting Them", *Journal of Air Transport Management*, 10, 51–60

Forsyth, P (2008) "Airport Slots: Perspectives and Polices", in A Czerny, P Forsyth, D Gillen and H-M Niemeier (eds), *Airport Slots: International Experiences and Options for Reform*, Aldershot, Ashgate, 379–406

Forsyth, P (2014) "Air Capacity for Sydney", in *Expanding Airport Capacity in Large Urban Areas*, Roundtable Report 153, Paris, ITF/OECD

Forsyth, P, C Guiomard, J Müller and H-M Niemeier (2021) "Changing Airport Governance and Regulation: The Regional Aspect", in A Graham, N Adler, H-M Niemeier, O Betancor, A Antunes, V Bilotkach, E Calderón and G Martini (eds), *Air Transport and Regional Development Policies* London, Routledge, 49–80

Forsyth, P and H-M Niemeier (2008a) "Setting Slot Limits at Congested Airports", in A Czerny, P Forsyth, G Gillen and H-M Niemeier (eds), *Airport Slots International Experiences and Options for Reform*, Aldershot, Ashgate, 63–84

Forsyth, P and H-M Niemeier (2008b) "Price Regulation and the Choice of Price Structures at Busy Airports", in A Czerny, P Forsyth, D Gillen and H-M Niemeier (eds), *Airport Slots: International Experiences and Options for Reform*, Aldershot, Ashgate, 127–148

Gillen, D (2008) "Airport Slots: A Primer", in A Czerny, P Forsyth, D Gillen and H-M Niemeier (eds), *Airport Slots: International Experiences and Options for Reform*, Aldershot, Ashgate, 41–62

Gillen, D and D Starkie (2016) "EU Slot Policy at Congested Hubs, and Incentives to Add Capacity", *Journal of Transport Economics and Policy*, 50, 151–163

Harris, P (2021) *Review of the Sydney Airport Demand Management Scheme*, Sydney, Australia, Department of Instructure, Transport, Regional Development and Communications, February

IATA (2017) "The Dangers of Slot Auctions", *Airlines International*, March, available at https://airlines.iata.org/analysis/the-dangers-of-slot-auctions

InterVISTAS ACI (2022) *The State of Play: Competition, Regulation, and Airport Charges* Montreal, ACI World Research Report

Kahn, A (1999) *Keynote Address, Airports Council International*, 8th Regional Conference, October 15, available at https://reason.org/aviation-policy-news/aviation-policy-news-air-travel-chaos-global-airport-privatization-recovery-and-more/

Little, I and K McCleod (1972) "The New Pricing Policy of the British Airports Authority", *Journal of Transport Economics and Policy*, 6, 101–115

Morrison, S (1982) "The Structure of Landing Fees at Uncongested Airports: An Application of Ramsey Pricing", *Journal of Transport Economics and Policy*, 16, 151–159

Morrison, S and C Winston (2008) "Delayed! US Aviation Infrastructure Policy at a Crossroads", in C Winston and G de Rus (eds), *Aviation Infrastructure Performance: A Study in Comparative Political Economy*, Washington, Brookings, 7–35

National Economic Research Associates (NERA) (2004) *Study to Assess the Effects of Different Slot Allocation Schemes A Final Report for the European Commission DG Tren*, London, NERA

Niemeier, H-M (2021) "Is Economics Good for Aviation Policy? Some Problems in Bridging the Gap Between Theory and Policy", *Journal of Air Transport Management*, 96, 102–107

Productivity Commission (2019) *Economic Regulation of Airports*, Inquiry Report No 92, Canberra, Productivity Commission, June

Rees, R (1984) *Public Enterprise Economics*, 2nd ed., London, Weidenfeld and Nicholson

Ribeiro N, A Jacquillat, A Antunes, A Odoni and J Pita (2018) "An Optimisation Approach for Airport Slot Allocation Under IATA Guidelines", *Transportation Research Part B Methodological*, 118, 132–156

Walters, A (1961) "The Theory and Measurement of Private and Social Cost of Highway Congestion", *Econometrica*, 29, 676–699

Weitzman, M (1974) "Prices vs Quantities", *Review of Economic Studies*, 41, 477–491

Zhang, A and A Czerny (2012) "Airports and Airlines Economics and Policy: An Interpretive Review of Recent Research", *Economics of Transportation*, 1, 15–34

Part 2

Ownership, regulation and efficiency

5 Ownership, finance and investment

5.1 Introduction

"Sell airlines, buy airports" was the advice many banks gave to investors at the beginning of the 1990s. Investors largely seem to have followed this advice. The first privatisation of a (major) airport occurred in 1987, when the British government sold the three London airports together with the BAA's Scottish airports. The trend to privatise airports took off in the mid-1990s. BAA's performance and its rising share price were widely seen as a success, making it a role model for the privatisation of airports. The relatively stable and high profitability of airports made them an attractive object for investors to buy and for governments to sell. Profitability was certainly one of the driving forces of privatisation but it is an ambiguous indicator of performance. High, stable profits might be the result of efficiency gains, but they might be the result of the exercise of market power. We must therefore look closely at the effects of privatisation to answer the question as to whether and how privatisation improves management, efficiency and contributes to the welfare of the stakeholders.

Privatisation is "the transfer from government to private parties of the ownership of firms" (Vickers, 1997, p. 122). Competition and privatisation are logically distinct but related concepts. Logically, private ownership does not imply competition nor does public ownership imply monopoly. Practically, privatisation might lead to more competition, but also it might cement a monopoly.

To assess whether privatisation improves performance, we firstly outline the changing ownership patterns of airports around the world and identify those countries which have moved more towards privatisation. Secondly, we shall describe and classify the variety of institutional forms which have evolved from the privatisation process. Thereafter, we will turn to the main question of how privatisation affects efficiency. We shall analyse this problem in two steps. In Section 5.3 we look at the effects of changed ownership on the principal–agent relationship of a firm. Then, in Section 5.4, we apply this to the analysis of airports and analyse how privatisation changes the broad objectives of government ownership to the simpler ones of private ownership, in particular for cost efficiency and pricing.

In Section 5.5, the Chapter considers airport finance and investment. Airport investments tend to be very costly, and large-scale sources of finance are required.

DOI: 10.4324/9781003156901-7

The general record of airport investment decisions is poor, which suggests that the incentives for good investment are weak. In particular, an airport operator will often be both a promoter of a project and have a (conflicting) responsibility to analyse the project's merits. Section 5.6 discusses the main methods available to select good investments (considered more fully in Chapter 6). The different kinds of investments at airports are also discussed. Section 5.8 considers the ways in which airport investments might be paid for, which in nearly all instances will be by passengers using the airport.

5.2 Changing patterns of ownership

Airport privatisation was part of the general trend of privatisation of public utilities. The Great Depression of the 1930s was seen by many as a failure of capitalism, leading after the second world war to a consensus that favoured public ownership. Utilities such as telecommunications, postal services, electricity, airlines and railroads should be publicly owned, and in addition some "strategic" manufacturing industries like steel. In the US, the approach was different. There, the services of public utilities are provided by private firms' subject to economic regulation. In the US airlines were private but regulated up to the early 1980s. US airports and air traffic control were public and remained so, although privatisation has been suggested by many analysts. We analyse this exception in Box 5.1, "The US airport system".

For most economists, state ownership was not regarded as a major economic problem in the 1950s and 1960s. This changed as Vickers and Yarrow (1988, p. 139) pointed out: "1979 is a decisive breakpoint in the history of public enterprises in Britain". Margaret Thatcher, the British prime minister, started a privatisation programme. Up to 1983 firms in reasonably competitive industries, for example, British Steel and shipbuilding, were privatised. In 1984, British Telecom was privatised. For Vickers (1997, p. 124) this marks a "key shift in the nature" of privatisation since for such a natural monopoly, a regulatory system had to be developed. In 1987 British Airways was privatised, followed by British Gas (1987), water in England and Wales (1989), electricity (1990–1991) and railways (1996). The share of GDP of public enterprises fell from 11% in 1979 to less than 2% in 1997.

Western Europe slowly followed the UK in the 1990s. Very often, only partial privatisations were attempted. The EU Commission adopted the UK model of regulated privatised monopoly but faced resistance from individual States. There were also major setbacks to privatisation, like renationalisation of Air New Zealand (80% government stake) in 2001, the failure of private Railtrack in October 2001 in the UK, which lead to a renationalisation of Railtrack in form of a not-for-profit organisation, Network Rail, in 2001, and the postponement and final cancellation of privatisation of German Railways in 2006.

Airport privatisation began with the sale of BAA in 1987, but there was not much privatisation outside the UK. In the first half of the 1990s, minority shares of Vienna and Copenhagen airports were sold. A wave of privatisation occurred at the end of the 1990s: 18 major Australian airports (but not Sydney) were fully privatised and airports in Germany (Düsseldorf, Hamburg, Hannover), Italy (Naples, Rome),

New Zealand (Wellington), Malaysia, and South Africa were partially privatised. The crisis caused by 9/11 slowed down privatisation though a further wave occurred in the second half of the decade including Aeroports De Paris, Brussels, Pisa, Venice and Zurich airports were partially privatised. The Financial Crisis brought that stage to an end and also led to increased public debt. In southern Europe, the austerity programmes required the sale of public assets, among them airports. The Portuguese airport system ANA, with the main airports of Lisbon and Porto, was fully privatised in 2013 and the Spanish airport group AENA, with the hubs Madrid and Barcelona, were sold partially to private investors. The COVID-19 crisis has stopped privatisation, though with exceptions in Brazil and India.

Privatisation has taken many forms. Ownership can be transferred by share flotation or trade sale. In many cases, the public owner keeps the land and gives a concession to a private operator for 20 or 30 years or even longer. If, as in the case on Australia and Portugal the period is 50 years or longer, we treat them as being fully privatised. There are further forms of public–private partnerships (PPPs) and management contracts which do not discuss in detail (see Graham, 2018)

The speed and extent of privatisation differs between countries. Australia and the UK lie at one end of the spectrum and the US at the other. There are many motives for privatisation. Vickers and Yarrow (1988) distinguish for UK privatisation of public utilities the motives of improving efficiency, of reducing the public sector borrowing requirement and government involvement in enterprise decision-making, of easing problems of public sector pay determination, of widening share ownership and encouraging employee share ownership and of gaining political advantage. Here we focus mainly on economic efficiency. This does not imply that we think these other motives are less or of no importance. Quite the opposite, but research on the political economy of privatisation is less developed (Forsyth and Niemeier, 2022) so that we just note these factors when they become essential. In Portugal and Spain, they were. Achieving high prices and revenues from privatisation for the treasury is such an important motive. It is a motive that leads to monopolies and prevents the airport industry from being restructured and horizontally separated. While this was done in Australia where airports are far apart, it was not achieved initially with BAA's London airports which were broken up roughly 20 years after they had been sold as a single entity. In Portugal and Spain as well as in Paris with the two airports of Orly and Charles De Gaulle, and in Milan with Malpensa, Linate and Bergamo, a breakup was never a serious option. Private investors often demand that no airports should be built or operated in the catchment area of an airport or have the first option for a new airport. This prevents entry. Both indicate that the market structure becomes an endogenous factor in the privatisation process with the result that monopoly power becomes entrenched.

Privatisation can also fail. There are prominent examples of this. There were plans to privatise the Schiphol Group in the first decade of this century, but Schiphol remains fully controlled by the Netherlands government and the cities of Amsterdam and Rotterdam. At about the same time the Irish government had tentatively considered the sale of Dublin airport, but enthusiasm for privatisation cooled down and came never back. Berlin International Airport was supposed to be the first fully privatised German airport, but the sales process to investors was flawed so that it remained in public hands.

On a global scale, but even on a regional level, airport privatisation has so far not fundamentally changed the institutional form of the industry. With a few exceptions such as Australia, New Zealand, the UK and Mexico. Airports are still dominantly run by the state either fully or as minority or majority shareholders, as shown in Table 5.1. In Europe hub airports such as Amsterdam, Helsinki, Manchester and Munich are publicly owned. Vienna, Fraport and Zürich are only privatised with a minority private share. Copenhagen and Rome have private majority ownership.

Table 5.1 Ownership of 50 largest Airports in Europe in 2019 in terms of passenger numbers

Country	*Airport*	*Public*	*Private Minority*	*Private Majority*	*Private*	*Year of Privatisation*
Country	Heathrow Airport				x	1987
Country	Charles de Gaulle Airport		x			2006
Country	Amsterdam Airport Schiphol	x				
Country	Frankfurt am Main Airport		x			2001
Country	Madrid—Barajas Airport		x			2015
Country	Barcelona—Airport		x			2015
Country	Istanbul Airport	x				
Country	Sheremetyevo International Airport			x		2017
Country	Munich Airport	x				
Country	Gatwick Airport				x	1987
Country	Rome Fiumicino Airport			x		1997
Country	Dublin Airport	x				
Country	Orly Airport		x			2016
Country	Vienna International Airport		x			1992
Country	Zurich Airport			x		2006
Country	Lisbon Airport				x	2013
Country	Copenhagen Airport			x		2000
Country	Palma de Mallorca Airport		x			2015
Country	Manchester Airport		x			2013
Country	Malpensa Airport		x			2011
Country	Oslo Airport	x				
Country	Domodedovo International Airport	x				
Country	London Stansted Airport*		x			2013
Country	Brussels Airport			x		2004
Country	Stockholm Arlanda Airport	x				
Country	Athens International Airport		x			
Country	Düsseldorf Airport		x			1997
Country	Berlin Tegel Airport					
Country	Vnukovo International Airport		x			
Country	Helsinki Airport	x				
Country	Málaga Airport		x			2015
Country	Pulkovo Airport	x				
Country	Warsaw Chopin Airport	x				

Country	*Airport*	*Public*	*Private Minority*	*Private Majority*	*Private*	*Year of Privatisation*
Country	Luton Airport	x				
Country	Geneva Airport	x				
Country	Václav Havel Airport Prague	x				
Country	Hamburg Airport		x			2000
Country	Budapest Ferenc Liszt International Airport				x	
Country	Istanbul Atatürk Airport	x				
Country	Boryspil International Airport					
Country	Alicante Airport		x			2015
Country	Edinburgh Airport				x	1987
Country	Henri Coandă International Airport	x				
Country	Nice Côte d'Azur Airport			x		2016
Country	Orio al Serio International Airport		x			2011
Country	Porto Airport				x	2013
Country	Stuttgart Airport	x				
Country	Birmingham Airport			x		1997
Country	Cologne Bonn Airport	x				
France	Lyon—Saint-Exupéry Airport			x		2016

Note: Stansted was fully privatised as a BAA airport in 1987. In 2013 it was bought by Manchester which is an airport with a minority private holding.

Source: Authors' classification

An important characteristic of airport privatisation is the stable and almost typical form of partial privatisation. Why has no major airport in Continental Europe been fully privatised except Budapest airport and ANA (Aeroportos de Portugal)? Why have partial privatisations so rarely reached the next step of privatisation, namely majority private ownership and full privatisation? Politics play a role in this, as very often public owners declare the airport to be "strategically important" without explaining the meaning of these buzz words. Wolf (2002, 2004) offers an explanation from a different angle. In his view, private investors will only take the risk of full privatisation if a stable and independent regulatory system is implemented; otherwise, they will prefer that the state shares the risk and avoids behaving opportunistically after privatisation. Indeed, the pattern of partial privatised airports is so far consistent with the pattern of independent regulation in Europe.

5.3 Institutional forms of privatisation

The process of privatisation has led to a greater variety of governance structures than before. While airports used to be run as a public utility, privatisation has added different forms of partially and fully privatised airports, and furthermore, the organisational structure of public airports has become more differentiated. Some of these structures seem to be rather transitory but the majority seem to be stable institutions which might not be efficient, but nonetheless work.

In the public sphere, we observe different owners at the various levels of the state, from the level of the municipality to the region and up to the central government. At the lowest level, the city government is typically the owner of the airport. As many airports are located at the outskirts of a city and serve a whole region, very often the city government together with the government of surrounding cities own the airport. In countries such as Germany, the regional state also has a share in the airport. In France, the region is represented by the chamber of commerce, which owned many of the airports before privatisation. In many countries, airports are owned by the central government either fully, or partially. While there seems to be less change within the ownership of public airports the owners have nonetheless adopted new organisational structures over the past three decades.

Traditionally a public airport was run as a public bureau or department under the rules of public budget. This caused major management problems as investment had to be financed out of the public budget and depreciation of assets was not considered. An increasing number of public owners corporatised their airports by transforming them into firms with commercial accounting methods. The type of a limited company was often selected by the public stakeholders. More commercial freedom was given to the management and airports became more commercialised. They adopted private management tools for cost control and began to market themselves. Profit-making became an objective, among others, in airport management. However, some public owners transformed their airports from a public bureau form of a non-for-profit organisation which adopted commercial accounting methods, freed airports from restrictions in funding investment on the capital market and other private management methods. While in the 1960s the typical public airport was managed like a public department as a non-commercial entity, the typical current public airport is managed as a commercial entity.

As the sale of public airports led to new private owners, the old public owners very often retained a share. Fully privatised airports might be listed on the stock exchange with a diverse or concentrated ownership structure, or they might be sold

Table 5.2 Examples of ownership and organisation patterns of public airports

	Organisation		
Ownership	*Bureau*	*Corporatised firm*	*Non-profit Organisation*
National Ownership	CAA in Finland, Sweden or Greece	AENA	
Regional	Minneapolis St. Paul	German airports	
Municipality	US airports	Small regional German airports	Canadian airports
Chamber of Commerce	French regional airports		

Source: Authors' classification

to a strategic investor, for example, other airport operators or to financial institutions. Very often, full privatisation is restricted as the former public owners want to secure certain political interests to be guaranteed. At most airports, the private owner has a minority share; either a stake of up to 49%, with private and public shareholders roughly equal, or in the form of less than 25%, with medium to large airports.

Box 5.1 The US airport system

Most US airports are owned by cities or counties though a few are under state or federal ownership. They are operated either directly as public organisations or by a port authority. Most of the activities are outsourced by long-term contracts of 20–50 years to the airlines, the so-called "airport-use agreements". There is a majority interest clause for airport capital investment, so that the airlines have a substantial influence on the capacity and quality of airports. Investments are financed by government bonds with low interest or directly on the capital market, with a tax exemption supported by federal aid (Airport Improvement Program). Revenues for airports are also generated through user taxes (passenger facility charges and also fuel taxes). Airlines invest in terminals and other facilities. The degree of outsourcing is much higher than at public or private airports elsewhere.

Airport charges are set on a cost-recovery basis. Under the residual approach, the runway charges are high enough so that the whole airport breaks even. Under the compensatory approach the average cost of the runway determines this charge.

The US airport governance model is a surprise with "unique economic and financial characteristics" (Graham, 1992, p. 188). The surprise increases because Graham's 1992 analysis is still true today, as nothing essential has changed (Graham, 2018). In particular, privatisation has never taken off in the US, although among others, Poole, from the Reason Foundation has recommended it (Poole, 2021).

Privatisation of airports was mainly proposed to reduce the need for scarce public funds, dating from the case of John Wayne Airport in California. Selling that airport was discussed as a way to balance the budget and avoid bankruptcy. However, the airlines were opposed as they feared that revenues from the sale would be diverted to non-airport purposes. In the end, they blocked privatisation. The US pilot privatisation programme can be regarded as almost a complete failure, because out of 10 airports, only one airport in Puerto Rico was privatised (Graham, 2018; Poole, 2021).

5.4 Does privatisation increase efficiency?

The effects of privatisation on economic efficiency is among the most debated topics of research on privatisation. Economists disagree on whether a change in ownership as such improves the performance of firms. The worldwide trend of privatisation gives a considerable amount of material for studying the effects. Two major reviews of the empirical findings reach opposing views. While Megginson and Netter (2001, p. 380) conclude "research now supports the proposition that privately-owned firms are more efficient and profitable than otherwise comparable state-owned firms", Willner (2003, p. 71) is much more critical of the evidence and concludes "that there is no robust relationship between ownership and efficiency". The reason why it is so difficult to find robust relationships between changes of ownership and efficiency is, among others, the simple fact that the change in ownership is very often mixed up with changes in the forces of competition, regulation and other institutional and economic changes. In order to gain some guidance through these complexities, we first theoretically analyse how in general privatisation changes the objectives of a firm, and then relate these results to the question of how privatisation impacts the objective of airports.

According to Vickers and Yarrow (1988), privatisation affects efficiency in three distinct ways: firstly, by changing the principals (e.g., owners) and their objectives; secondly, by changing the means of monitoring and giving incentives and thirdly, by providing a new scope of action by the former principal. The principal–agent approach[1] is helpful here.

In the first place, privatisation changes the objectives in the direction of profit maximisation. A private owner without any ownership restrictions will typically try to maximise profits and produce with minimal costs, while public owners will emphasise the profit objective less, and have a wider range of objectives like maximising output, jobs, regional competitiveness and attractiveness. Secondly, the means of monitoring are changed through the forces of capital markets. Here it is important to note that privatisation, as such, does not change the nature of competition in the goods markets. Privatisation does change ownership, that is to say the players of the game, but not the rules of the game. If competition in the goods markets is strong then there is strong evidence that the combined forces of capital and goods market competition lead to increased efficiency, as costs and prices are lowered. In Figure 5.1, the cost reduction is represented by a shift of the marginal (and average) costs of the public firm (MC_1) to the lower marginal cost of the private firm (MC_2). This reduction is passed on to the consumer as perfect competition forces the private firm to offer the output Xc where price is equal to marginal costs. However, while in the first phase of privatisation the state sold off firms such as steel mills, shipyards, and banks, which all operated in quite competitive industries. Privatised public utility industries do not approximate the model of competition.

In monopolistic markets, firms will use their market power to increase profits as the capital market discipline leads managers to maximise profits. Prices above competitive levels will make the welfare gain less than in a move to a private competitive industry. A private monopoly would charge monopoly prices where marginal costs equal marginal revenue at the output level X_m so that welfare is decreased by the shaded triangle. Furthermore, the cost reductions forced by the capital markets might be less than under perfect market conditions as managerial slack and lack of effort to produce efficiently (X-inefficiency) are more difficult to overcome. Compared to a typical public utility with a uniform price structure at the level of high

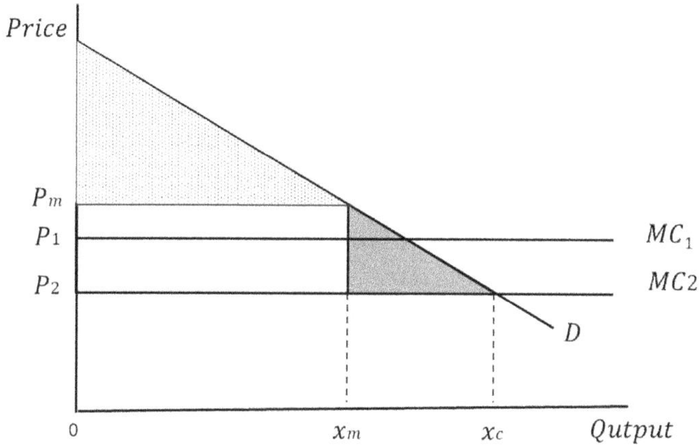

Figure 5.1 Effects of Privatisation

average costs, a private monopolised firm might have lower costs, but also higher prices. Overall, this might increase welfare because the increase in producer surplus is greater than the loss of consumer surplus. However, the situation could be further improved if goods competition forces the private firm to lower prices to marginal costs.

Privatisation as such also does not change other rules of the industry—in particular it does not change economic regulation. If regulation perfectly mimics the forces of competition, the joint forces of capital market discipline and regulatory discipline would force the private firm to minimise costs and price the lowered level of marginal costs. However, as with perfect competition, the real world of public utilities regulation exhibits various forms of imperfections leading to unexploited cost reductions and prices above marginal costs (see Chapter 6).

Privatisation gives the old principal new scope for public policy. The public owner can abstain from direct market intervention and depoliticise the industry. Furthermore, it can create more competition and/or regulate the industry to prevent the abuse of monopoly power. However, privatisation as such does not logically determine how well the old principal plays its new role. While the UK combined the privatisation of its natural monopolies with a new type of incentive regulation, other European countries were less willing to reform regulation and tried to shelter privatised industries from competition of new entrants. Even New Zealand, a country which had privatised its public utilities radically and followed a market-based policy more than any other country in the 1980s and 1990s, intervened in 2001 by buying 80% of Air New Zealand shares. Privatisation might lead to more competition, better regulation and less intervention, but there is no inevitability about this. Even proponents of the efficiency thesis of privatisation acknowledge that "a paradox of privatisation plans is that a policy which is intended to reduce government involvement and to depoliticise will invariably be designed and executed by government" (Robinson, 2003, p. 50).

How privatisation changes the objectives of airports

Ownership, together with competition, regulation and economic policy of the state, sets incentives for the airport to behave in a specific way. These factors lead to airports which maximise different objectives. In this section, we shall analyse changes in objectives brought about by privatisation, though the effects of privatisation do not lead to clear-cut results. Welfare can be maximised under different regimes. We shall start with two limiting types, namely a welfare maximising public airport, and a profit-maximising private airport. Then we describe other types of objectives and relate them to the ownership structure.

The welfare maximising airport

There are two models for achieving a welfare-maximising airport with different ownership forms. One is a public airport with welfare maximisation incentives, and the other is a private airport which is either disciplined by perfect competition or by effective regulation. The public welfare-maximising airport is the typical public utility of public interest regulation theory. According to this approach, a natural monopoly with sunk costs should be operated by the state. It is assumed to produce with minimal costs and charge optimal or second-best prices (see Chapter 4). The problem with this model is its normative character. It describes more how an airport should behave but not how it does behave. In reality, the public owners are faced with strong principal–agent problems, leading to cost inefficiencies and price structures which inefficiently allocate capacity. The approach tends to degenerate into an airport with no clear objectives. Because of the rather loose incentives, the UK government privatised natural monopolies in the mid-1980s in combination with the introduction of incentive regulation. In theory, privatisation, together with effective incentive regulation, results in airports maximising welfare. How close airports come to this model depends on the strength of the capital market discipline and the effectiveness of regulation.

The profit maximiser

A manager of an unregulated private airport has incentives to minimise costs and charge monopoly prices. Effective capital market discipline will set incentives to keep costs low and high prices will be restrained only by general competition law. The New Zealand airports up to 2010, when the government introduced light-handed regulation, might come close to this. In principle, a government, seeking cash or dividends, can also set incentives to induce its airports to maximise profits. In many cases, these incentives are probably not so strong as those from the capital markets because politicians will face the political countervailing power of airlines if an airport charges monopoly prices. There is also evidence that small airports which have problems covering costs face also a tight budgetary constraint from their public municipalities which are not allowed to increase their debt.

Maximising economic activity

Maximising the economic activity of a specific area is a possible objective of a public airport. From the viewpoint of the city or the region, the airport is seen as an instrument or a catalyst for increasing economic activity in the local region (see Chapter 9). The airport might maximise the number of passengers and freight, and the number of destinations (connectivity). The focus can be either on business travellers who view good quality of connections as vital for their business or on incoming tourists who demand cheap flights. As airports are depicted as "job machines", the emphasis on cost efficiency is not strong. Larger airports could break even, but small airports might be subsidised to attract regional carriers for business or low-cost carriers for tourists. Furthermore, the objectives might be contradictory if low charges and low costs are needed to attract low-cost carriers but high labour intensity is implied by the goal of job creation.

In addition, other objectives may be in play. The airport is sometimes regarded as a gateway to international markets and as a symbol of the city or the region. Here, the objective is to provide high quality at reasonable cost. The airport should break even, but up to a certain level, subsidies are paid by the owners. Very often the owners of an airport do not define objectives and find it too costly to monitor them. In such cases, the management and workers can enjoy a quiet life with relatively high salaries and wages. The airport is run with managerial slack. It has relatively high costs and charges but nevertheless functions well in a world with little incentives from the owners and from competition and regulation. Such an airport might arise with a public utility vision by its public owners, or it might be privatised under a cost-plus regulation regime.

Privatisation and performance of airports

In order to analyse the effect of airport privatisation on net social benefit or economic welfare it is necessary to analyse the cost and benefits of such a policy change (Florio, 2004). This could be done by quantifying the impact of costs and the impact of airport charges. Have the theoretically expected cost savings from privatisations been passed on to the users or have they been partly or fully eroded by price increases? These are the basic welfare effects of privatisation. Florio goes further and analyses the privatisation effects on taxpayers, owners, managers and workers. To measure the basic and full welfare effects it is necessary to isolate effects from privatisation from other changes, in particular from those in competition and regulation. This can be done by either comparing airports before and after privatisation, or by comparing airports under different ownership. The studies of airport privatisation have used both approaches.

The majority of benchmarking studies show that privatisation increases efficiency, but some find no relationship, or even a negative one. For example, Parker (1999) and Yokomi (2005) analyse the performance of BAA before and after privatisation and compare the BAA airports with the public UK airports for roughly the same period. While Parker finds no significant difference before and after privatisation, Yokomi's results show that BAA airports perform better. It is quite difficult to judge which study is correct as both use different methods with different inputs and outputs. Another study supports Yokomi—See and Li (2015) find that "privately owned airports tend to be more productive than airports under public and mixed ownership" (p. 9). For other countries, the results are not so clear. For example, Scotti et al. (2012) found that in Italy public airports are more efficient than private airports.

Another result (Oum et al., 2006, 2008) is that partially privatised airports perform less efficiently than fully public or fully private. This is a result of high policy relevance as we have seen that partially privatised airports are very often the chosen form of privatisation, especially in the European Union. It is a puzzling result as public airports also perform efficiently. However, the public airports in the benchmarking sample are almost exclusively US airports which are public in a very specific way (see Box 5.1) and which are internally subsidised to an unknown but relevant degree. The public airports are not of the corporatised type typical for Europe and elsewhere. Hence, these studies should be read as a warning against mixed ownership, in particular with minority private shares.

How can we explain that so many governments choose to partially, but not fully, privatise their airports? One explanation might be that the public owner wants to pursue its regional economic policy targets but needs a private investor in order to achieve a certain amount of cost control. Private investors signal to the management and the workers the importance of cost control, low wages and efficient operation. External management know-how might put pressure on former public managers to improve. On the other hand, private investors might seek less risky investments with safe profits. If so, the interest of the private investor is to limit competition from other airports, and to limit competition in commercial activities, for example, for off-site parking. The private investor might also seek a quiet life and tolerate inefficiencies, in particular if the higher costs can be passed to the users as under cost-based regulation. More entrepreneurial investors in airports typically have preferred full privatisation, or at least majority private ownership. Public and private owners differ in their interests. They also differ in their culture and management styles. All this might lead to costly conflicts in the management of the airport resulting in poor performance.

However, these studies neither isolate the effect of privatisation from changes in regulation and competition,[2] nor assess them in terms of basic and extended economic welfare (Niemeier, 2021). A notable exception is Adler and Liebert (2014) which benchmarks 48 European airports and three Australian airports (Melbourne, Perth and Sydney). This shows that full privatisation increases cost efficiency but leads to higher charges unless regulation or (where possible) competition prevents the airport from increasing charges. This study comes as close as possible to an assessment in terms of basic economic welfare, and it opens directions for further research on the effects of privatisation on taxpayers, management and workers. This is unexplored territory for airport economics.

5.5 The finance of airports and pre-finance of major investments

Evaluation of investments is a crucial question for airport operators as well as for the economy, especially at large metropolitan and hub airports. The remainder of this chapter introduces some of the principal aspects of airport investment decisions and investment financing.

The costs of airport investments are substantial, especially on brownfield sites. Standard and Poor's, the ratings agency, reported in 2019 that a large majority of the biggest US hub airports had 5-year investment budgets that each exceeded $1bn and, in the case of Los Angeles International airport, reached $13bn (S+P Global, 2019). Typically, these expenditures are recovered over time through airport charges, so the scale, timing and financing arrangements of such investments are critical decisions for airport managers and users alike. Moreover, if airport expansions are started only after passenger traffic has already outgrown existing facilities, costs in the form of congestion and delays are imposed on passengers and airlines.

For the future, the lower rate of aviation traffic growth expected in Europe following the pandemic (Eurocontrol, 2022) implies a smaller capacity shortfall than previously projected, although this is subject to considerable uncertainty. Eurocontrol's assessment is that the capacity shortage is now concentrated on particular airports in Germany, the Netherlands, Spain and Turkey. In North America, and especially, in Asia, capacity shortfalls also exist.

In a world of perfect decision-making, airports would be built or expanded moderately in advance of traffic growth, at a carefully judged scale and cost and, where possible, in a flexible modular form. Meeting such goals is, of course, difficult in each respect. Future traffic levels are uncertain, therefore the timing and the scale needed can only be approximated. Without very careful management, cost control on large complex projects is difficult, and the record is poor. Finally, certain types of airport capacity cannot be constructed incrementally; in particular, a runway is indivisible (though aspects such as length and thickness may be varied). A new terminal might be delivered in stages in line with traffic growth provided the site was suitable and at an additional cost which could be material.

Privately owned airports finance investments from their revenues and, for substantial projects, from large-scale borrowing and bond issuance. Airports conducting major investments sometimes also levy a supplementary airport-improvement charge on passengers. An airport operating company might also raise additional capital from shareholders given its expanded balance sheet and increased risk. There are also government funds available in some jurisdictions including the US, Canada and the EU.

Megaprojects

The scale of many airport investments justifies their description as "megaprojects". Flyvbjerg et al. (2003) coined this term following an extensive investigation into multi-billion-dollar infrastructure projects: airports, tunnels, dams, bridges, motorway and railway networks. They identified a performance paradox—although such projects have become larger and more numerous, their cost and revenue performance has been strikingly poor. Significant problems have included substantial cost overruns and traffic and revenue shortfalls. These have frequently jeopardised the viability of projects and have also undermined public support for them. These problems existed in private as well as public projects.

Flyvbjerg et al. explain the disappointing performance of large-scale investments in terms of poor incentives which reward underestimated costs, overestimated revenues, undervalued environmental impact and overvalued economic development benefits. The authors point to central problems such as lack of accountability and inappropriate risk sharing. These could be lessened by reforming the institutional arrangements for decision-making and by instituting accountability at the project development and evaluation stages. Their conclusion was that a promoter's financial projections for a project should be treated as much too optimistic (see Chapter 9). As a consequence, a project's actual *outturn* might be negative in which case it should never have proceeded.

These problems are apparent in many airport investments. A new airport in Denver which opened in 1995 suffered a cost overrun of about 200% or $5bn; traffic in the opening year was only half the level projected (Chapter 2 discusses the problem of overly optimistic forecasts). In Mexico, a very large new hub airport due to cost over $10bn was abandoned part-built after a 2018 national referendum. In Europe, there is an exceptional case of the new Brandenburg Berlin International airport, which far exceeded its budget and far overran its deadline for opening (see Chapter 9). There were also serious operating problems on the opening of the new Hong Kong International airport in 1998 and London Heathrow's Terminal 5 in 2008; both disrupted the airports' projections of costs and revenues.

Part of the reason for the poor performance of airport investment is the inflexibility of traditional airport master planning exercises (Burghouwt, 2007). These tend to be quite rigid, make unrealistic assumptions about planners' access to necessary information, and about the predictability of future traffic. An alternative approach is sometimes termed a "no regrets" policy: where possible, projects should be selected that can be adapted to a number of possible future scenarios. Researchers have also advocated that airport planning take account of the value of "real options". In other words, uncertainty about the future increases the attraction of a "wait and see" approach. On this basis, a significant premium over net present value should be required of a project to compensate for sacrificing future investment flexibility. The cost of an early decision could turn out to be high.

Investment incentives

The incentives to invest at an airport are not straightforward and could go either way. A profit-oriented private airport operator, especially facing little competition, might delay investment and seek to raise charges (see Chapter 6). Alternatively, a public airport, or one with owners interested to maximise its size, may over-invest and unduly expand airport capacity. An airport might also build excess capacity to deter rival airports from expanding or potential rivals from entering the industry. On the airline side, incumbents might resist capacity expansions that would allow rivals to serve the airport, especially if continuing capacity shortages would enable incumbent airlines to charge a premium on tickets. The impact of price regulation is also uncertain.[3]

The rules for allocating scarce runway capacity are important too. When, as in Europe, runway use is subject to administratively assigned slots, the associated rent accrues to the incumbent airlines, not the airport, dampening the incentive for investment by the airport. If slots were traded—which is rare—it would indicate how much airlines would pay for use of the airport. This measure of unmet demand would inform the airport operator as well as policymakers of any incipient capacity shortage. The commercial case for airport investment depends heavily on a medium-term traffic forecast that is reasonably accurate.

Pre-finance

"Pre-financing" of large airport investments is often sought by airport operators and lenders in order to reduce the financial risk. It is widely used in the US. It is opposed by airline representative bodies like IATA. In a competitive business, say automobile manufacturing, a business investing in a new factory could not earn extra revenue until the factory was operational. On the same principle, a regulator might refuse to allow higher airport charges until passengers paying the charge had the use of the new facilities. A counter-argument is that pre-financing would act like a congestion charge—raising charges when capacity is scarce but not when new capacity is in use—as would occur in a competitive industry with temporarily insufficient capacity. Pre-financing could serve efficiency. As discussed in Forsyth (2017), pre-financing also has distributional effects. The passengers and airlines using the airport at the time of the charge might not be those using the airport when the facility was in use. Pre-financing of slot-constrained runways would also reduce airline rents.

5.6 How can we assess when more capacity is needed?

Given the large scale of capacity increases at airports, the substantial associated risks and the record of building excess capacity, what tools are available that would help to rigorously assess when additional airport capacity is justified?

Three broad types of techniques have been used (Forsyth et al., 2021). These are discussed in Chapter 9 and so only mentioned here. There is the sturdy workhorse of cost–benefit analysis (CBA) along with the more recent approach of Computable General Equilibrium (CGE). There are some similarities between CBA and CGE, but these are quite different from a third method, Economic Impact Analysis (EIA). The fundamental difference between the two kinds of approach is that CBA/CGE focus on an investment's effect on *welfare*: will a country be better off or worse off because of the investment? An EIA study cannot answer this question as it focuses on certain impacts such as additions to employment, production, taxes and so forth but not the overall net effect. The use of cost–benefit analysis for airport investments was pioneered by the Roskill Commission (1971) which evaluated the case for a third London airport. A CBA should show whether an airport investment, especially a large and costly investment, should proceed. A CGE exercise constructs a model of a national or regional economy, using a series of equations that are for the principal sectors in an economy and the main economic flows between them. Thus, the effect of more airport capacity is estimated not just for the airport sector but any impact on employment (for example) flow across the rest of the economy, hence, the description of general equilibrium. The CGE technique was used, for example, for the Airports Commission (see Box 5.2).

5.7 Investment in runways, in terminals and in quality

Airport investments may be designed to increase capacity, to improve quality or to lower operating costs.[4] An additional terminal should raise capacity and quality, especially since airlines switching services from an overcrowded to a new terminal will improve quality in both buildings.

There are some differences between investments in runways and in terminals. First, indivisibility or lumpiness applies to runways but somewhat less to terminals (without being completely absent). Second, the range of possible quality levels is greater for terminals. As a first approximation, a runway of a given length and width is a relatively standardised asset. But even if a terminal is not designed specifically for particular users (long-haul versus short-haul carriers), possibilities range from expensive architectural statements (with a "Wow!" factor) to a very functional design with lower costs. Room for different opinions on the required size of the terminal is also greater than for runway length. As a result, user support may be easier to obtain for additional runway than for additional terminal capacity. Provided the cost is reasonable, and existing runway capacity is starting to be scarce, airlines will be likely to support the building of an additional runway. But the same may not be true for a new terminal. In the EU, since 2009, airports are required by law to consult with airline users about new infrastructure investments and their impact on airport charges.

When a large new asset is built at an airport, there will often be a large programme of related investments without which the new facility would operate below full efficiency. A new terminal is likely to require additional on-campus roads and possibly new access roads too (if the new investments are built in a different part of the campus). The airport's energy and water systems may need to be upgraded to handle the expanded capacity. New passenger and staff parking facilities may be needed. And there could be expenditure on protecting the environment and local wildlife. Taken together these may not be a negligible part of the total cost.

Box 5.2 How to appropriately evaluate large-scale airport expansion? The Airports Commission (2015)

The many and wide-ranging impacts of a large metropolitan hub airport, and the investment evaluation implications, are illustrated in the 2015 report of the Airports Commission. This Commission was appointed to make recommendations to the UK government about how and where to add a runway in the southeast of the UK, where a new full-length runway had not been built since the 1940s. Of the numerous proposals received, three were shortlisted and these involved an additional runway either at Gatwick or at Heathrow airports.

The report illustrates the many aspects of airport capacity investment. Analysis is needed not only of the investment's economic effects on production, trade and productivity but also of noise, carbon emissions, surface access, employment, air quality and housing. Uncertainty requires that a number of different possible futures be considered; the Commission analysed five possible scenarios for traffic growth.

Throughout the analysis, the forecasts are consistent with a 2050 cap on UK aviation carbon emissions derived from the planning assumptions of the UK's climate-change advisory committee. The Commission applied two frameworks: climate capped and climate traded. In the first case, an absolute carbon emission ceiling would have to be respected regardless of developments in other parts of the economy. This could be achieved by a carbon price raised sufficiently high to keep traffic growth at the carbon cap. In the second case, trading of carbon permits would allow aviation companies to buy permits from other sectors and thus to operate flights additional to those possible under the carbon-capped approach. Internationally, the Commission assumed that the number of carbon permits made available was consistent with international climate goals.

The Commission sought in particular to resolve the issue considered to have been the main obstacle to airport expansion in the UK. This was the mismatch between the considerable benefits of airport investment, which would accrue widely, and the environmental costs, which would fall narrowly and locally. To make expansion more acceptable locally, it was recommended that there be: a ban on night flights, a legally-binding "noise envelope", a noise levy to fund increased local compensation and mitigation schemes, and measures to ensure acceptable air quality. A recommendation was also made that there not be any further runways at Heathrow.

Part of the Commission's work was to consider the respective merits of a new airport on a greenfield site against an additional runway at a brownfield site. Attractions of a new airport included a substantial noise reduction and land released for redevelopment on the old site. But a new airport would also bring major challenges including the need to close Heathrow airport to make a new airport commercially viable. The direct investment costs of a new airport would be very high and to this would be added spending on improved surface access. The new airport would be less convenient to the central business district of London.

The Commission's final report firmly recommended an additional runway at Heathrow which it considered could be delivered on a commercial basis.

5.8 Who pays the cost of the investment?

Who pays for airport investments? Sometimes it is taxpayers, especially if the airport is in public ownership or is a small regional airport important to the local economy and society. More usually, the cost is borne by airport users; this is appropriate provided the investment also confers benefits on users which they value.

Governments provide funds for some airport investments. In the US, there is a long-established government scheme to subsidise the growth of airport capacity. The Airport Improvement Programme funds eligible airport investment based on passenger numbers, but such grants may also be increased on a discretionary basis. In 2021, the scheme's expenditure amounted to some $500m. Larger airports can be reimbursed for 75% of the cost of eligible investments and smaller airports up to 95%. In 2021, Canada launched a similar but temporary scheme after the pandemic.

In the EU, grants are available from regional development funds. These monies are not always spent efficiently. A report by the EU Court of Auditors (2014) reviewed a sample of 20 airports that had received a total of some €650m in public funding. The report considered whether the projects were needed, were delivered on time and on budget, and afterwards were used. Pessimistic conclusions were reached on each point. Passenger traffic had increased at only half of the airports. Seven of the airports were not profitable and therefore faced an uncertain future.

Airport investments may also in some parts of the world be eligible for loans from government-owned financial institutions which charge interest below prevailing market rates. The European Investment Bank (EIB), for example, offers loans for infrastructure investments of certain kinds. Capacity expansions at airports are no longer supported, following the adoption of the EU Green New Deal. However, investments in decarbonisation at airports are eligible for support. Such investments will, in future, require financing on a large scale to meet airports' target of net zero carbon emissions.[5] Reduced interest rates on loans from public banks would, of course, lower the private costs of these investments. On the other hand, the expected need for airport investment spending in other areas, for instance, to harness the benefits of digitisation and related newer technologies, will be for airport operators to finance.

Most airport investments are paid for by airport users through the price of their airline tickets, since these include the airports' charges. The impact of a large investment on the level of airport charges then depends on such factors as delivery of the project on budget, passenger traffic growth, and the period over which the cost of the investment is recovered. On the last point, there is something of a paradox. A large increment of capacity is costly to build but may be lightly used for some years. Straight-line depreciation of the asset would inflate charges more in the early years just when an airport would want to attract new passengers. Provided financiers accept "back-loaded" repayment of loans, cost recovery can be structured to better reflect the growth of the use of the facility. In any case, passengers pay for the investment whether early users or later users. This factor is also a reason why airport operators are keen on pre-financing investments to avoid a possibly abrupt price increase on the opening of an airport extension.

Box 5.3 Controversies in Airport economics: The airport runway nobody wants?

The London runway problem is never far from controversy. In Box 5.2, we documented the way the Airports Commission had analysed the capacity needs of London and recommended that a third runway be built at Heathrow. This recommendation was accepted by the government, and planning has begun. But the project is still very controversial—seemingly almost nobody wants it.

The Airports Commission did an exhaustive modelling exercise to try to establish what the best course of action would be. However, there have been many criticisms of its work. John Kay, a well-known public policy economist, was critical of the forecasting, noting that it is very difficult to forecast a long time in the future (a situation of "radical uncertainty"), and suggested that it would be better to keep options open as long as possible, rather than commit to a very expensive single project. A new runway at Gatwick would cost about £8bn compared to the Heathrow runway which could cost £18bn. Transport economist David Starkie has argued for a shorter, less expensive runway, noting that Heathrow already has two long runways, and the need for a third long runway has yet to be established, given that a lot of Heathrow's traffic can be handled with a shorter runway. The runway has been opposed by environmental groups who argue that it will lead to more flights and more greenhouse gas emissions. British Airways, the largest user of Heathrow, has come out opposing the runway—through airport charges it would pay much of the cost of the new runway (and the value of its slots would fall sharply if the runway were built).

But it is an exaggeration to say that this is the runway nobody wants—the owner, Heathrow Airport Limited, is keen to build it. They are relying on the regulator, the CAA, raising price-caps which enable the airport to recover the costs of building the runway. This puts considerable responsibility on the regulator to ensure it does not underwrite an overly costly option.

5.9 Conclusions

This chapter has considered two aspects of airports. What are the ownership and governance arrangements that promote airport efficiency and service standards at reasonable cost? And are the current governance arrangements appropriate? Second, how should airport investment decisions be made? What assessment tools should be used and who should carry out the assessment, in order to improve the industry's mixed investment record? And do current approaches reflect best practice?

Historically, airports were in the public sector because of a belief that public ownership would promote the goal of public welfare. When the actual record proved disappointing, especially in terms of cost control on the operating and investment sides, airports began to be sold to private owners. The effect on efficiency has depended on the form of such privatisations and the resulting market structure in the industry. We argue that privatisation under conditions of weak competition and absent regulation may primarily benefit shareholders. Under more competitive conditions, efficiency improvements should be passed on to passengers in the form of lower airport charges. Research into the impact of airport privatisation on airport efficiency is not conclusive, other than the finding that fully private airports perform better than the commonly observed partly privatised airports. This loss of efficiency may reflect the political desire to retain some influence over airports as well as the wish of investors to hedge their risk.

The quality of airport investment is crucial to the financial health of the airport operator, the airlines and passengers using the airport, and for the overall economy where significant connectivity benefits occur. But the investment record is mixed with a number of very large cost overruns and delayed openings. The chapter proposed that the problem could be lessened by having an independent body carry out a cost-benefit assessment of significant projects. At the moment, too many investment projects are promoted by the airport's own operator. The incentive for airport operators to deliver timely investment in an efficient manner will also be affected by airport ownership and by airport regulation. But none of these options will necessarily deliver efficient investment. This is a significant issue when airport creation or expansion is on a multi-billion-euro scale, often termed "megaprojects". In nearly all cases, airport users pay the cost of investments which should therefore produce clear benefits and meet user needs and preferences.

Notes

1 The principal–agent approach deals with the situation in which a principal (a company board or a regulator) is less informed about what is going on in the firm or utility than the agent (manager). The agent is employed to manage the firm or utility. To get good performance from the agent, the principal needs to set incentives for the agent (e.g., a bonus conditional on good performance) or spend some resources to monitor the agent's actions.

2 While the earlier studies (see Liebert and Niemeier, 2013) treated privatisation implicitly as a conglomerate of changes in ownership, regulation and competition, the later studies also tried to analyse the other effects. Good examples are Assaf and Gillen (2012) and Assaf et al. (2014), which analyse combined effects of different ownership and different regulatory forms. This is certainly an important improvement, but they do not cover competition which is supposed to have intensified.

3 Investment incentives under regulation are discussed in Chapter 6.

4 These different types of investment are considered in the context of airport economic regulation in Chapter 6.

5 Airports' impacts on the environment are discussed in Chapter 8.

References

Adler, N and V Liebert (2014) "Joint Impact of Competition, Ownership Form and Economic Regulation on Airport Performance and Pricing", *Transportation Research Part A*, 64, 92–109

Airports Commission (2015) "Final Report", available at assets.publishing.service.gov.uk

Assaf, A and D Gillen (2012) "Measuring the Joint Impact of Governance Form and Economic Regulation on Airport Efficiency", *European Journal of Operational Research*, 220, 187–198

Assaf, A, D Gillen and E G Tsionas (2014) "Understanding Relative Efficiency Among Airports: A General Dynamic Model for Distinguishing Technical and Allocative Efficiency", *Transportation Research Part B*, 70, 18–34

Burghouwt, G (2007) *Airline Network Development in Europe and its Implications for Airport Planning*, Ashgate, Aldershot

EU Court of Auditors (2014) "EU-Funded Airport Infrastructures: Poor Value for Money", available at http://eca.europa.eu

Eurocontrol (2022) "Aviation Outlook 2050", available from www.eurocontrol.int

Florio, M (2004) *The Great Divestiture: Evaluating the Welfare Impact of the British Privatisations 1979–1997*, Cambridge and London, MIT Press

Flyvbjerg, B, N Bruzelius and W Rothengatter (2003) *Megaproject and Risk*, Cambridge, Cambridge University Press

Forsyth, P (2017) "Pre-Financing Airport Investments, Efficiency and Distribution: Do Airlines Really Lose?", *Journal of Air Transport Management*, 67, 259–267

Forsyth, P and H-M Niemeier (2022) "European Airport Reform: Slots and the Implicit Contract Between Airlines and Airports", in E Pels, P Forsyth, J Müller and H-M Niemeier (eds), *Economic Regulation of Urban and Regional Airports*, Cham, Springer

Forsyth, P, H-M Niemeier and E Njoya (2021) "Economic Evaluation of Investments in Airports: Recent Developments", *Journal of Benefit-Cost Analysis*, 12, 85–121

Graham, A (1992) "Airports in the United States", chap 9 in R Doganis (ed), *The Airport Business*, Abingdon, Routledge

Graham, A (2018) *Managing Airports: An International Perspective*, 5th ed., Abingdon, Routledge

Liebert, V and H-M Niemeier (2013) "A Survey of Empirical Research on the Productivity and Efficiency Measurement of Airports", *Journal of Transport Economics and Policy*, 47, 157–189

Megginson, W L and J M Netter (2001) "From State to Market: A Survey of Empirical Studies on Privatisation", *Journal of Economic Literature*, 39, 321–389

Niemeier, H-M (2021) "Is Economics Good for Aviation Policy? Some Problems in Bridging the Gap Between Theory and Policy", *Journal of Air Transport Management*, 96, 102–107

Oum, T H, N Adler and C Yu (2006) "Privatisation, Corporatization, Ownership Forms and Their Effects on the Performance of the World's Major Airports", *Journal of Air Transport Management*, 12, 109–121

Oum, T H, J Yan and C Yu (2008) "Ownership Forms Matter for Airport Efficiency, A Stochastic Frontier Investigation of Worldwide Airports", *Journal of Urban Economics*, 64, 422–435

Parker, D (1999) "The Performance of the BAA Before and After Privatisation", *Journal of Transport Economics and Policy*, 33, 133–146

Poole, R (2021) "Annual Privatization Report: Aviation, Reason Foundation", available at https://reason.org/wp-content/uploads/annual-privatization-report-2021-aviation.pdf

Robinson, C (2003) "Privatisation: Analysing the Benefits", in D Parker and D Saal (eds), *International Handbook on Privatisation*, Cheltenham, Edward Elgar, 41–59

Roskill, E (1971) *Commission on the Third London Airport: Report*, London, HM Stationery Office

Scotti, D, P Malighetti, G Martini and N Volta (2012) "The Impact of Airport Competition on Technical Efficiency: A Stochastic Frontier Analysis Applied to Italian Airport", *Journal of Air Transport Management*, 22, 9–15

See, K F and F Li (2015) "Total Factor Productivity Analysis of the UK Airport Industry: A Hicks-Moorsteen Index Method", *Journal of Air Transport Management*, 43, 1–10

S+P Global (2019) "When The Cycle Turns: U.S. Airport Balance Sheets and Exposures Increase with Traffic", available at www.spglobal.com/en/research-insights/articles/when-the-cycle-turns-u-s-airport-balance-sheets-and-exposures-increase-with-traffic

Vickers, J (1997) "Economic Perspectives on Privatisation", *The Journal of Economic Perspectives*, 5, 111–132

Vickers, J and G Yarrow (1988) *Privatisation, an Economics Analysis*, Cambridge, MA, MIT Press

Willner, J (2003) "Privatisation: A Sceptical Analysis", in D Parker and D Saal (eds), *International Handbook on Privatisation*, Cheltenham, Edward Elgar, 60–86

Wolf, H (2002) *Privatisierung im Flughafensektor Eine ordnungspolitische Analyse*, Heidelberg, Springer

Wolf, H (2004) "Getting the Institutions Right", in P Forsyth, D Gillen, D Starkie and H-M Niemeier (eds), *Regulation of Airports*, Ashgate, Aldershot, 201–212

Yokomi, M (2005) *Evaluation of Technical Efficiency at Privatized Airports: Case of BAA Plc*, Air Transport Research Society (ATRS) Conference, Rio de Janeiro, Brazil, July 3–6

6 Airport regulation and competition

6.1 Introduction

A major policy question is whether airports should be regulated, and if so, how. When airports were first privatised, it was considered that price regulation would be necessary to curb monopoly power. This chapter presents an account of how that view has since evolved.

The chapter reviews a number of rationales for airport regulation, the associated inefficiency problems, and how well the rationales accord with regulatory practice. The way airport slots can affect price regulation is also explained. The chapter considers also whether regulation should be carried out by government departments or independent agencies. This is important because the effectiveness of regulation is likely to be related to the independence from the industry and government of the regulatory agency.

Next, the chapter considers whether competition or monopoly best characterises the airport industry. In practice, there is no strict dividing line between competition and monopoly, so a careful judgement of the need for regulation arises. Available methods to assess the strength of competition are reviewed. If regulation is warranted, there are three main approaches that have been used, and these are described. Regulation of investment poses particular challenges, which are also discussed. This is followed by a section on the regulation of non-aeronautical services which includes a discussion of the concepts of airports as two-sided markets and by a section on the mechanics of implementing price regulation. The chapter finishes with a brief conclusion.

6.2 Regulation: What it is, and Who does it?

Most firms are subject to a variety of forms of regulation: environmental regulation, financial regulation, health and safety regulation and land use regulation. Some firms, such as airports, may also be subject to economic regulation, which is particularly focused on their pricing and quality performance, and this is what we concentrate on here. The main rationale for airport regulation is to guard against the possible use of their market power, though other rationales exist.

In general, larger airports tend to be regulated. Smaller airports are often local government owned, though some, especially in the UK, are privately owned. The

DOI: 10.4324/9781003156901-8

judgement is that often the smaller airports are often subject to competition or are government owned so that regulation is not needed. Prior to the 1980s, most airports were government owned, but from the 1980s onwards, governments have privatised airports, though more so in some countries than others. Is economic regulation warranted? Large privately owned airports tend to be subject to regulation, though some quite large airports (e.g., London Stansted in the UK) are judged to face sufficient competition so that regulation is not needed. Governments also often regulate public airports, such as Amsterdam Schiphol airport, Bordeaux airport, Dublin airport and Munich airport. In recent decades, there has been a move towards corporatisation, which seeks to have public bodies managed on commercial principles. The rationale is straightforward. In principle, the government could give instructions or set incentives for airports to perform well, but in practice, this is difficult to do and corporatisation, combined with regulation, is a better way of encouraging good performance.

Another question is who should regulate the airports. Governments could establish an independent regulator or give the regulatory responsibility to a government department (which may also be the official owner of the airport). Dependent regulators typically face a conflict of interest between looking after the government's interests as the airport owner (such as maximising airport profits) and the broader public duty to look after other stakeholders such as airlines and passengers. An independent regulator is also more likely to be transparent, to provide information to airlines and passengers, than a dependent regulator. By establishing an independent regulator, the government can guard against the airport becoming too close to the politics of the day and can encourage longer-term decision-making. An independent regulator will be more open to the public interest and at lower risk of capture by departmental interests or—most importantly—by the regulated airport (International Transport Forum, 2011).

There are examples of both independent and dependent airport regulators. In the UK, the main airport regulator is the Civil Aviation Authority (CAA) which is an independent regulator with a well-defined statute. Countries which follow the British approach to regulation, such as Australia and India, have opted for independent regulation. The European Commission has also espoused the idea of independent regulators for more than 20 years. While initially only a few countries, like Ireland and Netherlands, supported this concept, over time more and more countries, like for example Italy and France, established independent regulators, but the two large member states Germany and Spain resisted.

6.3 The rationales for regulation

The underlying rationale for regulation is to limit the use of market or monopoly power (due to the lack of competition). Many, though not all, airports have market power and an incentive to use this power in ways inimical to efficiency and other economic objectives. The clearest case is with private sector airports, which may use their market power to increase their profits. However, public sector airports also often have market power, and while some governments may apply regulation to reduce this market power, other governments use the cover of regulation to facilitate the exploitation of market power by airports that the government owns.

We distinguish three distinct rationales for regulation:

- To enhance allocative and productive efficiency;
- To achieve distributional or equity objectives, and
- To protect users from airport expropriation of the users' sunk costs.

The efficiency rationales

There are two, quite distinct, efficiency rationales for regulation. The allocative efficiency justification is often relied on, that is, minimising the deadweight loss from monopoly pricing, though quantitatively this may not be very significant. The productive efficiency argument is rarely presented directly, though it may be more quantitatively important. It is convenient to discuss both together.

An airport with market power is shown in Figure 6.1. For simplicity, suppose that the airport has spare capacity, and does not use all of its capacity, K. The minimum feasible cost is C_1, which is equal to average (AC) and also to marginal cost (MC). The most efficient price would be one equal to C_1 and, with demand of D, airport output would be X_1. However, if the airport is unconstrained, it can choose a higher price in order to obtain higher profits. The profit-maximising price is P_1, and the corresponding output X_2. There is no certainty that the airport would operate at a cost of C_1—it is perfectly possible for it to operate at, say, C_2, and still cover its costs

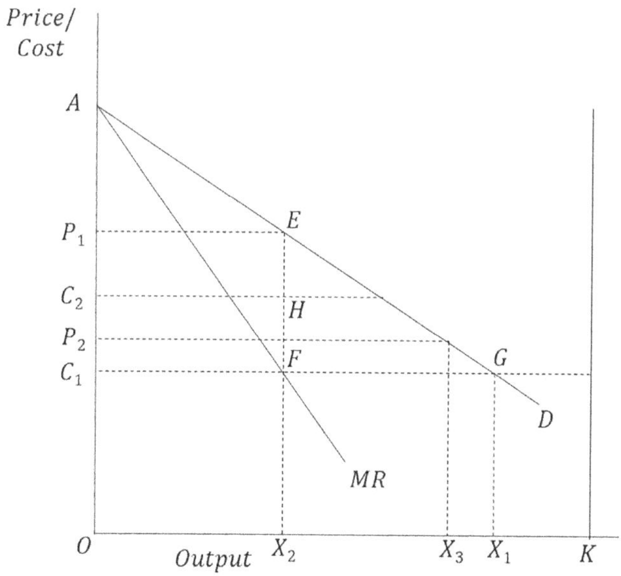

Figure 6.1 Airports with Market Power

and be profitable. The rationale for regulation is that the regulator would set a price of C_1 and force the airport to operate with an output of X_1, or, if there is doubt about the exact price which the airport can achieve, to set a price such as P_2, which is almost as good as C_1.

Firstly, consider the allocative inefficiency produced by a profit-maximising price and output decisions of the airport. At a price of P_1, there will be an inefficiency, or deadweight loss (DWL) given by the triangle EFG, if the airport is operating at a cost of C_1. But the airport is not obliged to have costs of C_1; at a higher cost level such as C_2 it could still cover costs and earn profits. A cost level of C_2 means an additional kind of inefficiency, namely productive inefficiency. This is given by the rectangle C_1FHC_2 in Figure 6.1.

The classic argument for regulation is to eliminate the first of these two inefficiencies (Armstrong et al., 1994). A private but productively efficient airport whose owners seek to maximise profits will set a price of P_1 which causes a deadweight loss (DWL) of EFG. But if a regulator imposed a price of C_1, this inefficiency would be eliminated. How big would the deadweight efficiency loss be? This depends on the size of the gap between the actual and the minimum feasible price, C_1, along with the elasticity of demand for the airport. It was argued in Chapter 2 that the elasticity of demand for many airports is quite low, so price increases would dampen demand only a little. This means that the airport could achieve quite high profits at a price well below the profit-maximising level. If the airport uses only some of its market power, it can gain high profits without the DWL being very large at all. If regulation can be achieved costlessly, it will be worthwhile regulating the airport. However, most regulation has a cost (to be discussed later), and so regulation may not be worthwhile. Furthermore, Figure 6.1 is a simple case which omits some important aspects of airport pricing. Most airports set weight-based or passenger-based prices, which lessens the DWL of higher prices (see Chapter 4). This further reduces the case for regulation if allocative efficiency is the primary objective.

But the rationale for regulation may be to lessen airport productive inefficiency. Airports may not be profit maximisers and may not seek to keep costs down to an efficient level. There are substantial holdings by local authorities and by pension funds in some private airports, and these owners are not always focused only on profits. Some owners are simply slack or dominated by executives interested in their own remuneration. These airports will have higher costs than the minimum feasible. If the airport has market power, it will use it to fund higher cost operations. If many airports operate at higher than minimum costs, carefully designed regulation could increase the airport's productivity efficiency.

Regulation is often presented as being aimed at reducing the use of monopoly power in the private sector. But it is often also used to change the behaviour of public airports. Why would this be necessary rather than governments simply requiring its airports to price and operate efficiently? Because doing so is not a simple task. Under public ownership, governments became dissatisfied with the performance of their enterprises, which had such significant levels of inefficiency that public enterprises became a by-word for inefficiency. Several responses were available: commercialisation, corporatisation and privatisation. Commercialisation meant making enterprises more commercially focused, and corporatisation meant making the enterprises similar to private, profit-seeking, firms. However, if the airport is corporatised, it *may* behave in much the same way as a private firm and this is where the need for economic regulation of public companies can arise.

Whatever the reasons, regulation is applied to many government airports. Airports in public ownership may still have market power and an incentive to use it, either to gain profits, or to cover inefficiently high costs. A corporatised public airport with high costs has an efficiency problem, and regulation may help to reduce it.

The equity or distributional rationales

Regulation changes who benefits from airport operations. An unregulated private airport with market power can earn high profits at the expense of airlines and their passengers. If the airline markets are competitive, high airport prices will be mostly passed through to the passengers. If the airlines mainly serve monopoly or oligopoly routes, an increase in airport prices will be paid partly by passengers and partly by airlines. Regulation can change this pattern of high airport profits paid mainly by passengers (Forsyth, 2001).

Regulators typically have several objectives. In addition to economic efficiency, another important objective may be to affect the distribution of the gains from operating the airport and this may be part of the regulator's terms of reference. The regulator might be expected to serve as an advocate for the consumer or be expected to set "just" or "reasonable" prices. The regulator may impose prices close to airport costs, thus maximising the gains to the airlines and their passengers. A regulator which keeps prices down will often be praised, but one which allows prices to be high (even if this is consistent with high efficiency) will often be criticised. An example of how high prices can be consistent with efficiency is where the airport is subject to excess demand, and high prices could be an efficient means of rationing the excess demand.

While higher regulated prices often fall on the passenger, this is not true when an airport is slot constrained. This case is presented in Figure 6.2. The airport is slot controlled at a capacity of K. Demand is as given by D, and this demand is allocated by price. A price of P_1 for the available slots would clear the market—demand for slots would equal the supply of slots. But the regulator may set airport charges much lower than this. Suppose that the average cost of the airport is C; if the airport is allowed to charge a slightly higher price P_2, the airport will gain a small amount of profit. If slots are traded (either formally or in grey markets—see Chapter 4), the airlines will reap slot rents of $CHEP_1$. If the airport is able to persuade the regulator to increase its price, for example to P_3, the airport will gain, but the airlines will lose to the same extent. Passengers will be unaffected. In this situation, the regulator is simply carving up the profits between the airport and the airlines. While the regulator will make statements about "protecting the consumer", in reality, it is protecting the airlines. At regulated airports that are slot constrained with excess demand, Figure 6.2 shows the reality for many airports, of which London's Heathrow airport is a very clear example.

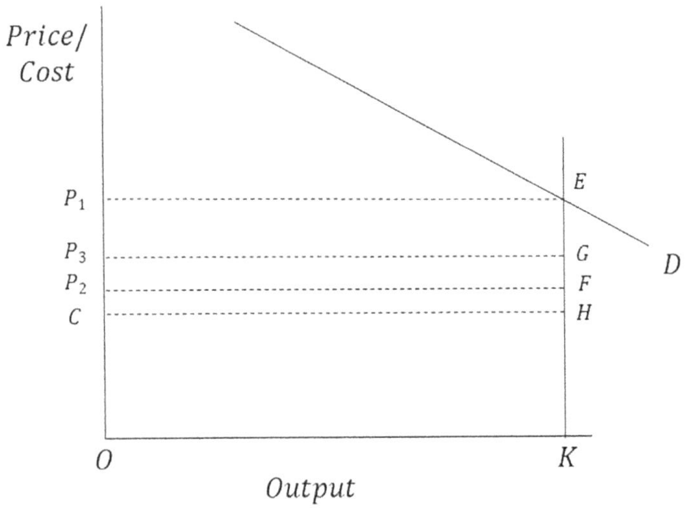

Figure 6.2 Slot Rents at Regulated Airports

The transaction cost approach and contracts

There has been recent interest in the transaction costs approach to regulation. This argues that regulation does not exist to avoid the deadweight loss of monopoly. Rather, regulation is there to protect (airline) users from having their sunk investments expropriated by the airport. When they use an airport, airlines need to make a number of sunk investments, these may include long-lived physical investments, such as terminals or investments to equip them, freight facilities, lounges and marketing campaigns. Once the airline has made the investment, the airport could take advantage of this and raise its charges. Regulation can be seen as a contract between the interested parties, the airport and airlines, to set the terms and conditions such that it is safe for the airlines to deal with the monopoly airport.

Proponents of the transaction cost approach argue that it is better able to explain several features of regulated airports (Biggar, 2012). One of these is that airports use slot mechanisms rather than peak pricing. While peak pricing allocates scarce capacity efficiently, the slot mechanism achieves the same objective but leaves airlines rather than airports with slot rents. Airlines are thus protected.

A related issue is the use of contracts. Whether the main rationale for regulation is efficiency, redistribution or protecting sunk investments, negotiated contracts can be used. The airport could offer the airlines a long-term price contract (say, for five years). Such a contract can avoid the risk of expropriation by the airport, since the airline does not have to accept the contract if it does not like the terms. But contracts on their own do not limit the use of market power; an airport can offer a take-it-or-leave-it contract at a high price. To limit market power, regulation may be needed with the function of an arbitrator, or the creation of a dispute resolution mechanism (this is close to light-handed regulation with arbitration). In themselves, contracts do not constitute regulation since they do not constrain airport behaviour. There can be advantages for both parties in concluding a contract, for example, an airline might choose a different structure of prices than the posted prices. There is some movement towards price contracting in regulated airports.

In summary, the most widely quoted rationale for regulation, that of lessening the DWL of monopoly power, is probably the least important in practice; productive inefficiency is more of a problem with airports, as documented in Chapter 7. Regulators often seek to keep prices close to cost, because this is what is politically acceptable, rather than for the efficiency implications. Looking further at how airports may use their market power, as the transaction cost approach does, explains much of what actually happens with regulated airports.

6.4 Competition or regulation?

Airports were initially considered to be natural monopolies, free from competitive pressures (see Chapter 3). Typically located in cities, airports were far from one another, making competition infeasible. More recently, however, there has been a realisation that competition is feasible in many circumstances (Starkie, 2009; Forsyth et al., 2010; Tretheway and Kinkaid, 2010; Copenhagen Economics, 2012; Wiltshire, 2018). There might be several airports in a region competing for traffic. A potent reason for increased competition between airports has been airline deregulation paving the way, especially in Europe, for new airports to enter the industry to serve LCC traffic. If this is so, the primary rationale for regulation is missing, since competition without regulation serves to stop airports from using market power.

Geography is a critical determinant of airport competition. In some countries, population density is high, while in others low. The UK has a high density, and in most regions, a traveller will have convenient access to several, perhaps three or five, airports. The density in other countries, such as Spain, France and Germany is lower, though many travellers still have convenient access to a few airports. In the US and China, densities are lower again, though particular regions have higher density, such as the US Northeast. Countries such as Brazil, Canada and Australia have very low densities, and for many regions, travellers have few options. Therefore, one of the best measures of competition is the number of other airports within the catchment area of an airport, or within a set radius. The radius might be expressed in distance (kilometres) or in time (number of minutes) to reach other airports. An airport might have two other airports within a distance of 80 km or travel time of one hour, or perhaps four airports within 160 km or two hours travel.

Airports can cater to different types of traffic, and this can also determine the effective competition it faces. There might be four airports within 160 km or two hours travel and all of these could provide competition in the leisure travel market, since leisure travellers may be willing to travel this distance to reach an airport. However, there may be no airports within this radius attractive to business travellers, who have a higher value of time. LCCs, operating from smaller airports, may provide considerable competition in the leisure market, but business travellers will mainly travel to the larger airports closer to the city centre, and the smaller airports may provide only limited competition in this market. This is reflected in pricing policies. The central city airport may be keen to attract all the traffic it can and will encourage LCCs to serve it. It may not overtly offer LCCs lower prices, but it will offer discounts on normal charges for airlines which offer new routes. These discounts can also be had by older established legacy carriers when they offer new routes, but most of their routes will have been operated for many years and will not qualify for discounts.

Another aspect of the level of competition an airport faces is hub competition. Larger hub airports may be in competition with each other even though located some distance apart. A traveller from Hamburg will have a choice of hubs to use when flying to Singapore—London, Frankfurt, Dubai or Paris. Bilateral service agreements limit competition—for example, Emirates does not have the traffic rights to serve Berlin. A number of airports including Singapore and Amsterdam Schiphol compete strongly for hub traffic. There are also large airports that are cargo hubs. Cologne, Leipzig and Memphis are large cargo hubs, and other airports mainly serving passenger traffic also have significant cargo traffic, such as Hong Kong. Cargo airports which are not geographically close may nonetheless be significant competitors for one another.

Competition also exists between destinations specialising in a particular form of tourism, such as beach or ski tourism. Airports may compete in as much as they provide access to the same type of destination. Airports on a Greek island, on the coast of Croatia and in Italy may all be competitors. One aspect of the business model of LCCs is an orientation towards providing travel to specific types of destination rather than travel between major population centres.

An important limitation to competition is a shortage of capacity, especially runway capacity. Several airports may be close together, but if they are all full, they will not compete effectively. This is so whether the airports are rationed by delays, as in the US, or by slots, as in Europe and Asia. A slot-controlled airport has a limited incentive to compete on price since more traffic pushes up the slot premium, and the airport becomes more expensive to use. In addition, airlines keep the slot premium, not the airport.

With many airports, there is no strict dividing line between "competitive" and "monopoly"—an element of both may be present. A city airport could be close to two or three smaller airports. Competition may then be moderately strong for LCC traffic but much less so for the traffic of legacy airlines. By offering discounts to some but not all airlines, an airport will be using its market power. It would have no market power only if competition forced it to offer all customers discounts. This raises a question for governments—what level of market power warrants regulation?

Measuring the strength of competition

With airports being so idiosyncratic, there is no easy or single way of measuring the strength of competition. But regulators have used several methods to estimate the strength of competition and we mention four.

The simplest method is to measure the number of other airports in the airport's catchment area, either in terms of distance or of a specific travel time. This is a relatively easy way to measure competition and it has been applied in a number of studies. It is, however, arbitrary. Should the access time be set at 2 hours (as in Copenhagen Economics, 2012), or, say, one hour? If travellers have a low value of time, as many leisure travellers do, two hours can be appropriate. If travellers have a high value of time, two hours is a long time, and most business travellers would not be prepared to travel two hours unless they had some strong incentive (say, very low prices). So, the strength of competition could differ according to the market segment considered.

Another possible method is to conduct a survey. This would ask potential travellers whether they would be prepared to fly from different airports and try to gauge the willingness to fly from the potentially competitive airports. Would the traveller be prepared to travel from a less convenient airport if the fare were, say, €10 less, or €20 less? One limitation of the survey technique is that respondents may not give accurate answers—they may "game" the answers (for example, if an airline is considering switching some of its flights to a less convenient airport). Another limitation is that surveys, if they are designed and administered carefully, can be expensive. This latter limitation may not be a problem if a regulator with adequate resources is considering whether an airport should be regulated. This issue is discussed in the example of the UK CAA and CMA studies of airport competition later in this chapter.

A third indicator of competition arises in the pricing behaviour of the airport. When conditions change, monopolies behave differently from firms subject to competition—observing behaviour will give the regulator some indicator of whether the airport is competitive or not. If there is an aviation crisis, such as that which occurred during the COVID-19 pandemic, and an airport raises its charges to cover its costs, this can be an indication that it is using market power. A competitive airport would be likely to reduce its charges, perhaps to gain more business, or not raise them (unless all of the airports in the region are increasing their prices as well). For example, if a city airport offers discounts to one market segment but not to others, this price structure suggests the presence of competition in some of its markets but not in all.

Airlines have argued that after the 2008 financial crash many airports raised rather than lowered charges (Wiltshire, 2018) and that as aviation re-opened following the pandemic, charges again rose at many airports that sought to recoup revenues lost during the COVID-19 crisis. In contrast, ACI, representing airports, rejected this interpretation, maintaining instead that average airport charges were falling in the five years to 2019 (InterVISTAS/ACI World, 2022) and that airports of all sizes face strong and growing competition which restricts their ability to raise charges (Oxera, 2017). A study of the European Commission reviewed data on the trends in airport charges in the EU in the years 2009–2016 and found an average increase in airport charges over this period of 23%.

A fourth approach is to use a modelling study to estimate the degree of substitution between specific airports. This has been done for the Greater London airports and for the San Francisco airports (Hess and Polak, 2010), though the technique can be widely applied provided data are available. A great advantage of this approach is that airport choice can be modelled along with route choice and information about the origins of passengers. Thus, for a resident of south London on a business trip, London Gatwick may be a good option but London Luton a poor option. Estimates can be made of overall substitution elasticities but also for specific types of travel. This approach does give the regulator a considerable amount of information, though it requires a considerable analytical effort.

Countervailing power and double marginalisation

Airports may have market power, but it is possible that their airline customers also have some market power. Airports may have countervailing power which they can use to drive airport charges down. If so, this would affect the case for regulation.

The idea of countervailing power is not a precisely defined one, and there are several situations in which the term is used. The clearest case is one in which both the airport and an airline have market power. There might be only one airline, in practice, which can serve the airport—this could be true of a dominant national airline with market power in serving regional airports (e.g., some regions in Australia and Canada). The airport may have a monopoly, but the airline has a monopsony (see Appendix) that it can use to push airport charges down. This is bilateral monopoly. There are some desirable features of this situation, especially that it reduces the monopoly welfare loss (the output loss is reduced compared to the output loss of a simple monopoly). Other implications are not so attractive. Prices to the airline passenger are not reduced under bilateral monopoly—the airport and airline share the profits. If regulators are concerned about overall efficiency, bilateral monopoly is desirable, but to the extent that they are concerned about prices to the passengers, bilateral monopoly does not help.

Sometimes the notion of countervailing power is taken to mean a situation in which airlines can choose which airport to serve, so the airline plays one airport off against another. In this case, the airports clearly have no monopoly, and there is effective competition. This can be the case when LCCs have several (probably small) airports which they can serve. There is competition between destinations, and passengers are not tied to a specific city (which business passengers are likely to be). In this environment, competition between airports is real, and there is no need for regulation.

The relative size of the airline and the airport is unlikely to be much of a determinant of countervailing power. It is often maintained that the airline is large, but the airport is small, and thus the airline must have countervailing power. However, even in those circumstances, if there is only airport at a destination that the airline wishes to serve, the airline has no option but to use that airport and pay its charges. Perth airport, which serves a large but remote city, has been involved in disputes with Qantas, a much larger company. Countervailing power is most likely in a location where there is a single airport but only one or two airlines that serve the route, at least in the short to medium term. These airports are likely to be small, and quite possibly marginal.

Another problem with countervailing power is that a "strong" airline counterbalancing the market power of an airport can lead to a situation of "double marginalisation". Double marginalisation means that an upstream monopolist (an airport), in order to charge monopoly prices, restricts output. Given this excessively low output, the downstream monopolist (the airline) also sets monopoly prices and reduces output even further. Compared to a vertically integrated monopoly (the airline and the airport acting jointly), output is further reduced and the welfare loss is increased. Such a situation can be interpreted as countervailing power. For example, the dominant national carrier, with its alliance partners, can counterbalance the main airport. If both reach an agreement, this is interpreted as a good outcome and evidence for countervailing power, although both parties have just double marginalised the market.

Competition and regulation—the case of the UK

The UK has a large number of airports, and most are not regulated. When some major airports such as London Heathrow and London Gatwick were privatised, they were regulated at first. Over time, however, the need for regulation has been questioned, and some have now been deregulated. The extent of competition has been assessed for the UK (Civil Aviation Authority, 2007; Competition Commission, 2009; Competition and Markets Authority, 2016).

At the time of their privatisation in 1987, the UK government subjected the three London airports owned by BAA to price-cap regulation, and the four Scottish airports owned by BAA, to a lighter form of regulation. The independently owned public Manchester Airport was also subject to price-caps. Prior to 1987, the government had also considered selling separately the London airports (Heathrow, Gatwick and Stansted) in order to foster competition, though it did not do so. Since then, the question of whether the airports faced enough competition to dispense with competition has been a live one. In 2008 the CAA determined that Manchester Airport faced enough competition and regulation was removed. In 2009 the principal competition body, now called the Competition and Markets Authority, recommended that the London airports be owned separately, and eventually, this took place between 2009 and 2013. Edinburgh airport was sold in 2012. Then in 2014, London Stansted Airport was judged to face sufficient competition to remove regulation, and the independently owned London Gatwick airport was subject to a lighter form of regulation, leaving only London Heathrow with full price-cap regulation. Recently, it has been suggested that Manchester airport retains market power, and the CAA has commenced a market power assessment at Manchester airport, though this was put on hold due to the COVID-19 crisis.

Thus, the CAA, combined with the Competition and Market Authority, has a track record in evaluating the degree of competition which airports face, and the need or not for regulation. The CAA has published detailed issued guidance for market power assessments, consistent with the Competition and Market Authority's approach; the SSNIP test (small but significant non-transitory increase in price) is used to test for market power. This method estimates the demand response to a hypothetical price increase (usually of 5–10%). In some cases, the response is assessed using survey results. In the case of Stansted airport, which mainly serves LCCs, the CAA relied to some extent on evidence of the buyer power of airlines such as easyJet and Ryanair (Stansted's two main customers). While in most countries the decision whether competition is strong enough to dispense with regulation has been made in ad hoc fashion or even not assessed at all, the UK has taken a very rigorous approach.

In a very small number of other jurisdictions, assessments of market power have been conducted, though not all investigations have been equally comprehensive. The Australian Productivity Commission's most recent assessment concluded that the four main Australian airports possessed market power but had not systematically exercised that power (Productivity Commission, 2019). In 2009, the Dutch competition authorities commissioned an assessment of market power at Schiphol airport (Müller et al., 2010). The study concluded that competition from other airports was weak. Full-service carriers needing the services of a hub airport would be unlikely to switch from Schiphol so that an increase in airport charges would be profitable for the airport operator. Maertens (2012), in his assessment of airport market power for the 50 largest European airports, concluded that most of them have persistent market power.

6.5 Types of regulation

Three main types of regulation have been applied to airports. The first is cost-plus regulation, which permits the airport to charge average prices equal to the airport's estimated average costs (including a return on capital). Usually, the regulator allows a slightly higher price to allow for contingencies, such as when the costs are underestimated. A second approach is incentive regulation, which directly recognises the problem of ensuring efficient production. A third approach is that of light-handed regulation, of which there are a few, but growing number, of examples. We discuss these in turn.

Cost-plus regulation

This is a general term for a system of regulation in which the regulator allows the airport to recover its costs from its customers, mainly the airlines. The most common form of cost-plus regulation is rate-of-return regulation, which is applied at many airports. Cost-plus regulation dates back to the 19th century in the US, where it was applied to private firms judged to have significant market power, such as railways, water companies and gas utilities. This system of regulation became more developed as regulators and courts determined what costs could and could not be counted in the firm's cost base. In the US, it gradually evolved into rate-of-return regulation. When airports were being corporatised and privatised it was natural that many countries moved towards cost-plus regulation where the airports were thought to possess market power.

A rate-of-return type of regulation might seem appropriate for airports. Airports are capital intensive forms of infrastructure, and capital costs loom large in total costs.

Thus, the regulator would need to develop a rule to assess which costs were allowable and which were not. The idea of average cost is quite broad and, to be more specific, rate-of-return regulation was adopted. Like other regulated industries, the airport would be permitted to earn its cost of capital (or slightly more)—this would set a limit on the prices that it was allowed to charge.

While this may seem reasonable, rate-of-return regulation suffers from a number of serious flaws. One of these is that it gives an incentive to over-capitalise. As long as the airport is earning more than its cost of capital, it has an incentive to expand its capital base (Averch and Johnson, 1966). The larger the capital base, the greater the return earned. Airports were able to over-invest because they had market power and could cover costs with higher prices. Over time, this was recognised as a major drawback of rate-of-return regulation, which was confirmed by empirical studies. In the case of airports, it led to "gold plating" and "Taj Mahals" terminals.

A further drawback is that cost-plus regulation generally does not impose much discipline on the firm to keep its costs down. A firm such as an airport can simply allow its operational costs to rise as long as they will be included in the cost base. This is something which regulators gradually became aware of. At the start, say before the end of the 1950s, regulators tended to accept the costs as reported to them. The firm would seek a price increase of 4% to cover its costs and the regulator might allow 3.9%. But by the 1970s a number of empirical studies of regulated industries had started to appear which indicated that many were producing at far above minimum cost (studies of productive efficiency at airports suggested that many airports are not efficient—see Chapter 7). Cost-based regulation provides no incentive for the airport to adopt efficient price structures, such as peak pricing (see Chapter 4).

In spite of these limitations, cost-plus regulation is used for several airports, especially in continental Europe. It is an easy idea to sell—what could seem more reasonable than requiring airports to charge no more than their average cost? Nonetheless, the shortcomings of rate-of-return regulation have led it to be replaced in many industries and jurisdictions by incentive regulation.

Incentive regulation

Incentive regulation grew out of dissatisfaction with the performance of cost-plus regulation. Its genesis was both theoretical and practical. At the theoretical level, economists sought to design regulation to harness the objectives of private or government firms more effectively, and in particular, to give regulated firms some freedom to seek profits by reducing costs. The problem is a principal–agent problem (Armstrong et al., 1994) where the principal, the regulator, is trying to set conditions such as price, to promote efficiency and equity. The agent, the firm, knows more about its costs than the regulator and whether its minimum feasible costs are high or low. If profit were the only consideration, the regulator could set a high price to cover all possibilities and thus guarantee that the firm would be able to cover its costs. If the firm is able to achieve low costs it would then make large profits. But this may have a cost in terms of efficiency (prices being unnecessarily high) and equity (again, prices being too high). The regulator will seek to set a price that achieves a number of conflicting objectives. The regulator tries to make use of the incentive for the airports to gain profits as a way of keeping costs down, but it constrains the profit objective.

The theoretical models of incentive regulation would be difficult to operationalise, but they have greatly influenced practical solutions to the problem. The most widespread form of incentive regulation is CPI-X. The idea came from Beesley and Littlechild, who, in 1983, were looking for a means of regulating telecommunications when the UK embarked on a programme of privatisation (Vickers and Yarrow, 1988). They were aware of the problems of cost-plus regulation and were seeking to devise a better system of regulation (especially one which would give the firm more incentive to reduce its costs). CPI-X (or RPI-X) was a relatively simple way to do so and this model was applied to British Telecommunications in 1984. The regulator would set a maximum price for a specific number of years (say, five years). Since productivity was expected to improve, the price would be required to fall by a set factor, X. To allow for inflation, the firm was allowed to increase its prices by the consumer inflation rate (CPI). Thus, if X was 3%, and the CPI rose by 2%, the firm would be required to reduce its prices by 1%.

This new system was applied across the privatised industries in the UK, and in 1987, to airports. The BAA was privatised as a group of 7 airports and regulated by CPI-X price-caps (Vickers and Yarrow, 1988). Over time, the number of BAA airports subject to the price-cap was reduced, and now only London Heathrow is subject to the original form of CPI-X price-cap. When Australia privatised its airports, it initially chose to regulate them using CPI-X regulation, though more recently it has opted for light-handed regulation. There have also been a number of European airports capped in this way as well as some examples in other regions (such as Mexico).

A pure price-cap creates strong incentives for the firm to keep its costs down, since it keeps any extra profits it generates. A price-cap encourages productive efficiency. However, there are drawbacks related to the choice of X. The regulator is not well informed about airport costs. Suppose the regulator sets X at 3%, but the airport can operate at much lower costs; in this case, the airport would be very profitable. High profits can be very controversial (sometimes leading to resetting of the price-cap). But by revealing high profits, the firm also reveals its true costs to the regulator. In the subsequent regulatory period, the price-cap can be set with reference to the airport's actual costs, not the earlier overestimate. The opposite problem is much more serious, when the regulator sets a price path which is too ambitious, and the airport is unable to cover its costs. This happened in Australia over the 1997–2002 regulatory period, leading to the suspension of the price-caps in 2001, followed by the replacement of them by light-handed regulation. Similar problems have occurred in the California electricity industry, and, in 2022, in the UK and Australian electricity markets, leading to the collapse of several suppliers. The COVID-19 pandemic does not seem to have led to this type of problem with price-capped airports, however.

Incentive regulation is used in a significant number of airports though not in a majority (Forsyth et al., 2021). The regulatory approach described earlier is a "pure" form of regulation; actual applications reflect a number of compromises and are less than "pure". It is common for a system when it is first set up to be fairly pure, but over time, compromises are made, and the system becomes a "hybrid" system. For example, when the Australian airports were first privatised, they were subjected to a fairly pure price-cap, but had it been continued it probably would have veered towards a hybrid form.

There are several ways in which systems evolve towards hybrid regulation (see Baldwin and Cave, 1999). When first set up, a regulatory period is determined (say, five years) and the "X" may be determined by educated guesswork about what productivity gains are possible, along with some empirical observations. When the second regulatory period starts, a new "X" must be chosen, along with a new initial price. To set strong incentives, this would be done without reference to the airport's actual costs. In reality, regulators do take account of the actual costs which the airport has been able to achieve. This gives the airport an incentive to allow its costs to be higher than they need to be, to induce the regulator to set an easy "X" for the next period.

Another limitation of incentive regulation is that, in a simple form, it gives airports a strong incentive to lower the quality of service (Rovizzi and Thompson, 1992) which typically lowers the firm's costs. This became apparent when firms were first regulated by price-caps. One response is to link the price-cap to a set of quality standards. Thus, London Heathrow and Dublin airports are required to meet set standards (cleanliness, queue length, equipment availability, etc.). Airports subjected to light-handed regulation are also expected to conform to set quality standards. This can be effective to maintain quality, but results in the regulator becoming more prescriptive.

In price-cap regulation, how should the "X" be set? It would be possible to set the X based on the past performance of the airport, along with forecasts (i.e., guesses) about future performance. Doing so might not give very strong incentives. Alternatively, the regulator may look at the performance of other airports as a guide—and use "yardstick" or "benchmark" regulation (see more on benchmarking in Chapter 7). The idea would be to determine a group of airports whose characteristics are similar to that of the regulated airport, or alternatively, undertake an econometric study of a range of airports to assess the possible cost or efficiency levels which the regulated airport can achieve. While yardstick regulation is an attractive idea, it has not been as widely applied as it might have been. There is a real difficulty in comparing airports like with like, because airports are very heterogeneous firms. However, benchmarking has been used successfully to assess relative performance in specific processes of the airport.

The primary motivation for incentive regulation is its effect on productive efficiency since it rewards an airport that keeps its costs low. However, it can also have some effects on allocative efficiency. Three key aspects include: the price structures at airports with spare capacity, the price structure at congested airports, and the possible use of peak/off-peak pricing. An efficient pricing structure for airports with spare capacity would be weight-based prices, which is a form of Ramsey pricing (see Chapter 4). It has been argued that price-cap regulation induces the firm to use

Ramsey pricing but that is the standard basis for airport charges in any case. At busy congested airports, one would expect incentive regulation to cause the airport to move away from weight-based pricing and charge every flight the same price. This would be efficient, and also maximise airport profits, since the airport would maximise the use of scarce capacity by encouraging larger aircraft. So far, there has only been limited evidence of this happening in price-capped airports. London Heathrow airport has, for a number of years, been moving towards price structures which discourage smaller aircraft. The third aspect of allocative efficiency is peak pricing of busy airports. This happens when the airport is slot constrained, provided slots are traded, whatever the form of regulation. The price-capped airport of Rome is one of the few airports with a peak charge (Forsyth et al., 2021).

Light-handed regulation

There has been a move towards the light-handed regulation of airports in recent decades (Productivity Commission, 2002). This has been in response to problems with more formal regulation including the impact of airport investment decisions. Investment regulation can be like cost-plus regulation (with attendant weakening of incentives for efficiency). Airports can also encounter financial problems when regulators have set too stringent targets.

A key element of "Light-handed Regulation" (L-HR) is that it is not ex ante. It is a form of ex post regulation. One form of L-HR is based on monitoring; the airport's performance is subject to (fairly detailed) monitoring of its price levels, profitability, productivity, quality levels and investment programmes. Monitoring may or may not lead to further action by the government or regulatory body if the airport's performance is judged to be deficient. In some cases, regulatory bodies consider that detailed and transparent monitoring is sufficient to encourage good behaviour given that airlines will report deficiencies if they are adversely affected.

A possible structure for L-HR might go like this. The regulator informs the airport that there will be no ex ante regulation; however, the airport's performance will be reviewed after a set period. The criteria for adequate performance will be set out. These might cover pricing behaviour, and whether the airport has been abusing its market power. Other criteria could include productivity, profitability and quality performance. The airport is informed about what will happen if performance is judged to be deficient. For example, it might be that deficient performance would lead to the re-imposition of detailed regulation, or it might be that the airport is instructed to reduce its charges. After the set period has elapsed, the government or regulator conducts a review, and if performance is adequate, recommends to the government that the arrangements continue. The review body may take into account additional factors—in particular, it may assess the competition the airport faces, and it may recommend to the government that there is no further need for L-HR.

Another approach to light-handed regulation is to institute a dispute resolution mechanism. A key feature of L-HR is that the airport and the airlines are encouraged to, as far as possible, to resolve disputes by negotiation. Often disputes are resolved, but not always—in particular, it is difficult for the parties to agree on the level of charges. If the parties fail to agree, there is a provision for the matter to go to an arbitrator, which resolves the matter. The model of arbitration to resolve disputes is common in the US and Canada, especially in the case of railway rates (Littlechild, 2012; Arblaster, 2014). It is quite possible that the arbitrator will be the country's competition regulator, which may have its own set of procedures for arbitration.

One of the most detailed and long-running systems of L-HR of airports is that for the four major airports in Australia (Littlechild, 2012; Arblaster, 2014). This was introduced in 2002 after the airports had been privatised and initially price-capped. There have since been periodic reviews, the most recent in 2019. Some airports, such as Adelaide Airport, were initially subjected to L-HR, but after a review, the government decided they were subject to sufficient competition to not warrant L-HR anymore. The reviews have been carried out by the Productivity Commission, the government's main microeconomic policy adviser. The competition authority, the Australian Competition and Consumer Commission (ACCC), annually monitors airport profitability, prices and quality, which serve as inputs to the reviews. In each review to date, the Productivity Commission determined that the airports had not been abusing their market power. Both the airlines and the ACCC have argued that charges are excessive (see Box 6.1), and have lobbied for a dispute resolution mechanism, but the government, on the advice of the Productivity Commission, has not introduced one.

6.6 Investment under regulation

Since airports are capital-intensive industries, the impact of regulation on investment is important. Almost by definition, rate-of-return regulation deals with the investment question. Light-handed regulation was partly motivated by the need to work out a way to enable an airport to make the necessary investments. Incentive regulation, in its basic formulation, did not pay any specific attention to the need for investment—it can be adapted to allow the airport to make investments, though in so doing it becomes less hands-off and requires considerable intervention by the regulator.

There are several distinct reasons why an airport will need to invest, each resulting in a different response. Three reasons are of particular importance:

- Investment to reduce operational costs (possibly to take advantage of new technologies).
- Investment to increase quality of service, and
- Investment to increase the capacity of the airport.

These are discussed in turn.

Investment to reduce operating costs

This is the simplest case. Under cost-based and rate-of-return regulation, investment increases the asset base, but operational costs fall when the investment is completed. If the airport is subject to light-handed regulation, there will be no limit on cost-reducing investment, though the airport will be subject to periodic reviews to assess whether the airport is providing its services efficiently. If the airport is subject to incentive regulation, such as a price-cap, it will have an incentive to make those investments which are worthwhile and which lower costs, and thus enable the airport to increase its profits.

Investment to increase service quality

Under a system of cost-plus regulation, quality-improving investments can take place. Under a system of rate-of-return regulation, the airport can make an investment, which increases its asset base, and thereby, its profits. The main problem with rate-of-return regulation is that it can give raise to excessive investment. The more the airport invests, the larger the profit it earns, and there is no limit on the amount of investment undertaken. In practice, regulators often monitor the investment by the airport and try to guard against excessive investment, but they do not always do this effectively.

In the discussion of incentive regulation, it was noted that there was an incentive for the airport to reduce, rather than increase, quality. As with other regulated industries, the airport can be given an incentive to make worthwhile investments in quality—for example, if it makes a specific investment, be it a new terminal or a runway extension, it can be granted a higher price-cap. This happened when London Heathrow built Terminal 5, which increased capacity and quality. If the regulator chooses, the quality improvement can be quite specific. Thus, when the Australian airports were regulated, the regulator allowed price increases for a runway extension and for air bridges—it is here where a price-cap becomes hybrid.

This is a practical approach, but it does mean that the regulator becomes less "hands-off". The regulator determines what investments the airport may make and which it may not. This also poses the question of *how* the regulator decides what investments to allow. The airport knows more about the quality preferences of its customers, but it does not have an incentive to report these truthfully. The management might wish to build at too high a quality standard. To inform itself, the regulator will need to undertake a shadow investment evaluation, to guard against excessive investment spending by the airport.

One way in which regulators tackle this problem is to encourage greater negotiation between the airport and its airline customers. There is a clear conflict between the airlines and airport about the level of charges, but no such conflict over the quality level. It may be possible for the two parties to conclude an agreement over a specific aspect of the quality of the airport, such as the size of the terminal. However, even here there can be problems since the quality preferences of different customers will differ. The legacy carriers will want a large, spacious terminal, and the LCCs will demand a small, cheap terminal. Nevertheless, it is sometimes possible to negotiate and agree on clearly defined aspects of quality, and the regulator can allow for this in setting allowable charges.

Disagreements between airlines and airports over investment have been one of the reasons for the move towards L-HR. Airports have been frustrated by regulator's unwillingness to approve investments which they consider essential, or they have been frustrated by the complicated arrangements imposed by regulators when they do approve investments. With L-HR, the airports are free to make their own decisions about investments, subject to periodic reviews of their overall performance. After Australia moved towards L-HR, there have been relatively few complaints about the airport's choices over quality (but many complaints about the level of charges).

Investment to increase capacity

If the airport is subject to cost-plus regulation, it should not lack incentives to invest but there remains the danger of overinvestment. If the airport is subject to L-HR it can choose the level of investment needed. There is a chance that it will over-invest, driving up prices and profits. In this situation, the review body will need to check that this has not happened.

If the airport is regulated by incentive regulation, it matters whether "constant costs" exist at that airport, that is, *unit* costs do not increase as the airport expands or, in other words, costs double if capacity doubles. Under a price-cap, the presence of constant or increasing costs also matters. In the former case, there will be no need for price adjustment as the airport expands. This is shown in Figure 6.3.

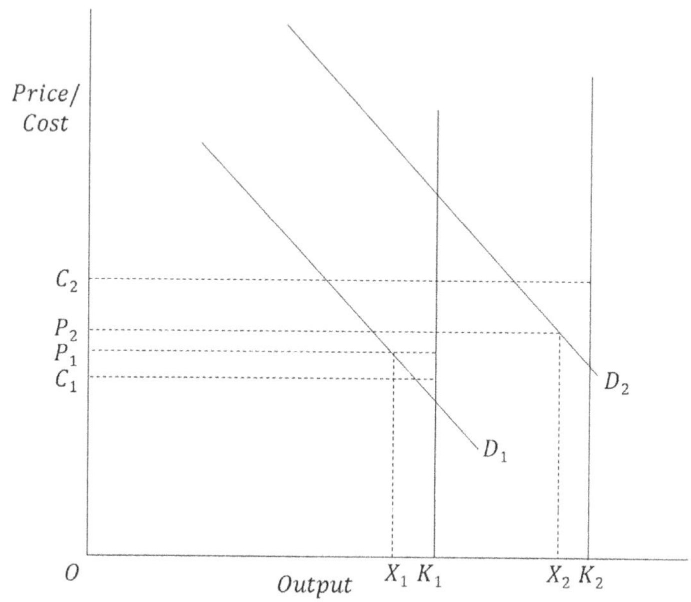

Figure 6.3 Price-Caps for Expanding Airports

The airport is subject to a price-cap of P_1, which is sufficient to cover its costs. As demand increases from D_1 to D_2, costs increase, but revenues increase to match, and the airport can still remain profitable.

However, some airports experience increasing costs. This is particularly related to the availability of additional land. With a restricted land bank, it can be very expensive to build new capacity. Major earthworks, or even land reclamation from the sea, may be needed in order to expand runway capacity. In this case, doubling capacity will more than double the costs. This will mean that at the old price level, revenues will not cover costs unless the regulator allows a higher price-cap.

This case is shown in Figure 6.3. Demand for the airport increases to D_2. When the airport expands beyond K_1, costs rise (say, a new, expensive runway must be built). Variable and marginal costs are C_1 up to K_1, and they rise to C_2 for the output levels beyond K_1. If the price-cap remains at P_1, the airport will fail to cover its costs and be unwilling to invest. The regulator can induce the airport to invest by raising the price-cap, to P_2, which is slightly above the average of C_1 and C_2. It is now worthwhile for the airport to make the investment and produce at X_2. This is a simplified representation of the problem facing the regulator.

Regulation is now moving away from a pure price-cap to a hybrid form of regulation. The price-cap aspect means the airport keeps the profits it makes by finding new efficiencies. However, the regulatory regime also allows for changes in costs, and specifically capital costs, to influence the price-cap and, in this respect, is like rate-of-return regulation (see Box 6.1).

Under all regulatory regimes, the airport may not deliver the investments, even though it collects higher revenues to finance them. This has happened, and it is difficult for the regulator to address this after the event unless the price-cap was conditional on delivery of the investment programme. Failure to deliver gives the regulator the option to adjust downwards the asset base in the next regulatory period and also to "claw back" the revenues the airport collected for the investment in the previous period. It is best if such an ex post response is explicitly advised to the airport and to users in advance of work starting on investments.

Major investments under regulation

Not all investments can be handled satisfactorily under a regulatory framework. Major airport investments can be very complicated, giving rise to environmental issues, including climate change, land use problems, access route problems and interactions with other airports. A solution may be made-to-measure evaluation. Major airports, such as London Heathrow and Amsterdam Schiphol are regulated by well-established regulatory structures. However, when it comes to large or complex investments, the regulator is bypassed, and a specific evaluation exercise is established. A good example is the Airports Commission in London, which reported on runway options for Heathrow and Gatwick directly to the government (Airports Commission, 2015; see Chapter 5).

6.7 Regulation of non-aeronautical services and airports as two-sided markets

A typical airport will produce both aeronautical (such as runway services, aprons and taxiways and some terminal services) and non-aeronautical services (which more or less covers the rent of their product mix, including retail services, car parking, offices and other services which vary from airport to airport (Graham, 2018)). A decision needs to be made as to how broad the coverage of the services to be regulated is to be. A regulator may simply restrict its attention to aeronautical services, and leave non-aeronautical services unregulated, in which it is said to be operating a "dual till", or it may seek to regulate all services provided by the airport, in which it is said to be operating a "single till". Regulators differ and neither single nor dual tills predominate. The literature on single and dual tills is one which generates more heat than light, and there is no convincing answer to the question of "which is superior?" There are several factors which affect the choice, and thus, "it all depends".

A starting point is to question whether there is a case for regulating non-aeronautical services. A government may consider that the regulation of an airport is warranted, but does this mean that all services of the airport should be regulated? If there is strong market power in non-aeronautical services, there can be a case for regulation. An airport might have market power in retail (the prices of the coffee or the burgers are ultimately set by the airport, and McDonald's are franchisees). The price of car parking can reflect both locational rents and monopoly rents, depending on the airport. Non-aeronautical services can be very profitable, which might reflect monopoly pricing. As a result, the choice of some regulators is to opt for single till regulation. Other regulators conclude that regulation of non-aeronautical services is not worth the effort, and possibly harmful.

There are several conflicting aspects which are relevant in the choice. Airport regulatory systems are imperfect (especially those which have poor incentives for productive efficiency). If this is the case, the smaller the base for regulation is better, and dual till regulation is better. On the other hand, the wider single till can promote allocative efficiency, and induce prices which are closer to costs. With a dual till the airport has more incentive to innovate, since it enjoys the profits from doing so—why should an airport try hard to innovate if the profits go to reducing airport charges, as they do under single till (this said, BAA was a leader in innovating retail in the early days after privatisation even though it was regulated under a single till).

If non-aeronautical services are profitable (and they often are), the choice between single and dual till affects who pays what. A single till results in overall prices being kept low, and the aeronautical charges kept low by the profits of the non-aeronautical services. Not surprisingly, airlines are in favour of the single till.

It is one thing to note that airports provide a range of different products, but it is also the case that the pricing of one service can influence the use of another. Products are complementary. Starkie (1999) noted that this has implications for price regulation. If non-aeronautical services are profitable, an airport will have an incentive to lower the price for aeronautical services to attract more flights and passengers, who then spend more in the terminal. This is something which regulators would need to take into account, and they may be less likely to choose to regulate.

In recent years there has been an interest in the idea of "two-sided markets" (see Rochat and Tirole, 2006). This is a theoretical concept which describes interdependence between two groups of actors, such as the suppliers and users of credit cards. Credit card suppliers would like more consumers to use their cards, and consumers gain from their cards being more widely usable. There are many examples of two-sided markets, and it has been suggested that airports are a good example of them (Gillen and Mantin, 2013; and for a recent review, see Starkie, 2021). In particular, there are externalities which flow from the interaction between the parties.

The externality noted by Starkie is an example of importance of seeing airports as two-sided markets, with implications for regulation. Another application of the idea comes with single or dual till question. Malavolti (2016) suggests an argument for single tills in that they are better able to capture the externality between aeronautical and non-aeronautical services than dual tills. The two-sided market idea is something which has only recently been explored, but it promises to be a valuable insight into how airports operate and price their services.

6.8 The basic mechanics of setting a price-cap

How do regulatory agencies actually set a price-cap? Over the four decades since price-caps were first introduced, a methodology has been developed which is now rather well established and accepted. The method is applicable to airports that are corporatised and operated on a commercial basis, whether they are owned by public or by private interests.

The prevailing method is called the "building blocks" approach, which distinguishes certain types of cost (building blocks) and, in particular, between operating costs, investment costs and returns on assets. The regulatory body sets an allowance for each of these elements of cost, perhaps using benchmarking methods, at least in part, or consultancy advice, as well as engagement with both sides of the industry. Good price regulation would estimate the efficient levels of these allowances, in other words, the sums that an efficient airport operator would need to operate the airport at the required level of service and given expected traffic. Similarly, an allowance for the efficient cost of making investments in capacity commensurate with expected traffic and desired quality.

An allowance for the return on assets also needs to be decided. The total net value of assets is known as the Regulatory Asset Base (RAB). New investment is added to the RAB and depreciation is subtracted. The airport operator is allowed a return on these assets, usually equal to the weighted average cost of capital (WACC, discussed later). This is the allowed rate-of-return. Multiplying it by the RAB yields an allowance on historic investments. A depreciation allowance is also calculated, normally using standard accounting rules and assumed lives for the different classes of asset. Each allowance is typically set for each year of the subsequent price-cap, often five years. The sum of the allowances—the building blocks—is divided by the forecast level of passenger traffic to compute a price-cap per passenger per year. The price-cap is often presented in constant-price terms for a base year and then adjusted to current-price terms using outturn inflation rates.

Once the price-cap is set, the airport operator collects the revenues yielded by the price-cap multiplied by actual passenger traffic. The use of the revenues is a matter for the airport operator, as long as the airport continues to be operated and the investments are made. If the airport finds economies in operating or investment costs, it retains the savings for the period of the price-cap. But if its costs are higher than the allowances, the airport suffers a loss because, to give the airport the incentive to find economies and to operate efficiently, the price-cap is not adjusted ex post, at least under incentive regulation.

A significant cost for airports, especially those with a large infrastructure or planning significant investment, is the "cost of capital". Prior funding is needed to finance an investment; as new revenues are earned only after the asset is in use. There are two main sources of such funds: equity and debt, and most airports use a mixture. Each source of funding has a cost: shareholders need to be paid a dividend (the "cost of equity") related to the returns that are available elsewhere in the economy taking account of the riskiness of a given airport's business. Likewise, bondholders will earn a return (the "cost of debt") which is also related to the riskiness of an airport's business model.

The cost of equity can be decomposed into two parts: the risk-free rate (RFR) and the equity risk premium (ERP). Government debt is generally considered to be close to risk free and the return on such debt is usually used as a measure of the RFR. The ERP is estimated from share price movements at airports with publicly traded shares and is multiplied by a beta variable that measures the volatility of an airport's shares compared to the stock market. A beta value of less than one would represent less volatility than in the market generally (say, 0.75) whereas high volatility might lead to a beta estimate of perhaps 1.5.

The cost of debt is also composed of two parts: the RFR and the debt premium. The latter is estimated by examining the cost of issuing new debt by companies with a similar credit rating. For airports that are state owned, there are no shares to be traded on financial markets and therefore no direct data on share prices. In these cases, cost of capital estimates must be inferred from trends in the share price of privately owned airports.

The cost of equity and the cost of debt are then weighted by the percentage of equity and of debt in the airport's balance sheet to give the weighted average cost of capital (WACC).

Expressed as a formula, the cost of capital can be written in the following simple form[1]:

$$WACC = r_d \times g + r_e(1-g)$$

where g is the percentage of debt on the balance sheet, r_d is the cost of debt and r_e is the cost of equity. In this formula, taxation and other complications are disregarded.

Why does the cost of capital matter to an airport operator? Airports are capital intensive, so remunerating the capital they have invested can constitute a large—or even a predominant—part of an airport's cost base. For example, as mentioned in Chapter 3, a 2022 CAA regulatory decision concerning London Heathrow airport projected that, over the subsequent five years, capital costs (including depreciation) would reach a total of £8bn. compared to £6bn of operating costs. This reflects the fact that London Heathrow has an asset base valued at some £17bn (CAA, 2022).

The cost of capital matters for costs but also influences airport investment decisions and charges. In considering future investments, a corporatised airport will compare the returns expected to be earned from the project with the airport's cost of capital. An investment will only be profitable if the project's returns are expected to exceed the cost of capital. A higher cost of capital therefore constitutes a higher threshold for new investment and vice versa. Also, in regulated airports, the cost of capital is a "building block" that feeds directly into the price-cap; a higher cost of capital implies higher airport charges.

Box 6.1 Controversies in Airport Economics: are private, lightly regulated airports ripping off airlines and passengers?

Competition and regulation are at the core of one of the sharpest controversies in airport economics, namely that of whether unregulated or lightly regulated airports are abusing their market power. If an airport has several effective competitors, it will have little scope to use market power, and its charges will be moderate. If the market is not competitive, an airport will have the scope to use market power, and, among other things, will be able to have high charges. Here there would be a case for regulation to prevent the airport from using its market power.

There is sharp disagreement between airlines and airports when it comes to airport charges. Airlines are convinced that unregulated and lightly regulated airports are using their market power to increase their profits, at the expense of airlines and their passengers. They have particular concerns about privatised airports, and especially the more lightly regulated ones. By contrast, the airports claim that their charges are moderate, and do not show any evidence of monopoly pricing. Both parties back up their claims with empirical studies. Thus, IATA did a study of airport profitability, arguing that it had been rising, and Airlines for Australia and New Zealand (A4ANZ) did a study of airport profitability in Australia and other countries, arguing that profitability of the lightly regulated major Australian airports were higher than in other countries' airports (A4ANZ, 2018). In contrast, ACI recently produced a report on airport charges, arguing that charges at lightly regulated airports were lower than those at heavily regulated airports (InterVISTAS/ACI, 2022), and the Australian Airport Association (AAA) (2018) produced an inquiry submission refuting the claims of A4ANZ.

This is an ongoing controversy, and there are many reasons why the studies come to widely divergent conclusions. However, one of the critical reasons is to do with the profit measures used. Typically, airline studies of airport profitability take EBITDA (earnings before interest, tax, depreciation and amortisation) as a measure, while airport studies use a rate of return measure. Put simply, the EBITDA approach is misleading (see Productivity Commission, 2019). This is because airports are very capital-intensive firms, and this measure of profit does not include the cost of capital. The problem is particularly acute when airports are investing heavily, as many of them are, to handle the capacity crunch.

The airport charges controversy is yet to be resolved. What is clear, however, is that it will not be resolved using simplistic measures of profit which pose more questions than answers.

6.9 Conclusions

This chapter might be summarised as offering responses to three questions:

- Which airport markets are sufficiently competitive to dispense with regulation;
- Which types of regulation are best; and
- What are the characteristics of the different forms of regulation, and is light-handed regulation sufficient to avoid the problems of the use of market power and high charges?

The original way of thinking about airports was that they were natural monopolies which would abuse their market power if operated by the private sector. Thus, public ownership was appropriate. Privatisation in the 1980s changed this way of thinking. Private owners would, if unregulated, have the ability and incentive to set high prices. As a result, as airports became privatised, regulatory systems were designed for them, as was the case in the UK in the 1980s and Australia in the 1990s. In addition, regulation was extended to many public airports as a way of articulating objectives and monitoring performance.

Over the past 20 years the question of whether airports could be operated in competitive markets arose. If so, it would not be necessary to regulate them. The question then is—how do we determine whether an airport is operating in a competitive market? As the controversy about airport charges demonstrates, the measurement of airport competition, and thus the role of regulation, has yet to be resolved.

Currently, many medium to large airports are regulated. The original form of public utility regulation, that of rate-of-return regulation, was recognised as having major drawbacks, especially in terms of having poor incentives for productive efficiency, or cost minimisation, and possibly excessive investment. Incentive regulation tries to address this, and this approach accompanied early privatisations, as in the

UK. The objective of price-cap regulation is to give the airport an incentive to keep costs down. A more recent approach towards regulation is light-handed regulation, which has been applied to airports in Australia, New Zealand and the UK. The question of which is the best form of regulation has yet to be settled. While incentive and light-handed regulation appear to be good at keeping *costs* low, airports argue that incentive regulation is too bureaucratic, and airlines claim that *charges* are too high under light-handed regulation.

Note

1 The framework for the formal analysis of the cost of capital is a technical field in finance is called the Capital Asset Pricing Model (CAPM).

References

A4ANZ Airlines for Australia & New Zealand (2018) *The Performance and Impact of Australia's Airports Since Privatisation*, Melbourne, A4ANZ

Airports Commission (2015) *Airports Commission Final Report*, London, Airports Commission, July

Arblaster, M (2014) "The Design of Light-Handed Regulation of Airports: Lessons from Experience in Australia and New Zealand", *Journal of Air Transport Management*, 38, 27–35

Armstrong, M, S Cowan and J Vickers (1994) *Regulatory Reform Economic Analysis and British Experience*, Cambridge, MA, MIT Press

Australian Airports Association (2018) Submission to the Productivity Commission Inquiry, *Economic Regulation of Airports*, Canberra, Australian Airports Association

Averch, H and L Johnson (1966) "Behaviour of the Firm Under Regulatory Constraint", *American Economic Review*, 52, 1052–1069

Baldwin, R and M Cave (1999) *Understanding Regulation Theory, Strategy and Practice*, Oxford, Oxford University Press

Biggar, D (2012) "Why Regulate Airports? A Re-Examination of the Rationale for Airport Regulation", *Journal of Transport Economics and Policy*, 46, 367–380

Civil Aviation Authority (2007) "De-Designation of Manchester and Stansted Airports for Price Regulation- The CAA's Advice to the Secretary of State", available at www.caa.co.uk

Civil Aviation Authority (2022) "Economic Regulation of Heathrow Airport: H7 Final Proposals—Summary", CAP2365A, available at https://publicapps.caa.co.uk/docs/33/CAP2365A%20H7%20Summary.pdf

Competition Commission (2009) *BAA Airports Market Investigation*, London, A Report on the Supply of Airport Services by BAA in the UK, March 19, available at www.competition-commission.org.uk

Competition and Markets Authority (2016) *BAA Airports: Evaluation of the Competition Commission's 2009 Market Investigation Remedies*, London, CMA

Copenhagen Economics (2012) *Airport Competition in Europe*, Copenhagen, ACI Europe

Forsyth, P (2001) *Airport Price Regulation: Rationales, Issues and Directions for Reform*, Clayton, Submission to the Productivity Commission Inquiry: Price Regulation of Airport Services, Department of Economics, Monash University

Forsyth, P, D Gillen, J Mueller and H-M Niemeier (eds) (2010) *Airport Competition the European Experience*, Aldershot, Ashgate

Forsyth, P, C Guiomard, J Müller and H-M Niemeier (2021) "Changing Airport Governance and Regulation the Regional Aspect", in A Graham, A, N Adler, H-M Niemeier, O Betancor, A Antunes, V Bilotkach, E Calderón and G Martini (eds), *Air Transport and Regional Development Policies*, London, Routledge, 49–80

Gillen, D and B Mantin (2013) "Transport Infrastructure Management: One and Two-Sided Approaches", *Journal of Transport Economics and Policy*, 47, 207–227

Graham, A (2018) *Managing Airports: An International Perspective*, 5th ed., London, Routledge

Hess, S and J Polak (2010) "Airport Choice Behaviour: Findings from Three Separate Studies", in P Forsyth, D Gillen, J Mueller and H-M Niemeier (eds), *Airport Competition: The European Experience*, Aldershot, Ashgate, 177–196

International Transport Forum (2011) *Better Economic Regulation: The Role of the Regulator*, Discussion Paper 2011, 03, Paris, OECD

InterVISTAS/ACI World (2022) *The State of Play: Competition, Regulation and Airport Charges*, Research Report, Montreal, ACI World

Littlechild, S C (2012) "Australian Airport Regulation: Exploring the Frontier", *Journal of Air Transport Management*, 21, 50–62

Maertens, S (2012) "Estimation the Market Power of Airports in Their Catchment Areas—a Europe-Wide Approach", *Journal of Transport Geography*, 22, 10–18

Malavolti, E (2016) "Single or Dual Till at Airports: A Two-Sided Market Analysis", *Transportation Research Procedia*, 14, 3696–3703

Müller, J, V Bilotkach, F Fichert, H-M Niemeier, E Pels and A Polk (2010) *The Economic Market Power of Amsterdam Airport Schiphol*, Amsterdam, Study Commissioned by the Netherlands Competition Authority

Oxera (2017) "The Continuing Development of Airport Competition in Europe", available at www.oxera.com

Productivity Commission (2002) *Price Regulation of Airport Services*, Inquiry Report No. 23, Canberra, AusInfo, January

Productivity Commission (2019) *Economic Regulation of Airports*, Inquiry Report No 92, London, Productivity Commission, June

Rochat, J and J Tirole (2006) "Two-Sided Markets: A Progress Report", *Rand Journal of Economics*, 37, 645–667

Rovizzi, L and D Thompson (1992) "The Regulation of Product Quality in the Public Utilities and the Citizen's Charter", *Fiscal Studies*, 13, 74–95

Starkie, D (1999) *A New Deal for Airports?*, London, Beesley Lecture Series on Regulating Industries, October

Starkie, D (2009) "The Airport Industry in a Competitive Environment: A United Kingdom Perspective", in *OECD/International Transport Forum, Competitive Interaction Between Airport, Airlines and High-Speed Rail, Round Table 145*, Paris, OECD, 67–94

Starkie, D (2021) "Two-Sided Airport Markets Reprised", *Journal of Transport Economics and Policy*, 55, 1–15

Tretheway, M and I Kinkaid (2010) "Competition Between Airports: Occurrence and Strategy", in P Forsyth, D Gillen, J Mueller and H-M Niemeier (eds), *Airport Competition: The European Experience*, Aldershot, Ashgate, 119–136

Vickers, J and G Yarrow (1988) *Privatisation: An Economic Analysis*, Cambridge, MA, MIT Press

Wiltshire, J (2018) "Airport Competition: Reality or Myth?", *Journal of Air Transport Management*, 67, 241–248

7 Airport performance

Efficiency and quality

7.1 Introduction

Achieving satisfactory levels of efficiency and quality are critical aspects of airport performance. In Section 7.2, we define the different aspects of airport efficiency, the data necessary for performance measurement and the different performance-measurement methods that are available. Low levels of efficiency might matter especially at airports that face weak competition as an airport operator could pass the excess costs onto airport users. (Forsyth, 2000). We also discuss airport performance benchmarking in the context of price regulation. Section 7.5 turns to airport quality and its measurement. The evolution in the methods used to measure airport quality is described. Evidence on airport quality is also reported before a brief conclusion.

7.2 Measuring airport efficiency

Airports provide infrastructure which is then used to produce air transport services. Is airport infrastructure provided using the minimum of resources? Are terminals and runways of a broadly appropriate capacity, avoiding prolonged overcrowding or significant underutilisation? Are the facilities operated at a reasonable cost? Do the services offered by the airport correspond to those that the airport's customers seek?

To answer these kinds of questions, an airport's performance needs to be defined and measured. In the 21st century, there is also a focus on the environmental impact of airports, and whether they are managed in such a way as to reach airport carbon neutrality in the coming decades.[1]

From a technical economic viewpoint, efficiency has three aspects. Productive or cost efficiency is the absence of waste and requires that an airport produce a given level of service at minimum cost.[2] Allocative efficiency requires that all consumers who are willing to pay a price at least equal to the (marginal) cost of production are offered the good or service in question. Dynamic efficiency refers to making investments at an appropriate scale and at the right time, whether these are to increase airport capacity or quality or to achieve savings in operating costs. Previous Chapters have examined allocative and dynamic efficiency and we turn attention here to productive efficiency. (The Appendix discusses the different efficiency concepts and related issues.)

DOI: 10.4324/9781003156901-9

How is efficiency measured and what do such measurements show? Quantitative measurement methods fall into several broad categories, with increasing degrees of sophistication and usefulness:

- very simple partial measures of efficiency based on certain ratios;
- aggregate productivity indexes; and
- methods derived from econometrics and mathematical programming such as stochastic frontier analysis (SFA) and data envelopment analysis (DEA).

The first set of measures is simple to calculate, and data are generally available. While such ratios are probably useful for airport managers monitoring internal efficiency, or to set managerial KPIs, they do not measure the overall efficiency of an airport and neglect the wide range of resources jointly needed to produce airport services. A second approach to efficiency measurement aggregates all the inputs and outputs to generate an overall measure of airport efficiency. A third method involves calculating an airport's efficiency in relation to an "efficiency frontier", estimated from data on firms' input/output combinations using standard technical assumptions. An airport's distance from the frontier represents estimated inefficiency.

Simple performance measures

Simple measures such as ratios of aircraft movements per runway, or of square metres of terminal space per passenger, or staff numbers per passenger, are easy to understand. These give a broad picture of efficiency and may identify gross levels of inefficiency. However, on their own, they are insufficient as an indicator of efficiency.

Simple measures of differences in airport performance can be very stark. For example, Kamp et al. (2007) found that in 2000–2001 Frankfurt airport processed an average of 4,000 passengers per staff member whereas in 2003 Atlanta airport processed almost 100,000 passengers per employee. While some of this gap probably reflects a difference in efficiency, other explanations include the nature of the traffic mix (low cost or full service), the degree of outsourcing and the scale economies available at larger airports.

Investment will also affect productivity ratios; as a first approximation, an airport with newly opened (and initially underused) infrastructure will appear less efficient than it would have seemed just before the building of the new infrastructure. On the other hand, service quality should be improved by investment. Measured airport efficiency will also be affected by many airport costs being fixed over certain traffic ranges. Airport traffic growth that can be accommodated by the existing infrastructure will therefore improve measured efficiency (and vice versa). Finally, changes in the structure of the aviation industry, such as airline mergers, could shift traffic between airports, affecting their measured efficiency.

A very important challenge to performance measurement is airport heterogeneity; beyond basic operational functions, airports differ substantially. Some directly provide security, air traffic control, ground handling, car parking, duty-free shops, and undertake aircraft maintenance, while others contract out these functions to specialist firms. In the limiting case, terminals may also be leased, as in the US.

One approach to airport heterogeneity is to isolate the costs of providing aeronautical infrastructure—land, runways, terminals and space for concession activities—to compare the cost of "core" services. However, taken too far, such estimates of core costs may be very different to an airport's actual costs that enter into the charges paid by users.

A number of publications report data on simple performance measurements. One such report was originally developed by TRL (Transport and Road Research Laboratory, various years) and has since been continued by Jacobs (2021). The TRL/Jacobs reports present many performance indicators for a large number of airports from different regions of the world. In calculating these results, publications face a number of measurement challenges. One of these is that of having access to sufficient data.

An important shortcoming of measurements based on ratios is that they do not take account either of all the resources used at an airport or of all of the service outputs produced. This can lead to what is known as the Fox paradox. Fox (1999) showed that it was possible for a multi-product firm to be more productive in each of its activities than any other firm and yet not to have the highest overall productivity. This might arise if different firms produced very different mixtures of services. For example, when an inefficient firm mostly produces the service where its efficiency gap is least, but the efficient firm mostly produces services where its efficiency gap is greatest, the firm that is less efficient at each task might be measured at the most efficient firm at an aggregate level. So, while simple ratios may be useful as descriptive statistics, they are unsuitable for performance benchmarking.

Total factor productivity indexes

Total Factor Productivity (TFP) calculations add up all of an airport's inputs and outputs and measure efficiency as a ratio of output to input. To generate the aggregate measure, the input quantities are weighted by their cost shares and the output quantities by revenue shares. Comparisons between airports of very different sizes are difficult unless it is assumed that there are constant returns to scale. Otherwise, performance may be attributed to managerial skill when in fact at least some is due to the difference in size.

In an early study, this technique was used to assess the performance of major Australian airports (Hooper and Hensher, 1997). The authors measured airport output as the revenues from aeronautical and non-aeronautical airport services. The inputs included capital, measured on the perpetual inventory method, labour, in terms of expenditure on salaries and wages and a third operating cost input which is measured by residual expenditures. A much more recent application of TFP is that of See and Li (2015) which measures the productivity of 22 UK airports over a nine-year timeframe up to 2009. The paper found that there was an annual average 0.32% increase in productivity over the period, mainly due to efficiency improvements, with larger airports more productive than smaller ones.

The methods and data used to assess airport performance can differ quite considerably from study to study and sometimes so do the conclusions. Kamp et al. (2007) compared the different performance findings at some European airports and found quite different rankings in the various studies. They concluded that more attention needs to be given to separating managerial performance from the different scales and scopes of airport operations.

All performance studies require extensive data, measured reliably and consistently. Measurement of capital inputs poses a particular problem given that airports use incommensurable inputs including terminals and runways. A good measure of capital would be the value of the total asset base just as total wages and salaries are used to measure labour input. However, this asset value is not always available for airports. There is also the issue of how to measure non-labour non-capital inputs such as services and materials. Measurement challenges also exist on the output side. It is possible to consider at least the following as airport outputs: aircraft movements, passenger numbers and cargo tonnage. Indicators of service quality, such as delays at airports, are also an important aspect of performance.

The Air Transport Research Society (ATRS), in its annual reports of airport productivity, measures airport output in terms of passenger numbers, cargo tonnage, aircraft movements and non-aeronautical revenues; inputs are measured by employee numbers, purchased inputs and, as measures of capital, the number of runways, the number of terminal gates and total terminal size. TRL/Jacobs measures output as passengers and cargo, workload units (a combined measure of passengers and cargo) plus non-aeronautical revenues. Jacobs also publishes an ATU (airport throughput unit) statistic that includes passengers, cargo and flights (Air Transport Movements). The TRL/Jacobs reports measure inputs such as staff numbers, operating expenditures, depreciation charges and taxes.

Econometric measures

Econometric studies go one stage beyond productivity indexes. For example, the annual reports of the ATRS cover over one hundred airports across the globe. The approach begins with a basic aggregate productivity measure and then uses regression analysis to adjust the basic result for a range of factors which influence productivity, including airport size, average aircraft size, the share of international traffic, the share of non-aeronautical revenue and the degree of competition in the industry. These are all factors outside the control of airport managers and their removal gives a residual measure of managerial performance. This approach yields an adjusted productivity estimate, namely Residual Variable Factor Productivity, which can be ranked to identify good or poor airport performance.

DEA and SFA

Data Envelopment Analysis (DEA) and Stochastic Frontier Analysis (SFA) are the two main contemporary methods used to benchmark airport performance. Initially, they were used almost exclusively by academics but now they are undertaken more widely, for instance by the Italian airport regulator. Like TFP, they are total measures and do not rely on KPIs. Hence, they avoid the Fox paradox and give a more complete picture of airport performance.

Both methods assess airports relative to an efficiency frontier. The frontier can be defined in terms of technical or cost efficiency. The distance between a specific airport and the efficiency frontier is a measure of that airport's inefficiency. DEA utilises multiple inputs and outputs without attaching ex-ante weights to each indicator. It is nonparametric and assumes no specific functional form for the production function. SFA models consist of an underlying estimated production function, a random effect term reflecting the efficiency of the individual airport and a random error component which accounts for the combined effects of various types of errors. In comparing both methods, the principal advantage of DEA is that it does not need the specification of a functional form while SFA has the advantages that it accounts for statistical noise and can be used to conduct hypothesis tests (Coelli et al., 2005; Liebert and Niemeier, 2013).

Both methods seek to explain performance differences using regression analysis. Results have to be carefully interpreted to draw the correct lessons for management and policy. Both methods are often used by researchers. Managers can sometimes be irritated that the two methods do not necessarily lead to the same results, but as the methods differ so may the results. Efficiency is a theoretically well-defined concept, but its measurement might differ as the performance is influenced by so many factors. Skilfully applied with good data both methods produce reliable results or at least guide research to understand the differences in performance better. Of course, data quality remains a challenge. And very often airport data are not disaggregated, for example, in the cases of the Paris airport system and AENA airports in Spain.

Much research focuses narrowly on technical and cost efficiency. Questions of allocative efficiency, for example, how scarce capacity is managed in the short and long run, are not assessed. Cost efficiency improvements lead to welfare gains, but changes in governance have effects which go beyond cost efficiency. For example, privatisation increases incentives to raise prices leading to a decrease in welfare. Most studies do not cover this aspect. Furthermore, privatisation affects taxpayers, workers and managers. These effects have not been analysed at all. Widening the scope of DEA and SFA studies to cover the full welfare effects would increase their policy relevance.

7.3 Determinants of airport performance

As in other parts of the economy, the ownership status of the companies in the industry and the number of competing companies—the industry structure—are important influences on airport performance.

Private owners are presumed to appoint managers who pursue profits by containing costs and looking for opportunities to increase revenues. However, airports were traditionally in the public sector (Forsyth et al., 2021), owned by a government and operated by managers who respond to the political objectives of the owner. On that basis, airports may be operated to break-even financially, or to earn only modest profits. If not motivated by profits, airport operators will not be required to the same degree to control and minimise costs. Instead, they might favour expansion and act as size maximisers.[3] Since the 1980s, outside North America, there has been a worldwide evolution towards private airport ownership. It would be consistent with this change to expect to see an improvement in airport efficiency over recent decades. Apart from pure public and private forms of ownership, other structures are also found, especially for small airports. These may be owned by local communities or by local governments. Canadian airports, including the larger ones, are owned by not-for-profit entities.

A second important influence on efficiency is the degree of inter-airport competition. Competition gives firms an incentive to pursue efficiencies in order to attract business away from competitors. But airports may not operate under competitive conditions and so may fall significantly short of full efficiency. A lack of effective competition can mean that airports are able to increase profits by limiting capacity and raising prices. In these circumstances, air transport is underprovided and passengers willing to pay the (marginal) cost of service are not provided with the service.

Competition is thought to have a larger influence on efficiency than ownership. In the UK, in 2007, the Office of Fair Trading investigated the possible loss of airport efficiency arising from there being a dominant owner in the industry (OFT, 2007). At that time, the BAA airport group owned all three large London airports, plus both Edinburgh and Glasgow airports in southern Scotland, and other airports besides. These airports accounted for over 60% of UK air passengers in 2005. The OFT investigation concluded that the common ownership structure restricted airport competition and hampered the delivery of sufficient airport capacity, especially in the southeast of England, and that the quality of airport services had also suffered. The OFT argued that competition would increase under separate ownership and improve incentives for efficient capacity expansion focused on user needs. As a result of a subsequent decision of the UK Competition Commission, the airport operator was required to sell two of its three London airports and one in Scotland. In London, the operator retained ownership of Heathrow airport and sold Gatwick and Stansted airports.

This example demonstrates the possible links between ownership, competition and efficiency. On its own, a change to private ownership may not be sufficient to improve efficiency and attention also needs to be paid to the structure of the industry. A retrospective analysis by the UK Competition and Markets Authority (Competition and Markets Authority, 2016) judged the BAA break-up to have produced substantial benefits. These included stronger traffic growth, increased investment, improved operational efficiency and service quality, and better relations between the airports and their airline customers including, at Gatwick and Stansted, long-term agreements on airport charges. For Scotland, following the sale of Edinburgh airport, Pagliari and Graham (2019, 2020) concluded that there were indications of improvements in efficiency and service quality at Edinburgh and Glasgow airports.

Studies such as those just discussed are somewhat descriptive or use partial efficiency measures. This analysis of industry ownership and structure is supplemented by econometric techniques (DEA and SFA, as already mentioned) which estimate managerial performance taking account of such influences as ownership, regulation, the extent of competition, the level of service quality, externalities and other relevant variables. Some representative examples follow.

We argue that the effects of policy (privatisation, regulation, competition) should be assessed in terms of economic welfare. Have there been gains from better governance in the form of reduced costs and have these savings been passed on to airlines? To answer this question the effects of privatisation, regulation and competition need to be separated. Although this is not always done, some conclusions may be drawn from the benchmarking literature.

Partial privatisation does not improve cost efficiency. Full privatisation raises efficiency but in the presence of market power it needs to be combined with effective regulation as otherwise the savings are kept by the airport and charges are not lowered. The efficiency effects of regulation depend on whether or not the airports have persistent market power and whether the regulatory regime gives good incentives. In particular, Adler and Liebert (2014) have shown that where airports have overlapping catchment areas, competition has positive effects on cost efficiency and regulation is unnecessary. This confirms what one would expect from a theoretical analysis.

From theory, we also expect that cost-based regulation does not set the right incentives but could lead to overcapitalisation (called the Averch–Johnson effect) and gold plating. Incentive regulation seems to be superior to cost-based regulation. In practice, the difference between cost-based and incentive regulation is not so clear cut and there are forms of incentive regulation which have weak and strong incentives for efficiency. Adler et al. (2014, and in particular 2015) find that incentive regulation reduces the operational costs of airports relative to cost-based regulation. Whether light-handed regulation would improve on price-caps is yet to be fully analysed. Future research is also needed on the impact of regulatory independence.

Does increased competition raise efficiency, as would be expected? Adler and Liebert (2014) find this, but for airports the results are not that clear. If airports are too close to each other, traffic might be cannibalised and efficiency might be decreased. There is some evidence of this at small regional airports (Scotti et al., 2012). For large airports, the effects of the break-up of the London and Scottish BAA airports are of interest. Some other findings of the DEA and SFA literature are that outsourcing, in particular of ground handling services, increases cost efficiency, as does hubbing. The impact of slots and congestion are not sufficiently incorporated into such analyses.

An important aspect of economic welfare and airport performance concerns external costs ("bads") such as noise or air pollution. These are shown to matter significantly for airport performance rankings by Martini et al. (2013). That paper studied the impacts of aircraft fleet mix, airport ownership and the presence of LCC airlines on the efficiency of 33 Italian airports using data for 2005–2008 while also allowing for two airport externalities, namely noise and local air pollution. Inclusive of external "bads", public airports are found to be more efficient than private ones, possibly because local governments are more attentive to environmental concerns. The presence of LCCs does not appear to affect efficiency, whereas without the inclusion of noise and pollution, an LCC presence improves measured efficiency.

However, it is difficult to judge if these results also hold outside Italy as Italian airports have no noise and emission charges which some other private and public airports in Europe have. Thus, this is a tentative conclusion.

7.4 The role of benchmarking in regulation

In addition to the airport efficiency studies just discussed, from time to time there are benchmarking studies carried out in the course of regulatory reviews of airport charges. Regulators aim to set charges with reference to the level of costs that an efficient airport would incur. Data on airport performance is thus of considerable interest to regulators. Setting a price-cap on the basis of data external to the firm is the core element of incentive regulation since external benchmarking gives a firm a strong incentive to pursue efficiencies (see Chapter 6). Against this background, the benchmarking literature asks the question: are there methods and sources of independent data that could be used to set benchmarks for future cost allowances? An early discussion of airport benchmarking is CAA (2001).

Benchmarking approaches to assessing airport efficiency include "top-down" modelling as well as "bottom-up" process or activity benchmarking. A mix of the two approaches allows a cross-check on each set of findings. Top-down approaches include SFA and DEA methods, and total or partial productivity studies. Bottom-up approaches focus on individual activities and processes of the regulated firm and depend in part on judgements by experts familiar with the activity being reviewed. Such exercises can make reference to data on similar activities performed by other companies, or the modelling may attempt to develop an idealised cost structure for the activity under review. Bottom-up studies are vulnerable to the criticism that the sum of the parts from such an exercise may bear little relationship to what is achievable in practice.

Especially in a regulatory setting, airport benchmarking studies can give rise to considerable controversy. Airports may consider that studies that show them in a poor light are invalid. Indeed, they may offer adjusted measurements that indicate a different result or ranking. Agrell and Bogetoft (2017), in a discussion of the applicability of benchmarking to economic regulation, warn that care is needed in regard to data validation, model specification and outlier detection. Concerning regulatory benchmarking, data are scarce as airports, good or bad performers, are reluctant providers of information. Regulators must expect to have to do their own information gathering and assessment, if they are to have reasonable confidence that costs and thus prices have been set on a broadly efficient basis.

Box 7.1 Can airport performance be benchmarked? Dublin airport 2014

An example of a top-down airport per-passenger cost exercise, conducted in respect of Dublin airport in 2014, offers some insight into regulatory benchmarking. Given airport heterogeneity, the regulator decided to include in the benchmarking exercise every European airport listed on Ryanair's and Aer Lingus' route maps that were served from Dublin. The data came from published annual accounts or regulatory reports. Information was collected for 69 airports, including 43 of the approximately 90 European destinations served by Ryanair and 47 of the 80 or so destinations served by Aer Lingus.

Airports were compared on the basis of operating costs per passenger. The benchmarking reveals different performance gaps by reference to different subsets of the full sample. So, the figures indicate Dublin's per-passenger operating costs in 2012 were:

- 1% below the sample average
- 7% below the average of airports with 10–35 million passengers per annum
- 5% below the average for destinations served by Aer Lingus
- but 10% above the average for Ryanair destinations.

It is clear that a given database of airport costs can point in quite different directions depending on how the figures are analysed. The airport argued that the regulator's benchmarking exercise was flawed in approach, contained errors and that a lower level of costs was not achievable.

Many airlines took the opposite view and doubted that the benchmarking exercise had sufficiently challenged the airport operator's costs. Some airlines expressed nervousness that a tight operating expenditure settlement might jeopardise operational features of the airport that were important to them (e.g., smoothly functioning security). This view was partly shared by economic development and business representative bodies which sought a careful balance between the pursuit of efficiency and reliable service quality.

7.5 Measuring and achieving quality

Airports differ not only in the range of services they provide but also in the quality levels at which these services are delivered. The development of low-cost travel has led to more diversity of passengers and airlines. Airports serving LCCs aim for more basic and less costly infrastructure than would be sought by full-service airlines serving the same routes. Changes to airport ownership. and increased competition at least in segments of the airport industry, has made airports more commercial and less like utilities, and has oriented them towards meeting user needs rather than their less responsive previous stance.

Historically, at the infrastructure planning stage, the level of service (LoS) provided at passenger terminals was defined in very basic terms as the average floor space available to passengers (Ashford, 1988). IATA published an Airport Development Reference Manual (ADRM) which defined an LoS of between A and F that prescribed average floor space for the arrivals concourse, baggage drop, departure gate area, and so forth. IATA recommended LoS 'C' for developing new terminal facilities or for rating existing terminals. Where relevant, standards were also expressed in average waiting times for certain services, for instance, check-in, security searches, and immigration. Since passenger flows vary over the day and the year, the measurements are conventionally those for a "typical busy day/hour", often a very busy day in the summer high season.

Since 2014, airline and airport representative bodies, IATA and ACI, have worked jointly on airport standards moving away from the mechanical space-based LoS definitions. Service levels are now assessed with reference to a matrix defined over available space and maximum waiting time. An airport is then categorised as: over-designed, at the optimum, or sub-optimum or under-provided (Renner and Wielgus, 2015).

Beyond physical planning standards, quality assessments now rely on passenger surveys that seek to identify passengers' views on airport quality. ACI, representing airports, conducts a large quarterly survey asking passengers about their experience with airport ground access, check-in systems, passport control and security checks, food and beverage services, as well as questions about ease of wayfinding in the airport, cleanliness and the overall quality of airport facilities and ambience. The ACI Airport Service Quality (ASQ) Monitor reports quarterly performance by airports for these metrics (ACI, 2021). However, these reports are not public and are available only to subscribing and participating airports.

IATA, representing airlines, also conducts an annual Global Passenger Survey to assess airport metrics similar to those of ACI (IATA, 2021). IATA also reports to airlines on the results of a survey of the levels of passenger satisfaction with airlines (IATA, 2021) but these reports are also available only to subscribers. A third evaluation of airports is carried out annually by Skytrax using inspections and assessments made by professional audit teams. Skytrax then rates airports (and airlines) on a five-star rating scale, distinguishing by airport type and by geographical region (Skytrax, 2021). In 2021, it reported that 17 airports globally reached a 5-star standard which, it said, required that an airport meet global best practice in staff service and product standards for every element of the rating.

Airport economic regulators increasingly make a price-cap conditional on an airport's delivery of certain specified service levels. When these standards are not met, airports are allowed to collect less revenue. This prevents price-regulated airports from maintaining profits by degrading quality while continuing to charge up to the full price-cap. The focus on service quality reflects an evolution in airport regulation towards explicit consideration of the airport passengers' interests rather than a sole focus on prices. The CAA defines service standards for Heathrow Airport (CAA, 2021). There are entire sets of metrics relating to passenger views, queuing times, and equipment and facilities. The passenger surveys include questions about queueing at security processes and immigration. Equipment availability is measured for lifts, escalators, check-in desks, baggage carousels and, on the airside, parking stands and minimising deferrals of runway movements. In addition, carbon emissions are required to be measured and reported. Both penalties and bonuses are applied. In total, some 7%

of Heathrow's charges revenue is contingent on meeting these standards (CAA, 2014, Appendix C). Service quality terms have long been part of the CAA price-cap regime, but their number and complexity have increased rather considerably over time.

The treatment of service quality in the context of airport regulation in Europe is discussed in Forsyth et al. (2021). Of eleven European countries, only Germany, Austria and Switzerland did not have a system of penalties and bonuses to give incentives to deliver service quality. In Australia, which does not rely on formal regulation but rather on a light-handed approach, the Australian Competition and Consumer Commission (ACCC) collects and publishes many different measures of the level and the trend in service quality at the four largest Australian airports. A further tier of five Australian airports is required to report service quality and other data on their own websites. Service quality is based on both passenger and airline surveys as well as objective measures of airport quality such as airside and terminal facilities. These measures are used by the Australian Productivity Commission (PC) to assess service quality at Australian airports, as part of the PC's reviews of the performance of Australia's approach to regulation.

To sum up, airport quality issues have gained increased attention and importance as airports have shifted towards more commercial thinking and as airports perceive themselves to be subject to an increase in competitive pressures.

Box 7.2 Controversies in Airport Economics: Why do airlines complain about low-cost airports that have high profits but not high-cost airports that have low profits?

In evaluating airport performance, the attention of the public and of politicians often focuses on the level of airport profits. Large profits lead to suspicions of overcharging. But it is the contention of the authors that attention should be paid to airport charges rather than airport profits.

The relationship between profits and charges can take very different configurations. The scale of profits—the difference between revenues and costs—may be attributable to cost control or to excessive charges. A reduction in profits brought about by an airport allowing costs to rise would be of no benefit to airport users if charges were unchanged.

On efficiency grounds, it is desirable that costs be low (waste minimised) even if this means high profits. Also on efficiency grounds, charges should be close to costs which, other things equal, would keep profits broadly in line with those made elsewhere in the economy. Profits, whether larger or smaller, are only part of an airport's cost base and high overall costs that lead to high charges rightly attract airline objections. Provided charges are reasonable, profits are not very objectionable especially insofar as they are the reward for cost control.

7.6 Conclusion

This chapter considered airport performance in terms of efficiency and service quality. From an economic perspective, airports should deliver facilities and an airport experience in line with user wishes and trends in traffic growth, and at moderate cost. Traditional features of the airport industry have, however, not been the most conducive to efficiency. Public ownership has reduced the incentives for operational and investment efficiency. Weak competition has been magnified by airport operators owning a number of large airports in metropolises (including New York, Paris and London)—population centres sufficient to support a number of competing airports. Only in the UK has there been an airport restructuring to improve efficiency.

In recent decades, as passengers and airlines have become more differentiated, airports more commercialised and regulators more attentive, quality issues have gained increased importance and quality indicators have become more sophisticated and more widely available. Although still at an early stage, assessments of overall airport managerial performance now take account of service quality and environmental impacts. Inclusion of these variables can change an airport's performance ranking as well as the set of influences that affect measured performance. As further studies are produced, they can be expected to identify policies that will help to improve airport efficiency in the future, and as well as being useful to airport operators wishing to improve their own performance relative to other airport operators.

Notes

1 Environmental issues at airports are discussed in Chapter 8.
2 The subject of airport costs is discussed in Chapter 3.
3 Airport objectives are discussed in Chapter 5.

References

Adler, N, P Forsyth, J Mueller and H-M Niemeier (2015) "An Economic Assessment of Airport Incentive Regulation", *Transport Policy*, 41, 5–15

Adler, N and V Liebert (2014) "Joint Impact of Competition, Ownership Form and Economic Regulation on Airport Performance and Pricing", *Transportation Research Part A*, 64, 92–109

Agrell, P and P Bogetoft (2017) "Regulatory Benchmarking: Models, Analyses and Applications", *Data Envelopment Analysis Journal*, 3, 49–91

Air Transport Research Society (ATRS, annually) (n.d) *Airport Benchmarking Report: Global Standards for Airport Excellence*, Vancouver, Canada and Daytona Beach, FL, Embry-Riddle Aeronautical University

Airport Council International (2021) "ASQ Global Traveller Survey", available at www.aci.aero

Ashford, N (1988) "Level of Design Concept for Passenger Terminals", *Transportation Research Record*, 1199, 19–32

Civil Aviation Authority (2001) *Use of Benchmarking in the Airport Reviews, Consultation Paper*, London, Civil Aviation Authority, available at webarchive.nationalarchives.gov.uk

Civil Aviation Authority (2014) *Market Power Determination in Relation to Heathrow Airport—Statement of Reasons*, CAP1133, London, Civil Aviation Authority
Civil Aviation Authority (2021) *Statement of Measures, Targets and Incentives*, London, Civil Aviation Authority, available at www.caa.co.uk/
Coelli, T J, D S P Rao, C J O'Donnell and G E Battese (2005) *An Introduction to Efficiency and Productivity Analysis*, New York, Springer
Competition and Markets Authority (2016) *BAA Airports: Evaluation of the Competition Commission's 2009 Market Investigation Remedies*, London, CMA
Forsyth, P (2000) "Models of Airport Performance", in D Hensher and K Button (eds), *Handbook of Transport Modelling*, London, Elsevier, 621–632
Forsyth, P, C Guiomard, J Müller and H-M Niemeier (2021) "Changing Airport Governance and Regulation: The Regional Aspect", in A Graham, N Adler, H-M Niemeier, O Betancor, A Antunes, V Bilotkach, E Calderón and G Martini (eds), *Air Transport and Regional Development Policies*, London, Routledge, 49–80
Fox, K (1999) "Efficiency at Different Levels of Aggregation: Public vs. Private Sector Firms", *Economics Letters*, 65, 173–176
Hooper, P and D Hensher (1997) "Measuring Total Factor Productivity of Airports—an Index Number Approach", *Transportation Research Part E*, 33, 249–259
IATA (2021) "Global Passenger Survey (GPS)", available at www.iata.org/gps
Jacobs (2021) *Airport Performance Indicators*, London, Jacobs
Kamp, V, H-M Niemeier and J Müller (2007) "What Can Be Learned from Benchmarking Studies? Examining the Apparent Poor Performance of German Airports", *Journal of Airport Management*, 1, 294–308
Liebert, V and H-M Niemeier (2013) "A Survey of Empirical Research on the Productivity and Efficiency Measurement of Airports", *Journal of Transport Economics and Policy*, 47, 157–189
Martini, G, A Manello and D Scotti (2013) "The Influence of Fleet Mix, Ownership and LCCs on Airports' Technical/Environmental Efficiency", *Transportation Research Part E*, 50, 37–52
Office of Fair Trading (2007) "BAA—the OFT's reference to the Competition Commission", OFT 912, available at webarchive.nationalarchives.gov.uk
Pagliari R and A Graham (2019) "An Exploratory Analysis of the Effects of Ownership Change on Airport Competition", *Transport Policy*, 78, 76–85
Pagliari R and A Graham (2020) "Airport Competition Within the Scottish Lowlands Region", *Research in Transportation Economics*, 79, 100760
Renner R and M Wielgus (2015) "Improving and Optimising the LOS of an Airport", *International Airport Review*, 19(5), available at www.internationalairportreview.com
Scotti, D, P Malighetti, G Martini and N Volta (2012) "The Impact of Airport Competition on Technical Efficiency: A Stochastic Frontier Analysis Applied to Italian Airport", *Journal of Air Transport Management*, 22, 9–15
See, F and F Li (2015) "Total Factor Productivity Analysis of the UK Airport Industry: A Hicks-Moorsteen Index Method", *Journal of Air Transport Management*, 43, 1–10
Skytrax (2021) "Ratings of Airports", available at www.skytrax.com

Part 3

Environment and impacts

8 Airports and the environment

8.1 Introduction

In the 21st century, environmental challenges have climbed steadily up the public and political agenda, and with it the question of aviation's environmental impact, especially its contribution to climate change as well as airport noise.

These two primary environmental impacts of aviation differ in an important way. Aircraft noise is specific to air travel and localised to aircraft flight paths in the vicinity of airports. The analysis of noise is a central issue for airports, especially at times of investment and expansion. Climate change is a global challenge and most, if not all, human activities give rise to harmful carbon emissions. The analysis of climate change is only partly an aviation issue and the contributions of airlines and airports are distinct, at least in principle. Though most emissions associated with aviation are produced by airlines, airports in their own right also account for a proportion of emissions in particular related to energy generation and the surface movement of passengers and staff.

It could be argued that airports, by providing the essential take-off and landing infrastructure for airlines, are responsible for airline emissions also. More airport capacity, at least in a region, means probably more emissions. This aspect is a difficult one to analyse. For the purpose of this chapter, we consider airports mainly in their capacity as direct contributors to environmental problems. Aside from noise and carbon, there are other important pollutants from airports that affect local air quality, in particular nitrogen oxides (NOx). NOx and related pollutants are regulated in the US, EU and the UK where governments have set clean air standards which are monitored and enforced. These pollutants are not however the primary focus of this chapter.

In the next section of this chapter, we present the problems of noise and carbon emissions as examples of an externality. We then set out how noise is measured and discuss the tools that are available to mitigate noise. We review academic estimates of the cost of noise to local communities. The second part of the chapter considers airport carbon emissions. Airports must first measure emissions as a benchmark against which to pursue reductions. The policy emissions-reduction framework of airport operators is described and the actions needed to decarbonise airports. We mention a July 2021 suite of European Union policies to reduce carbon emissions. Finally,

DOI: 10.4324/9781003156901-11

we consider the implications of climate change for the future of airports. Both noise and carbon emissions, as they relate to airports, are quite well-understood issues and are, at a cost, capable of being considerably moderated.

8.2 Types of environmental externalities

Airports produce large externalities, both positive and negative. A negative externality is a harm caused by an economic activity (e.g., air transport) but not paid for by the producer and therefore not counted among the private costs of that activity.

In the early years of air transport, when flights were few, the local cost of noise was ignored, meaning the airports' total social costs were understated and the price of air transport was too low (as aviation did not need to collect revenues sufficient to pay for its noise costs). The polluter did not pay. Although policies have since been designed that could mitigate noise, these are only rarely deployed and even then, not sufficiently to cause polluters to pay for their noise pollution. The cost of carbon emissions is a second unpriced cost of aviation. While these are now receiving considerable though belated attention, and policies to reduce them are being developed, a lot remains to be done. Fundamentally, it is necessary to introduce or expand economic measures to assign a monetary value to emissions. This internalisation of emission costs ensures that producers explicitly take these costs into account in their business decisions. It incentivises producers to reduce their emissions. It also means that passengers are presented with the correct price "signal". The correct price includes the costs of the passengers' carbon "footprint" and allows passengers to identify the most environmentally sustainable travel choice.

Not all airport externalities are negative; benefits can also occur. Airports produce such benefits locally and nationally (discussed in Chapter 9). These include increased inward tourism and increased connectivity; the latter helps to make markets more competitive, allows cities and countries to specialise, workers to more easily reach productive centres of activity and firms to draw employees from a wider catchment area (Venables et al., 2014).

Positive and negative airport externalities are separate issues that need separate responses; the positive and the negative do not offset each other. The "polluter pays" principle requires that each "unit" of pollution should attract a penalty designed to induce less polluting behaviour. Positive airport externalities often arise at the time of decisions about airport capacity (such as regional capacity or capacity additions at congested airports) that need to be made taking account of external benefits.

8.3 Noise: How can this be measured?

Aircraft engine noise, although much reduced in modern engines from the levels of the first jet aircraft, is still an important and often controversial issue, especially for people living in the neighbourhood of airports. Its importance derives from the fact that excessive noise (from any source) may have many substantial negative effects for the populations affected, including for health, productivity, learning and quality of life. Extensive research has established a connection between noise and sleep disturbance, loss of hearing, raised blood pressure, damage to mental health as well as learning impairment in children. There may also be a loss of productivity due to loss of sleep, poorer health or workplace distractions. More subjectively, airport noise also causes annoyance to many people exposed to the sound of aircraft movements.

Noise is measured in decibels (dB). The scale is log linear; 10 dB is ten times louder than near-silence (0 dB), 20 dB is 100 times louder than 0 dB, 30 dB is 1,000 times louder and so forth. Since the human ear does not hear all sound frequencies, the decibel scale is adjusted for frequencies to give a weighted measure, dB(A).[1] dB(A) values range from 30 in a quiet library, to 80 at the side of a busy road, to 130 at the threshold of pain.

Noise effects are measured in many different ways, depending on whether the focus is on the maximum level of the noise event, the frequency of events, their duration or the time of the day when they occur. Noise may also be expressed in terms of its energy equivalent averaged over a certain period of the day. While such a measure combines many noise events into a single statistic, people living in the neighbourhood of an airport do not experience noise in this averaged fashion.

The appropriate counterfactual for noise measurement must also be chosen, especially in comparing options for airport expansion; should the reference be the absolute noise level or the level compared to a benchmark? And should adjustments be made for the scale of an airport's operations? Policy towards noise impact also requires consideration of whether lower levels of noise dispersed over a wider population is to be preferred to fewer people exposed to higher noise levels, or the reverse. Each aspect of noise has its own metric and these can be combined into various summary measures. A noise "footprint" is also often plotted, and sometimes reported on airport websites, that indicates the area (and population) experiencing noise above a certain threshold.

By law, certain airports are required to produce periodic noise studies. Noise emissions have been regulated in the EU for many years. Maximum noise limits for motor vehicles and for outdoor equipment date back to the 1970s. These rules have since been extended to production facilities and to airports. In the EU, the Environmental Noise Directive (Directive, 2002/49/EC) requires airports with more than 50,000 movements per annum to publish every five years noise contour maps, as well as plans for noise management. In other jurisdictions, including the US and the UK, regulations are broadly similar, although noise thresholds and definitions differ.

Prompted by government policies, aircraft manufacturers have made technological improvements that have reduced noise levels. Recent generations of aircraft, such as the Boeing-737 MAX and the Airbus A-350, produce noise "footprints" some 40–50% smaller than similar aircraft in current use. Data from the UK civil aviation authority used by the Airports Commission, indicate that today's jet aircraft produce 75% less noise than jet aircraft used in the 1960s, though the earliest jets were extremely noisy. These improvements are expected to continue into the future, perhaps at a slower rate (Airports Commission, 2013). Technological improvements are for a given aircraft type; larger aircraft and increased numbers of flights cause an overall increase in noise.

Noise standards, technological investments, retirement of older noisier aircraft and in some instances redesigned airport operations, have resulted in reductions in many localities in the total number of people exposed to significant aircraft noise. But even at these reduced levels, noise remains an external cost of aviation and a very important issue for those communities that are exposed to aviation noise or to increased noise when airports grow especially if new airport runways are built.

8.4 Noise mitigation policies: noise standards, budgets and noise charges

There are international frameworks for airport noise management, including that of the UN's International Civil Aviation Organisation (ICAO) and of the EU's European Aviation Safety Agency (EASA). At a global level, ICAO's 'Balanced Approach' is based on identifying the source of airport noise and then reducing it by means of four possible sets of actions.

The first element is technological improvements to reduce airport noise at source. ICAO sets noise certification standards: in effect, a maximum 'noise budget' for a given generation of aircraft designs. These standards have been adopted by most countries and require that designs for new aircraft submitted for ICAO certification must incorporate certain noise-reduction standards. Thus, each new generation of aircraft is less noisy than the one before (even if the older noisier aircraft remain in service for a considerable time). The Airport Council International (ACI) operates a similar Aircraft Noise Rating Index but currently, this is not widely used in Europe.

The first ICAO noise standard ("Chapter Two") was adopted in 1972. But ICAO certification has not kept pace with technological improvements. In the half-century since 1972, ICAO has set new noise standards only three times. The noise standard set in Chapter Three in 1977 was not updated until 2006. A more sophisticated noise standard, updated regularly, would better distinguish aircraft according to noise emitted and expose them to higher noise surcharges at airports where these apply.

Regulatory control measures such as those of ICAO are "one size fits all" and do not take account of the fact that noise abatement costs are different for different generations of aircraft. Therefore, the ICAO standards are not the lowest-cost way to reduce noise. ICAO standards also reflect compromises among stakeholders, making it unlikely that the standard fully reflects the best available technology (Fichert et al., 2020).

A second ICAO approach relates to land use. This works by limiting new house and school developments to locations away from airports. A third element concerns airport operational procedures, decided in conjunction with ATC bodies. This includes mandating appropriate flight paths that minimise overflight of residential areas by selection of runway and by directing aircraft away from noise-sensitive areas. Take-off and descent procedures can also be changed to steeper ascent and descent trajectories that reduce the time aircraft are close to the ground near airports. A final element of the ICAO approach involves airport operational restrictions such as restrictions on night flights.

The ICAO Balanced Approach is criticised for not being the best way to reduce noise. A more effective policy would apply to all aircraft generations and penalise aircraft with reference to noise emitted. A better policy would also rank the different policies under the Balanced Approach according to the noise reduction to be achieved for a given application of resources. The ICAO classification also suffers from other important weaknesses. It is expressed per ton of aircraft weight rather than absolute noise emitted so it does not reflect that heavier aircraft are noisier.

Noise budgets

A noise budget (or envelope) limits the overall noise impact of an airport and acts as a restriction on the airport's capacity. It may take the form of a movement cap (a crude proxy for noise) or as a limit on the sound energy that an airport is allowed to emit. In the former case, each flight would count towards the cap, regardless of noisiness. In the latter measure, a larger number of quieter flights or a smaller number of noisier flights would be compatible with the cap in energy-equivalent terms.

A night curfew could be regarded as a zero-noise budget for the relevant time period and such curfews are set for many airports including Frankfurt, Zurich, Dublin, London City and Sydney airports. However, an absolute ban on night-time flights does not take into account how noisy a given flight is. A noise budget specific to night-time would allow for an overall limit with some flexibility for low-noise flights.

As regards economic efficiency, noise budgets and movement limits are quite different. A noise budget could be an efficient instrument to reduce noise to an optimal level, that is, where the marginal benefit of reducing noise equals the marginal abatement cost. However, movement caps are not defined in terms of noise (but rather movements) and therefore incentivise flights using relatively loud aircraft. Noise caps have been implemented at Hamburg, Amsterdam Schiphol and Zurich airports, but without seeking to set them at the optimal level. These caps rather reflect political decisions to limit noise to a level accepted by stakeholders including households living in the neighbourhood of the airport.

A noise budget at an optimal level could be managed like a cap-and-trade system of tradable permits though no such system has yet been implemented. A cap-and-trade system might however be subject to industry lobbying for a large number of permits which would undermine the effectiveness of the scheme (not unlike the early phase of the EU Emission Trading System for carbon emissions).

A noise budget at a time of airport expansion could require the airport not to increase its footprint beyond a given number of square kilometres. Different possible investment plans, especially regarding runway use and runway building, may also be assessed in terms of their impact on the airport's prior noise footprint.

Noise charges

A second tool to mitigate the noise externality is to structure airport charges to penalise noisier aircraft and encourage airlines to retire louder aircraft and purchase quieter aircraft. Such a charging structure—if seriously applied—would strengthen the incentive for manufacturers to seek lower noise emissions from new aircraft designs. In terms of economic efficiency, the noise charge should be set at a level equal to the marginal external costs of noise so that, together with the airport charges set at marginal private cost, the total airport charge would be at the optimal level.

Outside Europe, few airports apply noise charges; in Europe, only some half of the hundred busiest airports do so. No airport in Italy, Portugal, Greece, Norway or Ireland applies noise charges (EASA, 2019).

Box 8.1 Airport Noise and Night-time Charges in 2022 at London Heathrow airport

In 2017, Heathrow airport restructured its charges to discourage older and noisier aircraft by substantially widening the differential between landing charges for new and older aircraft. The 2022 landing charges are set by aircraft age (ICAO Chapters) and are reported in Table 8.1 where the final column reports the peak night-time movement charge for the aircraft.

The night charge for Chapter 3 aircraft is prohibitive and even in daytime the movement charge for Chapter 3 aircraft is more than ten times the charge for the least noisy Chapter 14 aircraft. This charging structure gives airlines some incentive to retire their oldest aircraft and (if slots are available) to schedule services outside the night-time period.

Table 8.1 Heathrow Airport 2022 Charges by aircraft ICAO Chapter

Landing/Take-off Movement charges (rounded to nearest £)	*Peak (£)*	*Super Night Peak (£)*
Chapter 3 (pre-1977 aircraft)	11,917	59,584
Chapter 4 Base (pre-2001 aircraft)	3,774	18,868
Chapter 14 Base (pre-2017 aircraft)	1,601	8,004
Chapter 14 Low	961	4,806

Source: Heathrow Airport (2021, p. 33)

In a similar way to London Heathrow, Amsterdam Schiphol airport has had a surcharge since 2019 for older aircraft. In 2022, the basic movement charge was €2,757 for an aircraft weighing more than 100 tonnes (before passenger, parking, or other charges were applied). The noisiest aircraft was charged 200% of the basic charge for daytime, and up to 600% for night-time movements. The least noisy aircraft paid only 40% (daytime) or 75% (night-time) of the basic charge (Amsterdam Schiphol Airport, 2021). Both the Heathrow and Schiphol noise charging structure is defined per movement, which reduces their effectiveness.

Noise charges give stronger incentives in Germany where they were first introduced in the 1970s (Fichert, 1999). Today, according to the German air traffic act, noise surcharges are mandatory at German airports (and emission surcharges "shall" be levied). Over time, the design of the noise surcharges has been strengthened. The first schemes simply set lower charges on the basis of aircraft weight for Chapter 3 aircraft, the most modern at the time. In the 1990s, the least noisy modern aircraft in the Chapter 3 category received a further incentive in the form of an additional "bonus".

More than a decade ago, some of the larger German airports replaced weight-dependent schemes with noise surcharges based on average actual noise emissions of each aircraft type as measured at the respective airport. Using these actual noise emissions, aircraft are grouped into "categories", that is, all aircraft with noise emissions between x and y dB belong to category "a". At some airports, a distinction between emissions during take-off and landing is made. In recent years, the width of the categories has been reduced, and at most airports it is now one dB. When compared to a continuously increasing tariff, which is the ideal solution for noise surcharges, one advantage of this stepwise function is to provide strong incentives to replace specific aircraft.

A disadvantage of noise surcharges based on actual average emissions is that they are independent of the technological standard of an aircraft. Assume, for example, that the noise emissions of an old narrowbody aircraft are as high as the noise emissions of the most modern widebody aircraft. In this case, an airline would have to pay the same surcharge for both aircraft. However, it would be possible to carry the same number of passengers with a more recent narrowbody aircraft, thereby reducing aircraft noise per passenger. Consequently, some airports have introduced an additional element into their noise charging scheme which is based on the technological standard of the aircraft, usually the difference between the (weight-based) standards and the certified noise emissions of the aircraft. Noise surcharges are then reduced based on the difference between permitted and certified noise emissions. Whereas the incentives sketched here are designed in a revenue-neutral way, some airports levy an additional charge for financing noise monitoring and noise insulation programmes.

Box 8.2 Noise Charges at Frankfurt Airport

Frankfurt airport is an example of a sophisticated noise-surcharging regime (Fraport, 2022).

In total there are 15 noise categories, and aircraft are assigned to these categories separately for landing and take-off. For example, the surcharge per take-off during daytime is €89.48 (Cat. 1, e.g., A320 neo), €148.70 (Cat. 4, A 320), €805.80 (Cat. 10, e.g., B747–800), and €1,442.99 (Cat. 12, e.g., B747–400).

During night-time (10–11 pm and 5–6 am) there is an additional noise surcharge (65% of the daytime surcharge), and for (exceptional) movements during the curfew time (11 pm–5 am) the additional surcharge is tripled. Furthermore, all surcharges are increased by 50% for aircraft certified according to Annex 16, Chapter 3 (and even higher during night-time for aircraft that only marginally comply with this standard). Finally, the noise surcharge is reduced between 5% and 14% if the so-called noise rating index (i.e., the difference between the Chapter 3 standard and the certified noise emissions of the aircraft) is above 15 EPNdB, again using a stepwise approach.

Unfortunately, at very congested airports, a charging structure of these kinds will not be very effective due to the interactions between charges and slots (see the discussion in the next Box).

The recent structure of noise charges at London Heathrow, Schiphol Amsterdam, and Frankfurt airports is not found at many other airports, where the level of noise charges is too low and not sufficiently differentiated. Some noise charges are based on the cost to airports of providing noise protection and monitoring, in other words, on the airport's internal costs. But the cost of noise to the local community—the external cost—will certainly be a lot higher and it is on these external noise costs that noise charges should be based. To date, there are not many estimates of these external costs (but see Table 8.2).

The umbrella body for EU airport price regulators (Thessaloniki Forum, 2021) and the UK CAA have both recently reviewed the use of noise-related airport charges. The CAA study advocated that noise charges be defined consistently across airports and applied to all aircraft types, not just the noisiest. The study also argued that to be effective noise-based charges should comprise a larger portion of overall airport charges, and the differential between the noise charge levied on different aircraft types should be much larger. At price-regulated airports, new or higher noise charges could be accommodated by reductions in other airport charges to respect a given regulatory price-cap. The EU regulators' report confirmed that environmental charges at airports were compatible with the rules of the EU Airport Charges Directive and would not constitute discrimination between airport users.

Table 8.2 Some estimates of the external costs of noise and local emissions

Study (year)	*Airport*	*Method*	*Noise per LTO cycle*	*Local air quality per LTO cycle*
Schipper (1999)	European Airports	HP for noise	555€ for B737–300 (150seater) 150€ for B757–200 (200 seater) 275€ for B767–300 (275 seater) 420€ B747–400 for 420 seater	Not applicable
Pearce and Pearce (2000)	Heathrow	HP for noise	108€ for B737–400 (150 seater) 148€ for MD 82 (150 seater) 140€ for B757 (200 seater) 108€ for A310 (220 seater) 106€ for B777 (350 seater) 538€ for B747 (420 seater	Data for short- and long-haul flights published. LTO cycle in the range of Dings et al. (2003)
Dings et al. (2003)	European Airports	HP for noise	180€ for 40 seater 300€ for 100 seater 600€ for 200 seater 1,2000 for 400 seater	33€ for 40 seater 119€ for 100 seater 241€ for 200 seater 631€ for 400 seater
Grampella et al. (2017)	Italian airports 1999–2008	Based on Dings et al. (2003)	External costs of noise per average movement 110€ (type not specified)	External costs of noise per average movement 60€ (type not specified

Source: Based on academic articles as published.

Compensation is sometimes paid by airports to local communities for noise levels above a certain threshold or grants and finance provided to insulate buildings. Compensation schemes operate at a number of European airports (including in London, Amsterdam and Frankfurt). Non-cash programmes of acoustic revitalisation of buildings are used in the US and to a more limited degree in the EU (e.g., Brussels and Barcelona airports; Batog et al., 2019).

Box 8.3 Airport charges and environmental charges

Chapter 4 set out a number of principles for efficient airport charges. Returning to these principles, consideration is given to how to integrate them with pricing of environmental externalities. In what follows, it is necessary to distinguish airports with excess capacity and those with excess demand.

Begin with an airport's private costs. For an airport with excess supply, charges should equal short-run marginal costs, MC (see Figure 8.1). In case

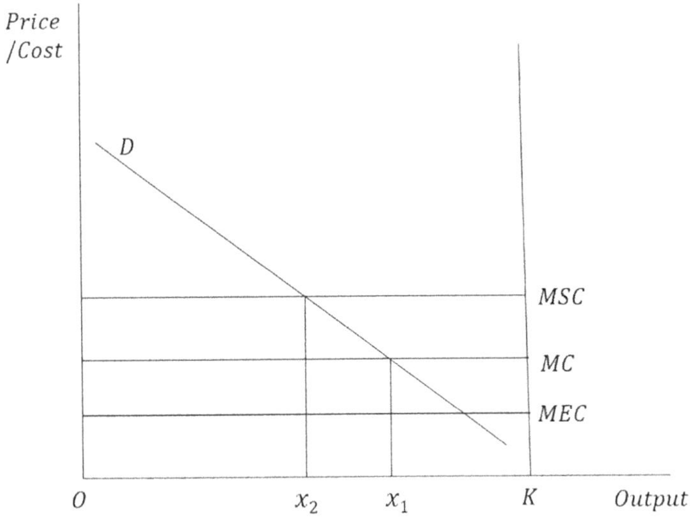

Figure 8.1 Externality pricing for airports with excess supply

this would not cover average costs, the airport should apply Ramsey pricing, that is set charges at marginal cost but for users with inelastic demand, set charges above marginal costs. Weight-based charges would broadly do so. Next, consider marginal external costs (MEC), which for simplicity are assumed to be constant. In terms of efficiency, the airport should add to the marginal external cost the marginal private cost and set charges accordingly. In Figure 8.1, this would reduce output from the level of x_2 to x_1 movements. The airline would pass this on to the passengers and the external environmental costs would be reflected in the airfares. In case the charge does not cover the costs, the airport can continue with Ramsey Pricing, but on a higher level. Depending on the size of the externality, prices inclusive of external costs might mean that the airport would be profitable so that a Ramsey adjustment would not be necessary. How to treat profits is discussed later.

How can airports achieve such an efficient outcome? If an airport does not use a slot system to ration demand, then the optimal congestion charge has to be increased by external environmental costs. This is theoretically easy, but in practice, no airport has done so. For US airports, optimal congestion charges have been recommended by many economists (e.g., Morrison and Winston, 2007), but never implemented. The same holds true for optimal congestion charges inclusive of environmental externalities.

If an airport does use slots to ration demand, then increasing charges to reflect the external environmental costs will not work (see Figure 8.2). If the

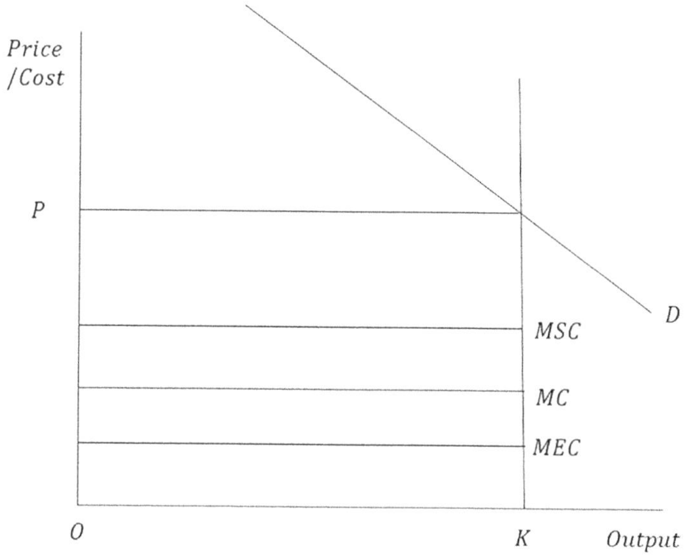

Figure 8.2 Externality pricing for airports with excess demand

airport adds to marginal private costs (MC) the marginal external cost (MEC) and sets the charges accordingly, it does not affect the price P which clears the market. The increase in airport charges just reduces the slot rent by the marginal external cost. The same effect occurs with an air passenger tax. Under slots, the better way to achieve efficiency is to set the slot constraint lower, to allow fewer flights. Again, this is theoretically easy, but in practice has not been applied.

This analysis, for simplicity, assumes all flights are homogenous in terms of noise and other emissions. But if noise and other emissions differ between flights, there is a reason to differentiate airport charges according to the noise of the aircraft, for instance, based on a sufficient number of noise classes.

How should the additional revenues for airports generated from environmental charges be used? In terms of simple economic efficiency, it does not strictly matter; the important thing is to set the prices correctly. But in practice it does matter. If the additional revenues are retained by the airport operator, that operator has an incentive to set its charges to include the cost of the externality. If the additional revenues are not retained, that incentive is lost. If the additional revenues must be used for noise insulation programmes and other projects in the airport's neighbourhood, there are incentives for excessive noise-mitigation programmes.

8.5 Measuring the external cost of noise and other local emissions

It is possible to put a value on the damage from noise either directly or indirectly. The direct method calculates the costs of medical services, along with estimates of lost working time and higher death rates in terms of opportunity cost and lower productivity. This method would however seriously underestimate the cost of noise as, for example, the cost of a headache might be valued at just the cost of an aspirin tablet. Therefore, this method is not much used.

The indirect method is based on the willingness-to-pay principle. One application is to calculate the expenditures of those affected by noise to protect themselves from noise, for instance by better insulation. Another is to compare otherwise equivalent house prices in noisy and quiet areas. This so-called hedonic pricing method (HP) is a very commonly used method. Both methods analyse market data to calculate what people are willing to pay for less noise. A third method tries to estimate the direct willingness-to-pay by conducting a survey and asking people. This is the stated preference technique (SP) which is used, though less often than the hedonic pricing method.

Research in this area dates back to the first major plan to expand airport capacity in the London area in the 1970s. Early studies focused on noise and the cost of noise. Airport prices were to be set inclusive of the costs imposed by the negative effects of air transport at a local level, and especially in regard to noise. Based on this approach, studies followed that focused on noise (but also on air quality). The results of some of the main studies are summarised in Table 8.2.

Overall, there are relatively few studies of the local external costs of air transport. In particular, the marginal external noise costs of different aircraft and at different airports are not well understood.

From such studies as have been conducted, the following results emerge. First, external noise costs are much higher than the external costs of poor local air quality. Depending on the aircraft, noise costs exceed air quality costs by between 2 and 5 times. Second, the external costs of poor local air quality are not negligible as some early studies and policy papers had suggested. Dings et al. (2003) show that NOx is important because of its magnitude and fine particularity because of their serious health consequences. As only a few European airports have emission charges sufficiently high, the external costs of poor local air quality are borne by the local residents, not by airport users. Third, the difference in external noise costs between noisy and less noisy aircraft are smaller than the differentials in some noise surcharges. This is because airport noise surcharges penalise loud aircraft a lot, rather than all aircraft proportionally to their noisiness. A further implication is that for modern aircraft, the external noise costs are higher than the noise charges. Fourth, results are relatively aggregated and do not distinguish sufficiently between landing and take-off and daytime and night time.

All the studies in Table 8.2 conclude that external costs are not internalised. However, it is not clear how this translates into a reduction of noise and an improvement of local air quality. For Schiphol airport, Lijesen et al. (2010) have calculated an optimal noise level which is recommended to be lower by 3dB, a substantial reduction. All methods that seek to estimate the external costs of noise, or other emissions, face the problem of making a calculation for which there is no information from a market transaction. The methods try to get around this problem and have made progress in this respect, but we should interpret the results with caution.

External costs as measured are relatively modest compared to congestion costs or to airport charges that reflect the private costs of operating the airport. The marginal noise costs per passenger are in the range €2–€9, and between €1.4 and €1.6 per passenger for landing and takeoff (LTO) emissions in 2002 prices. Average airport charges per passenger in Europe in 2005 were about €20 and had reached some €34 in 2014. From this perspective, it looks as if there is a large gap between measured costs and the extent of local opposition to airport expansion at many airports. Noise, in particular noise at night time, is regarded as the most important obstacle to expanding capacity. Yet, if an additional slot is worth so much, then it ought to be possible to reduce noise by internalisation of externalities. This would require higher airport charges, but the impact would not be so large if the policy were applied at many airports or even for all transport modes, as indicated by the EU's transport policy goals.

Another explanation for the divergence could be that the studies underestimate the environmental costs, but so far this does not seem to be the view of researchers. A final explanation might be that airport expansions have become so politicised and, in some cases, polarised that the political process has gained its own momentum and airports have lost the acceptance of their neighbourhoods.

Box 8.4 Controversies in Airport Economics: Why are economists the only people who think that airport noise is a minor problem?

Airport noise is localised, primarily in the vicinity of the flight paths of aircraft using an airport. The number of people affected by significant noise levels can be locally significant but nationally modest. Airline passengers are numerous nationally, and if they do not live near an airport, they do not experience much airport noise. The passenger who benefits from air travel may have little to say about airport noise whereas those experiencing high noise levels in the airport's neighbourhood will be loud in their opposition, especially towards airport expansion. Those exposed to significant levels of airport noise legitimately consider it to be a major problem.

Economists observe that studies of the cost of airport noise have, at least to date, found those costs to be modest. Readers will recall that studies indicate that the marginal noise costs per passenger are in the range €2–€9 in 2002 prices, suggesting a considerable gap between estimated noise costs and the degree of local opposition to airport expansion. At the same time, noise charges at airports are too rare and too low. In Europe, average airport charges were about €34 per passenger in 2014; within this total, noise charges—in the few airports where they apply—are well below the estimated cost of noise.

But airport slot values can be very high, as much as €100–€150 per passenger at the busiest airports. This implies that the value to passengers of expanding such an airport's runway is more than enough to pay higher charges sufficient to cover noise costs. This "internalisation of externalities" is the economist's recommended policy response to noise. Such an approach would make the (noise) polluter pay, rather than have the cost fall on the local community.

8.6 Emissions and the carbon neutral airport

For airports, climate change will act in both directions; airports at present contribute to climate change, but in future are likely also to suffer some of its effects. A 2021 study (Egis and UK Met Office, 2021) foresees climate impacts in the form of more frequent short-term closures of lower-lying airports due to flooding attributable to higher sea levels and to stronger storm surges. The report estimated that the number of airports at risk from severe flooding (mostly smaller airports) would increase by 15–20% over this century and that some two-thirds of coastal and low-lying airports would be at risk of some degree of runway flooding. Flight disruptions would spread across the entire air traffic network.

The airport industry defines carbon "neutrality" as absolute carbon reductions combined with measures to offset continuing emissions (Dube, 2021). "Net zero" is a more demanding target, defined as reducing emissions to a very low level while removing from the atmosphere carbon equal to an airport's continuing emissions. Many airports consider carbon neutrality to be attainable in the medium term, and net zero to be necessary by mid-century.

Airport emissions may be classified with reference to the accounting scheme in the Greenhouse Gas Protocol used in many industries (GHG Protocol). It offers a three-way classification of GHG emissions, based on the degree of control by a company (such as an airport) over the source of emissions.

Scope 1: emissions from sources that are owned or controlled by the airport operator, such as airport-owned energy generation plants, vehicles that use petrol or diesel, or ground support equipment using diesel fuel. In these areas, an airport operator could act directly to limit or reduce emissions.

Scope 2: emissions from services purchased by the airport operator from off-site suppliers, for example, purchased energy. Emissions from such sources depend on the fuel used by the power company from which the airport operator obtains its energy supply.

Scope 3: indirect emissions the airport does not control but may influence, including emissions by tenants of the airport, by aircraft landing, taking off, taxiing or parking, and emissions from processing and disposal of airport waste. A substantial part of Scope 3 emissions is due to passenger and staff vehicles arriving or departing the airport.

Scope 3 accounts for nearly all airport emissions; see Table 8.3 for estimates relating to London Heathrow and Gatwick airports. A first step in reducing airport emissions is to take an inventory of carbon emissions using internationally approved methodologies such as those produced by ICAO or Airport Council International. After identifying the baseline levels and sources of emissions, airports can develop a plan to reduce or eliminate them. A baseline may also be used to estimate the carbon implications of airport expansion and investment.

A baseline of this kind was prepared for the Airports Commission (2015) which evaluated a number of possible projects to deliver an additional runway in the London area. Table 8.3 reports the baseline before an additional runway. An estimate was then prepared of the additional emissions over the period 2025–2085 from an additional runway, distinguishing air travel, surface travel, airport operations and runway construction (Jacobs, 2014, Tables A2 and A4). The table shows that either of the runway projects would increase airport emissions over six decades by approximately one-quarter. But the absolute increases from the Heathrow runway project are three times larger than those for Gatwick, which is mainly explained by Heathrow serving more long-haul (higher carbon-emitting) flights than does Gatwick.

Table 8.3 Baseline emissions from airport operations at London Heathrow and London Gatwick airports, and the additional emissions from a new runway at either airport

	Gatwick airport	*Heathrow airport*	*Shares (%) of additional emissions*	
	2025–2085: millions of additional tonnes CO_2	*2025–2085: millions of additional tonnes* CO_2	*Gatwick*	*Heathrow*
Air travel (net change)	68	237	89%	97%
Of which: airside ground movements	4	13	5%	5%
Passenger surface movements	7	6	9%	2%
Airport operations	1	2	1%	1%
Total operational emissions	76	244	100%	100%
Construction of infrastructure	4	11	-	-
Baseline operational emissions	259	1109	-	-

Source: Jacobs (2014).

The inclusion of in-flight emissions gives a wider measure of emissions than under the GHG Protocol. In-flight air travel accounts for more than 90% of the additional emissions from a new runway. For airports serving short-haul flights and for regional airports, the in-flight share would be expected to be lower. The presence or absence of public transport links to the airport also affects emissions shares. Emissions at the airport due to a new runway are almost fully accounted for by aircraft landing and taking off (LTO) and by surface passenger movement. Emissions from the airport's own operations (Scope 1 and 2) are small relative to these other sources of emissions.

The climate policies of airports

Many airports have developed environmental plans to reduce and eliminate by mid-century their carbon emissions. These plans are usually found on the websites of airport operators. The global airport representative body, Airport Council International (ACI), manages a global Airport Carbon Accreditation (ACA) scheme. The scheme began in 2009 with 17 participating airports. By 2020, member airports exceeded 300 that served 45% of global air passenger traffic.

The ACA scheme primarily addresses Scope 1 and 2 carbon emissions while encouraging airports to seek reductions by parties responsible for Scope 3 emissions. Some observers argue that airports could act as enablers to encourage and facilitate airlines and others to decarbonise. This could be pursued through a revised structure of airport charges, relating them to variables with emissions implications—load factors, aircraft types, fuel shares. Slot rules and tenders for ground handling services could also be revised to reward lower-carbon suppliers. Airlines respond that it is more appropriate and consistent for aviation environmental policy to be decided at a national or international level. A common methodology for including emissions costs in airport charges would have the important benefit of creating a uniform carbon price; this would mean that decarbonisation would be most attractive at airports where it was less expensive.

The ACA framework classifies participating airports into six levels. Certification at the first level requires the airport to measure its emissions and to carry out annual follow-up audits that are independently verified; the second level requires a carbon management and reduction programme with demonstrable targets for reducing emissions; the third level requires that airports engage with third parties such as airlines, ground handlers, suppliers and surface-access providers to reduce emissions across the airport community. At level 3+ ("Neutrality") airports must have reduced carbon emissions and offset remaining emissions on the basis of internationally verified offsets. For levels 4 and 4+, an airport's emissions reduction programme must cover Scope 3 emissions and reduce the absolute level of emissions to a very low level and consistent with the Paris Climate Change Agreement's aim to keep the global temperature increase to well below 2 degrees above pre-industrial levels.

The carbon-free airport

To decarbonise, airports will need to replace current power supplies with non-carbon sources of energy, either by means of on-site energy generation or by contracting with suppliers that provide electricity from renewable sources (Janic, 2011). The size of airport campuses means that, in certain countries, solar panels could be deployed on a large scale. Other measures include support for the extension of railways between airports and cities; incentivising a switch to car-pooling or public transport for airport employees; facilitating or investing in access to sustainable fuels for airlines using the airport; support for ground handlers to electrify their vehicle fleets; and optimisation of airside ground movements by aircraft and other vehicles. EV chargers will need to be installed for electric vehicles using the airport.

In the case of buildings, new facilities will need to be designed on a near-zero energy basis and existing buildings to be better insulated; heating and ventilation and baggage handling to be provided by more efficient technologies; existing lighting to be replaced by low-energy systems. Operational efficiency will be a primary consideration for airports to limit energy use. Future investment assessments must include a carbon price to allow the selection of the most environmentally sustainable investment option.

How are such airport environmental investments—which will be costly, at least in the aggregate, and may need to last for decades—to be paid for? A distinction is needed between environmental investments that lower airport operating costs and those that do not. Insulating buildings, switching to electric vehicles and deploying renewable energy reduce both the airport's emissions and its operating costs once the investments have been delivered. Thus, once the investment costs have been paid, the airport's operational costs are lower. The cost of these investments should be included in airport charges that would decline in the medium term to reflect reduced airport costs.

Where environmental costs are incurred by airports but benefits accrue to society generally (by moderating climate change), the means to recover investment costs will be more controversial. For example, charges at price-regulated airports are set now by regulators at levels broadly equal to the efficient level of private costs incurred in providing services. These charges should include the aviation externality (see the discussion in Box 8.3) but this has rarely happened to date. In the EU, the body that represents airport regulators (the Thessaloniki Forum), found that EU airport charges regulations are consistent with the inclusion of the costs of airport externalities.

Airlines argue that where environmental investments produce social gains, the costs should be borne by the public purse, not airport users. But even if this were to be agreed, the large scale of required environmental investments across society in coming decades, much of which will be paid for from public sources, is likely to rule out public funding being available on a large scale for airport decarbonisation. Governments at national and EU levels will offer substantial funds for research into low-carbon technologies that will be important for those parts of aviation that are currently hard to decarbonise.

8.7 The European Commission's 2021 aviation policy proposals: implications for airports

Given the expected increase in the use of air transport, the EU Commission in July 2021 made a series of proposals to reduce emissions from aviation. These formed part of a larger set of emissions reduction measures ("Fit for 55") with the goal to achieve EU climate neutrality by 2050. An intermediate target was for a net reduction of at least 55% in emissions by 2030. It makes sense to consider developments in Europe when discussing airport emissions as Europe is the continent which has gone furthest in policies to reduce emissions. Other regions will have the European model to consider when they are developing their own plans.

Box 8.5 describes the EU's main decarbonisation policy, the Emissions Trading Scheme (ETS). The ETS will affect airports insofar as, for example, their energy consumption causes carbon emissions. But airports outside the EU, the US, the UK and New Zealand do not face a specific obligation to reduce their emissions, although, as shown by global Airport Carbon Accreditation scheme, many seek to do so voluntarily.

Box 8.5 The EU Emissions Trading Scheme (ETS) and airports

The ETS is cap-and-trade, whereby a ceiling (cap) defines total permitted annual carbon emissions. Emitters must surrender allowances equal to their previous year's CO_2 emissions. Each allowance is equal to one tonne of CO_2. Aviation has been included in the ETS since 2012. Progressive reductions in the cap move emissions towards levels consistent with climate policy goals. As allowances become scarcer, they become more expensive, giving polluters stronger incentives to reduce emissions.

The trading of allowances defines a price for carbon and requires companies to include the emissions cost (valued at the carbon price) in their cost base; the polluter must pay to pollute. By limiting the number of allowances, the cap on emissions must be met, while leaving companies free to find the lowest-cost way to pursue decarbonisation.

Flights are responsible for the bulk of aviation carbon emissions so the ETS mainly affects airlines. For airports, some permits will be required to cover emissions from their power plants and other Scope 1 activities. The likelihood of substantially costlier allowances means that the carbon price will have some impact on airports' future operational costs, their investments and the evolution of passenger traffic.

The aviation elements of the package are three-fold and concern the ETS, sustainable fuels, and the taxation of aviation. Policies that affect airlines will of course also indirectly affect airports, but some Fit for 55 policies affect airports directly.

First, the number of free ETS allowances allocated to aviation emitters are to be reduced by 25% per annum to eliminate them by 2027, at that stage leaving all allowances to be allocated by auction. Furthermore, the total supply of allowances is to fall by 4.2% annually rather than the current 2.2% annual reduction. A market stability reserve (MSR) will remain available to mop up excess allowances. Second, under a ReFuelEU regulation, aviation jet fuel supplies would be required to be increasingly blended with sustainable aviation fuels and made available to be uploaded at EU airports. This sustainable aviation fuel (SAF) share will rise from 2% in 2025 to 20% by 2035 and to over 60% by 2050. To make blended fuel readily available, there will be an obligation for EU airports to invest in the necessary infrastructure to deliver blended SAFs for aircraft refuelling. Third, the current exemption whereby aviation fuel is not subject to standard fuel taxes would be removed.

As part of a broader European Green Deal, a policy of Sustainable and Smart Mobility envisages zero-carbon airports on the basis of electrification. Other proposals might affect the number of passengers using airports in future. In particular, airports and airlines may be required to inform passengers about the carbon footprint of their trip and EASA required to develop an environmental labelling programme for European aviation.

8.8 Climate change and the expansion of airports

As we have seen, airports themselves do not account for a large share of aviation's carbon emissions. But a major challenge is that while individual flights will become more carbon efficient, the worldwide expansion of the industry (forecast at 4% per annum before COVID-19) would dominate per-flight or per-passenger efficiency gains, causing an absolute increase in the level of aviation emissions, and an even larger proportional rise as other sectors' emissions fall.

There are moves to address airline emissions through controls at the level of the airports. Some climate policy advisory bodies have recommended a cap on aviation emissions. The UK Committee on Climate Change (CCC) has recommended an annual air travel emissions limit of about 37 million tonnes. This compares to a post-COVID aviation emissions level of about 35 million tonnes. The same committee recommended that in the 2030s there should be

> no net expansion of UK airport capacity unless the sector is assessed as being on track to sufficiently outperform a net emissions trajectory that is compatible with achieving Net Zero alongside the rest of the economy and is able to accommodate the additional demand and still stay on track.
>
> (Committee on Climate Change, 2020)

The Netherlands is currently analysing caps on aviation emissions. The Dutch government's civil aviation policy memorandum for 2030 includes a target to bring

Dutch aviation emissions down to, at most and excluding offsets, the level of 2005. Options under consideration included an emissions ceiling at Dutch airports, an emissions trading scheme specific to airlines using Dutch airports, or a ceiling on the use of airline fossil fuel (Kingdom of the Netherlands, 2022). In June 2022, citing noise considerations, the Dutch government announced its intention to reduce the annual ceiling on runway movements at Amsterdam Schiphol airport in two stages from 500,000 to 440,000, a 12.5% decline.

Policy commitments by many governments are starting to be used in legal challenges to airport expansion plans in a number of jurisdictions. In 2020, the UK Court of Appeal rejected London Heathrow airport's plans for a new runway on the grounds that the additional flights would jeopardise Britain's commitment to net-zero GHG emissions by 2050. The ruling required Heathrow airport to revise its plans to show consistency with climate commitments. Subsequently, the UK Supreme Court reversed that decision and found that a new runway would not breach policy commitments on climate grounds, allowing the airport to apply for planning permission. Nonetheless, the court's judgement demonstrated that international climate objectives may begin to have significant implications for the development of airport infrastructure with long-term climate costs.

In a separate court case in 2020 involving a proposed expansion of Bristol airport, the local planning authority rejected the project because the CBA in the airport's application had not priced carbon emissions using an appropriate carbon price. Proper valuation of emissions in CBA studies would undoubtedly improve the accuracy of measured net benefits and in some cases perhaps showing the net social benefit to be negative.

It is to be expected that air travel will become more expensive in the coming decades due to: application of standard taxes to aviation fuel, charging VAT on airline tickets, and counting international aviation emissions in national carbon-reduction plans which will push up the price of ETS allowances. Many observers favour, in addition, direct demand-management limits, whether by means of carbon taxes or air travel ceilings in some form. All these factors act to slow future air passenger growth, and need to be allowed for in airport traffic forecasting and capital investment planning in future.

8.9 Conclusions

Airports produce large externalities, primarily noise and carbon emissions. How should these external costs be moderated considerably? And are current policies adequate?

A noise budget, defined in terms of the total noise occurring in a given nighttime period, set at a level where the benefit of noise abatement matched the cost of noise abatement, would be an effective tool to reduce noise. But this is done at very few airports, is generally defined in the wrong way (by aircraft movements and not noise itself) and is not set at the optimal level.

An alternative tool, applicable throughout the day, is noise charges. These would discourage flights by noisier aircraft and accelerate fleet modernisation and should be based on noise actually emitted by a given aircraft. Set at the right level, they would act to dissuade operators of noisy aircraft. But noise charges are absent from many countries and, in others, they are too low to reflect the cost of the noise emitted.

Because the policy tools that are available and that could be effective are hardly used, the cost of local noise does not fall on those who cause airport noise—it is not internalised—but instead that cost falls on local communities.

The situation is very similar for a second, and much larger, airport externality: airport carbon emissions. In this case also, a price should be paid for emissions at a level to properly incentivise the decarbonisation of airports. This could be done directly by a carbon charge (or tax) or indirectly through a cap-and-trade system such as the EU Emissions Trading Scheme. In its absence, carbon emissions costs are also not internalised and not paid by the polluter.

So far, there are few policies to stabilise, reduce and eliminate carbon emissions by mid-century, though the problem is now receiving serious attention. With sufficient investment, decarbonisation of direct emissions (Scope 1 and 2) is feasible at airports though at a cost, using available technologies, primarily electrification. For airports, the upfront investment costs of decarbonisation, and the obligation until then to purchase ETS allowances, will tend to raise airport costs and charges. As decarbonisation obligations spread generally throughout the aviation value chain, the prospective growth in passenger demand for airport infrastructure may prove lower than in recent decades, especially in the developed world.

Given the large benefits and costs of airports, internal and external, careful professional cost-benefit studies (see Chapter 5) which include the values of all major externalities as well as the full social benefits, will continue to be a critical tool to inform decision-makers about where and how much investment should take place to deliver the net social benefits of airports.

Note

1 db(A) is the noise measure used in Europe; the US and ICAO use EPNdB.

References

Airports Commission (2013) "Discussion Paper 05: Aviation Noise", available at assets.publishing.service.gov.uk

Airports Commission—Final Report (2015) available at assets.publishing.service.gov.uk

Amsterdam Schiphol Airport (2021) "Charges and Conditions", available at https://schiphol.ne

UK Committee on Climate Change (2020) "Policies for the Sixth Carbon Budget and Net Zero", available at www.theccc.org.uk

Batog, J, I Foryś and J Konowalczuk (2019) "Airport Noise Compensation: Real Estate Perspective", *Journal of European Real Estate Research*, 12, 250–266

Dings, J M W, R C N Wit, B A Leurs, M D Davidson and W Fransen (2003) *External Costs of Aviation*, Berlin, Federal Environmental Agency, Umweltbundesamt

Dube, K (2021) "Climate Action at International Airports an Analysis of the Airport Carbon Accreditation Programme", in G Nhamo, D Chikodzi and K Dube (eds), *Sustainable Development Goals for Society*, Berlin, Springer, 237–251

Egis and UK Met Office (2021) "Climate Change Risks for European Airports", available at www.eurocontrol.int/publication/eurocontrol-study-climate-change-risks-european-aviation
EU (2002) "Directive 2002/49/EC (Which Was Replaced by Regulation 598/2014)", available at https://eur-lex.europa.eu/legal-content/EN/TXT/?uri=CELEX%3A32014R0598
European Aviation Safety Agency (EASA) (2019) "European Aviation Environmental Report", available from www.easa.europa.eu/eaer
Fichert, F (1999) *Umweltschutz im zivilen Luftverkehr*, Berlin, Duncker & Humblot
Fichert, F, P Forsyth and H-M Niemeier (2020) *Aviation and Climate Change Economic Perspectives on Greenhouse Gas Reduction Policies*, London, Routledge
Fraport (2022) *Airport Charges ACCORDING to Art. 19b Air Traffic Act (LuftVG)*, Frankfurt/M, Fraport
Grampella, M, P Lo, G Martini and D Scotti (2017) "The Impact of Technology Progress on Aviation and Emissions", *Transportation Research Part A*, 103, 525–540
GreenHouse Gas Protocol (n.d) available at https://ghgprotocol.org/about-us
Heathrow Airport (2021) "Airport Charges for 2022", available at www.heathrow.com
Jacobs (2014) "Carbon Assessment, Prepared for the Airports Commission", available at https://assets.publishing.service.gov.uk
Janic, M (2011) *Greening Airports: Advanced Technology and Operations—Green Energy and Technology*, London, Springer
Kingdom of the Netherlands (2022) *State Action Plan for the Reduction of CO_2 Emissions from Aviation*, Amsterdam, Ministry of Infrastructure and Water Management
Lijesen, M, W van der Straaten, J Dekkers, R van Elk and J Blokdijk (2010) "How Much Noise Reduction at Airports?", *Transportation Research Part D*, 15, 51–59
Morrison, S and C Winston (2007) "Another Look at Airport Congestion Pricing", *American Economic Review*, 97, 1970–1977
Pearce, D and B Pearce (2000) *Setting Environmental Taxes for Aircraft, a Case Study for the UK*, Norwich, Centre for Social and Economic Research on the Global Environment
Schipper, Y (1999) *Market Structure and Environmental Costs in Aviation: A Welfare Analysis of European Air Transport Reform*, Amsterdam, Free University
Thessaloniki Forum (2021) "Airport Charges and Environmental Issues and Considerations", available at www.ec.europa.eu
Venables, J, J Laird and H Overman (2014) *Transport Investment and Economic Performance*, London, Research Report for UK Department for Transport

9 Economic impacts, policy and COVID

9.1 Introduction

In this chapter, we examine two aspects of airports. The first concerns the impacts and benefits of airports. Airports are often claimed to create very large economic impacts and benefits. These claims need to be scrutinised, since they often are exaggerated, and concepts are misused. For example, a study by InterVISTAS for ACI Europe (2015) claims "European airports contribute to the employment of 12.3 million people earning €356 billion in income annually, and generate €675 billion in GDP each year, equal to 4.1% of GDP of Europe". A common mistake is to confuse economic impacts with benefits—both concepts are valid and have a role in policy evaluation, but they are different. We look at what techniques can be used to assess them. The well-established technique of cost–benefit analysis (CBA) can be used to evaluate the costs and benefits of an airport project or policy shift, though this can also be done using the newer technique of computable general equilibrium (CGE) modelling. This technique is also the recommended means of evaluating impacts, such as impacts on GDP and jobs. In recent decades, there has also been considerable use of a third approach of economic impact analysis (EIA), but this is a technique which has major problems and is not recommended. Over the past decade or so there have been developments in the measurement of the benefits of airport projects and policies. In particular, the idea of "wider economic benefits" (WEBs) or wider economic impacts (WEIs) has gained currency. These ideas are explained and the ways in which WEBs might be measured are explored. Section 9.3 provides a brief discussion of the uses of impact models. Secondly, we examine how the COVID-19 pandemic has affected airports. Demand for their services dropped sharply, and this leads to serious financial problems for many of them and we explore how best to handle these problems.

9.2 Impacts, benefits and connectivity

Estimating the impacts of airports, their benefits and their costs is a confusing and controversial area. It is often claimed (typically by the proponents) that airports create huge impacts and benefits, and that they are "job machines", and that the benefits from them far outweigh any costs they have, including environmental costs.

DOI: 10.4324/9781003156901-12

By contrast, other studies (such as those using a cost–benefit analysis framework, as used in Chapter 5), talk about benefits which are in the same order of magnitude as the costs of achieving them. To deal with these issues, it is best to start with some of the key concepts.

Concepts and measures

One confusion deals with the differences between impacts, benefits and costs. An impact of an airport investment, such as a new runway or policy, or of a noise price, concerns its effects on economic and other variables, such as jobs, output or GDP, consumption, greenhouse gas emissions or local road congestion. Some of these impacts are desirable, others not. A benefit is a very specific kind of impact and involves an assessment of how much better off the economy, or more specifically residents in it, are as a result of the investment or policy. In Chapter 5 there was a discussion of how much better off the economy would be as a result of expanding capacity, and this involved measuring gains to users or consumers, and comparing these to costs to affected parties, to produce a measure of net social benefit. If the airport investment results in benefits greater than cost the residents of the economy gain, but it is not clear whether the residents gain or lose if there are more jobs or GDP increases.

There are several ways in which we can measure these, but three are of particular relevance and use. Cost–benefit analysis has been used for many decades to assess the costs and benefits of a project, and it is a rigorous technique grounded in welfare economics. It cannot measure general impacts, however. Computable general equilibrium (CGE) modelling is a newer approach which can be used to estimate a wide range of impacts such as those on employment, output and GDP, consumption, possibly greenhouse gas emissions, though probably not the impact on noise or local road congestion (unless the model used is specifically designed to do this). Many, though not all, CGE models can be used to measure benefits and costs in the same way as used in CBA. Economic impact analysis (EIA) is used as a means of estimating impacts such as those on employment and output, though it cannot be used to measure net benefits (though sometimes it is, mistakenly).

Partial and General equilibrium refers to the capabilities of different measurement approaches. Partial equilibrium means that the approach only measures effects in the market directly involved (e.g., an airport market). Thus, with CBA, the direct benefits and costs of a new runway will be measured, but any broader effects such as on car and rail travel, other than those directly related to the airport, will not be. A CGE model is specifically designed to measure the full general equilibrium effects of a change, thus a CGE model can estimate the effects of a new runway on car and rail travel broadly and many other effects as well. EIA makes an estimate of the direct impacts on variables such as output and employment, along with an estimate of employment and output effects on *some* markets indirectly affected. It only measures some effects and should not be seen as a full assessment of benefits or impacts. To summarise, Table 9.1 sets out how different variables can best be measured.

Table 9.1 Measures and techniques

Ability to Measure	*CGE*	*CBA*	*EIA*
Economic impacts (e.g., GDP, Employment)	Yes	No. Very difficult to handle	Incorrectly
Welfare or net benefits	Perhaps. Needs to be specified in model- often not done	Yes	No
Local externalities (e.g., noise)	Perhaps. Externalities normally addressed outside the model, but environmental measures can be added easily	Yes	No
Impacts on National/ Global (e.g., greenhouse gas emissions)	Yes—if specified in the model	No. Estimates from CGE modelling can be added in in some cases	No
General Equilibrium Effects	Yes	No. Shadow pricing can measure some of these	No
Distributional impacts	Yes	No. Can measure only direct, not indirect incidence	No
Detail and disaggregation	Perhaps if disaggregated sub-models are used	Yes	Yes

Source: authors' analysis

What is recommended? Investment and policies

CBA was developed as a means of assessing investments, especially infrastructure investments such as at airports, from a national or social viewpoint (as compared to a financial or profit assessment) (Forsyth and Niemeier, 2021; Forsyth et al., 2021). It has been applied to airports from its early days in the 1960s. It can be applied to the assessment of whole airports or airport systems, parts of airports such as runways and terminals, and minor investments such as air bridges and car parks. It is also useful as a way of evaluating policies, such as the costs and benefits of a night curfew, a noise control measure, or moving a particular type of traffic from a specific airport, or a programme to reduce carbon emissions at an airport. It can also be used to assess the closure of an airport. Its techniques are well established, understandable and simple to use. It is a popular technique.

By contrast, CGE models have only recently been used to evaluate airports. Not all CGE models can be used for this purpose, since the model needs to have an economic welfare measure embodied in it. The types of information needed to develop such a measure, including demand and cost functions, are very often implicit in a good model. The principles are the same as those which underlie CBA. Thus, a CGE model can be used to estimate the net benefits of an airport investment in the same terms as a CBA assessment would. Recent major evaluations of airport investments, such as the evaluation of the Second Sydney airport (2012) and the Airports Commission (2015) have used CGE and CBA approaches.

The advantage of a CGE assessment is that it is a general equilibrium assessment, and this means that it will capture various costs and benefits across the full economy which are not captured fully, or at all, using a CBA. Many measures of costs and benefits will be much the same no matter which technique is used. A CGE estimate can capture effects which work through substitutes, such as passengers choosing road or rail rather than air. When taxes are used to finance the airport, a CGE model can be used to determine the overall cost of the taxes to the economy. On the other hand, there are limitations to using a CGE model. While CGE models are becoming more widely available, a suitable model may not be readily available. CGE models are more aggregate since they often model the whole economy, and this can be a source of inaccuracy (though this can be addressed by the use of sub-models). Just as CBAs can be poorly done, some CGE models embody questionable assumptions, which lead to unreliable results. While the use of CGE models as a means of assessing investments is in its infancy, they have potential to become a very useful technique.

CBA was not designed to measure broader economic impacts. By contrast, CGE models are specifically designed to assess the broader economy-wide impacts of policies and investments (Forsyth and Niemeier, 2021). They can be used to make estimates of the effects of an airport investment or policy on output and GDP, employment and output of other industries such as rail and road. They can be used to estimate the effects on the whole economy, and a regional model can be used to estimate regional impacts. For example, a model which includes several regions of a national economy can be used to assess the impacts of a major investment in one region on the traffic and outputs in other, competing regions (this was done for the (UK) Airports Commission in 2015).

A couple of examples can be used to show the usefulness of impact studies. In the earlier years of using CBA to evaluate airport investments, attempts were made to address distributional effects. However, it became apparent that CBA could only measure initial or direct incidence, which could be very different from the final incidence (and as a result, CBA studies rarely try to study incidence). However, if a CGE model includes different groups, such as different income groups, it can be used to study the distributional effects of investments. Another example of the use of impact assessments comes with measuring employment effects of investments. These can be important, especially when the economy is not close to full employment, though a CBA will be silent on these. A CGE approach can be used to assess the impact of an airport investment on employment. Building an airport will absorb skilled and unskilled workers away from other industries, both directly and indirectly (e.g., by reducing demand for other substitutes such as road and rail), and the final impact will be very different from the effect on direct employment of the project.

Examples of CBAs and CGEs

A good way to understand what is involved in a CBA or a CGE analysis of an airport is to consider some examples. In the case of a CBA this is easy, since CBA is well documented. In particular, the book by Jorge-Calderon (2021) provides a detailed guide, with worked examples, of how an airport CBA can be done. CBA involves setting out all of the costs and benefits of the project. To start with, demand, revenues and costs need to be forecast. The various elements of cost, such as the expected capital cost and operational cost need to be itemised, along with the costs which fall on the passengers and airlines, such as the cost of access and delay costs which need to be estimated. Revenues to the airport and benefits to passengers and airlines also need to be detailed. Many of the costs and benefits associated with airports are the costs of time spent or saved, and the value of time is a major parameter (time costs might be nearly 80% of total costs). These costs are at best only partially reflected in the financial statements. It is also important to estimate the externality costs of an airport, such as noise and emissions. These are also not included in the financial statement of an airport. A good CBA will identify the overall costs and benefits of the airport to all parties, as well as the financial costs and benefits. It can be the case that the net benefits of the airport are socially positive even if the airport makes a loss. The balance could also be the other way around because the financial costs do not include the costs of time spent or saved nor the external noise and emission costs.

It is more difficult to illustrate what is involved with a CGE assessment of an airport investment for a number of reasons, most notably because CGE models have only recently been used to assess airport investments. Furthermore, most of the CGE assessments have not done a complete assessment of an airport, but rather concentrated on specific aspects. Perhaps the most thorough assessment is for the Airports Commission (Airports Commission, 2014). This study focuses on the wider economic impacts of the airport proposals, though it also explores other aspects—it is a substantial exercise. It gives greatest emphasis to the impacts on GDP, though it also evaluates the impact of welfare (or net social benefit)—several CGE studies document GDP impacts but not welfare impacts. It also analyses the effects on employment and house prices, to name a couple. The assessment also considers several aspects of wider economic benefits (WEBs), such as benefits which come about as a result of imperfect competition and tax effects. It also measures benefits which come from greater connectivity. Beyond this, it also includes estimates of increases in consumer surplus (which are not normally regarded as a wider benefit). All in all, this is a thorough and extensive study which breaks new ground in measuring the impacts and benefits of an airport proposal, from which a lot can be learned. So far, many other airport CGE studies are less ambitious than this one.

Economic impact analysis—a roadmap to nowhere?

Thus far, we have mentioned but not recommended EIA as a means of assessing impacts or benefits. This is with good reason. In spite of its name, EIA does not enable us to measure the impact of investments such as airport investments. Furthermore, it is of no help in measuring the benefits or costs of investments or policies. In spite of this, it is very widely used in a number of assessment tasks, and over the past two or three decades in evaluating airport investment. Indeed, with some major investment projects, such as the new Berlin airport (BBI), it was the only form of investment evaluation used (Mueller, 2021). Not surprisingly, EIA is very popular with lobbyists or proponents of (airport) projects.

The best way of showing why EIA is of no value in estimating impacts and benefits is to sketch out what it involves. Firstly, a direct impact is estimated—this is a sum of resources directly used in the project, such as the (value of) the labour input, the capital input and so forth. An indirect impact is added to this. Using an input-output table, the use of other inputs which enter the project indirectly is estimated. Thus, the airport project uses concrete, IT services, plumbing and electrical services, glass and so forth. These are outputs of other industries. Typically, the total impact as estimated will be about twice the direct impact. There are sometimes estimates of further effects, and in particular, recent studies have estimated "catalytic" impacts of projects (these are discussed in the next section).

At best, these calculations could be regarded as an estimation of the resources used in creating the airport, nothing more (Niemeier, 2001; Huderek-Glapska, 2021). They do not measure the economic impact of the airport. For example, they do not measure the output of the airport—an airport may gain very little traffic and little measured output, yet it will be counted by an EIA study as having a substantial "economic impact". An EIA does not tell us where the resources come from, and it implies that they are effectively free. There will be a use of labour resources, but unless there is serious unemployment, these will come from somewhere else. It may be true that jobs are created directly by the project, but this does not mean that jobs in the economy have increased. An EIA only takes account of the resources directly used in the project, plus some used indirectly. If the airport project goes over budget, and costs rise, an EIA will conclude that its economic impact has risen. EIA studies very often claim that an airport investment will create significant "benefits", implying that residents in the economy will be better off as a result of it being made. But an EIA provides no measure of benefits in the way that a CBA study does, and the project might create large benefits for airlines and their passengers, or nothing much at all.

Jobs and GDP: What to do about them?

Jobs—are airports "job-creation machines"? One of the more popular claims about airports is that they are "job machines", and that this is a good thing. Airports are associated with increased employment when they are being built, and then when they are being used. When a large airport is being used there are many people working there, some of whom are directly employed by the airport, but most work for airlines, retailers and office staff. Airports will give rise to further off-airport employment in car parks and freight handling. It is clear where the idea of job machines comes from.

In spite of this, it may not be that an airport significantly increases overall employment in the economy or that it even increases it at all. If an economy is operating at close to full employment, the more employment in one sector of the economy, the less employment there will be in others as workers shift from one sector to another.

There may be a temporary impact on employment if an airport expands, but this will not last forever as the airport bids up wages (especially of skilled workers) and other industries are crowded out. An airport will have an impact on local employment, though not necessarily the wider economy, at least in the medium to longer term.

Things can be different if the general economy is operating at less than full employment, which can happen in developed economies, but especially in developing economies. Investing in the airport, or increasing its size, will have an impact on local employment. However, the impact on the national economy will be much less, as the expansion draws skilled workers away from other industries. CGE models can be useful in measuring the impact on economy-wide employment, focusing as they do on the relationships between industries and on aggregate supply and demand imbalances. This said, the labour market is a complex one, and the results of different models can differ widely.

Many studies report the impact on GDP (or related concepts such as GNP and National Income) of a policy change involving airports or as a result of an airport investment. These studies should preferably use a CGE approach to estimate this impact, though many studies of impacts use EIA. The impact on GDP as estimated by a CGE model is a relevant measure of impact on the regional or national economy. But it is not a measure of welfare, in as much as it does not tell us how much better off the residents of the economy are. A welfare measure, as used in a CBA, will typically be much less than the impact on GDP. In order to create more output, more resources of land, labour and capital need to be used, and these have a cost. Impacts on GDP and the measured benefit or welfare gain are different measures with their own role and should not be confused. It is a matter of comparing apples with oranges. For example, if there is a €500m investment in an airport, and it gives rise to a €1bn rise in GDP, one cannot claim that it is a good investment. It might be, but it is necessary to compare like with like, and compare the cost of the investment to the benefits it brings, not GDP or other macro magnitude.

The wider economic benefits of air transport

Over the past two decades or so, in the context of surface transport evaluation, there has been a recognition that traditional CBAs may not capture all of the benefits and costs which come about. CBAs may be missing important effects, such as the benefits from agglomeration, which can occur when firms cluster and generate external economies, and benefits and costs which come about because of market failures, such as the presence of market power and taxation. These effects have been called "wider economic benefits" or WEBs, though sometimes the related concept of "wider economic impacts" is used. Measurement of these effects is still in its infancy. In earlier days, it was often suggested that these WEBs could be an additional 40% of benefits, though recent work has suggested that they may be of the order of 10%.

More recently, there has been interest in the idea of wider economic benefits in aviation (Airports Commission, 2014; Forsyth, 2021). These can be similar to, though not the same thing, as WEBs in surface transport. Some WEBs of surface transport can be directly translated to aviation—perhaps the most important of these are the benefits and costs which come about through market failures. These can occur much as with surface transport. Their effects are different. An important source of benefits in surface transport can be agglomeration benefits which do not translate directly to air transport. There may be agglomeration benefits when businesses cluster around airports. However, there is a related effect which can be summed up as a "connectivity" benefit. We shall look in more detail at market imperfection and connectivity sources of WEBs later in this chapter. There has been a limited amount of study of the WEBs of air transport. The most significant study of WEBs or wider economic impacts (WEIs) in air transport has been that done for the Airports Commission (2014) which used both CBA and CGE approaches to get a handle on measurement. A related concept is that of "catalytic benefits" which is a term used in the EIA literature. This is not the same as WEBs which are associated with the CBA literature, though *some* of the effects are similar.

There are several market imperfections which can give rise to WEBs, and such benefits can arise in particular from market power and from taxes. There can be several air transport markets which can be subject to market power—for example, some air routes are monopolies or oligopolies. In this case, customers pay the market price, but this is above the (marginal) cost. While this affects airline markets directly, the effect filters down to the airport market. In this situation, the value of the additional output which airports create should not be valued by the price they receive, but by more, since the benefit to the airline customers is more. In short, there is a WEB created when the airport is used. The same sort of effect comes about through taxes. If an output of an airport is taxed, the airport receives less than the full value of the service it creates. Airports are subject to a number of taxes, from personal income taxes, corporate taxes, value-added taxes (VAT), and labour taxes. They can also be the recipient of subsidies.

Evaluating this type of WEB is relatively straightforward, albeit involved. To measure the market power benefit, it is necessary to find out what market power effects there are (e.g., oligopoly at the airline level), and what impact they have on the airport's costs and prices. There is a similar exercise needed when the effects of taxes are estimated. We need to know the level of the taxes, and relevant demand and supply elasticities. This is where a CGE model can be useful, since a detailed CGE model will have the main taxes in the economy built into it. In this case, it is a simple matter of running the model to estimate, for example, how large the WEBs from expanding the output of the airport are. CGE models have been used to estimate WEBs from labour taxes in surface transport in London by Venables (2007), and the principles can be readily applied to the airport case.

Analysts of air transport have been paying increasing attention to its role in facilitating connectivity. It is easy to appreciate that connectivity might be important, but rather more difficult to develop ways of estimating the benefits it brings. Air transport enables increases in the connections between cities and airports. A useful tool is that of connectivity indexes, which measure how connected cities or airports are, and show how connectivity can be increased (Burghouwt and Redondi, 2013). Direct flights between airports save time and money, giving rise to benefits from greater connectivity between cities. Greater connectivity leads to more interaction between people from different cities, facilitating business, increasing investment and promoting understanding. Not all aspects of connectivity are positive, however. It has become very apparent since 2020 that connectivity facilitates the transmission of disease, and governments around the globe were systematically *reducing* connectivity by putting up border restrictions.

While the benefits of connectivity can easily be appreciated, it is not easy to measure them in a reliable way. There have been a number of empirical studies of the relationship between measures of connectivity and indicators such as GDP, productivity of regions and business development (see InterVISTAS, 2006; Gillen et al., 2014). However, these studies need to be treated with care. For example, there is the causality issue—is it a matter of increased connectivity resulting in greater GDP or is it the other way around? GDP may increase in a region, but GDP is not a good measure of benefit. In short, increased air transport connectivity seems to be creating benefits but how big they are, at current state of knowledge, is a matter for conjecture.

In summary, the notion of WEBs of air transport is a good one, and airports have a role in facilitating them. WEBs have a role in the estimation of the benefits and costs of airport investments. The measurement of how big the WEBs are is only at the beginning. Some WEBs are straightforward to measure, but most are difficult to measure except in the broadest of terms.

Airport development gives rise to a range of impacts and benefits. Airports give rise to increased output and incomes in a city or region, are associated with increased employment in the region, and they facilitate increased connectivity. These are impacts of relevance to policymakers and businesses. They are not necessarily benefits in the sense that they lead to the residents of the economy being better off. One impact of an airport investment might be additional GDP in the region—this may be desirable, but the net benefit to residents from this would most likely be much less than the simple GDP gain. More jobs around the airport may sound impressive, but it may not yield any net benefit in the wider economy. With airports, if the impacts as measured are really large, and the benefits are great, then perhaps there is something wrong with the calculations.

9.3 Impact analysis and airport policy in practice

Impact studies now form an important part of the airport policy discussion. We look at two examples using these and highlight how this discussion has become more difficult, with a chasm between the studies using the traditional CBA framework and those using impact models suggesting very different results.

Airports as job machines

Recall the big numbers of the ACI claim from 2015. Airports were said to be responsible—directly, indirectly, and via induced and catalytic effects—for the employment of a total of 12.3 million people. To understand the policy message of such an EIA study, one needs to go back into the history of EIA and how it was adopted by airport councils and management. In the late 1980s US state-owned airports faced, for the first time, capacity problems and needed investment. Such investments were subject to CBA like other public investments with which they competed for scarce budget funds. In addition, airport investments faced in many cases opposition from the local communities. In this situation, the US Department of Transportation (USDOT, 1992) recommended EIA to support airport extensions and to overcome local resistance. The US DOT was aware that the EIA approach was at odds with CBA which, as argued earlier, should guide the public discourse, but nevertheless the DOT recommended the use of both methods. Exactly how to combine these methods was left open. The important thing was that EIA was established as a method for public discourse. ACI-Europe followed suit and recommended similar EIA guidelines for its members without mentioning or clarifying the relationship to CBA (York Consulting, 1998). At the same time, industry studies forecasted capacity crunches at a large scale, although in retrospect these never materialised.

The objective was to persuade policymakers that airports are job machines which solve the problem of unemployment. Any obstacle which prevented airports from expanding would destroy jobs. Airport capacity should be extended to such a degree that, even in the peak, capacity would be abundant. This strategy was partially successful; for example, Frankfurt airport got its runway approved and built. But this strategy did not persuade environmental groups or communities living in the neighbourhood of airports. In the UK, Friends of the Earth took Manchester airport to court for advertisements claiming that thousands of new jobs would be created by a new runway.

The early EIAs relied on direct, indirect and induced effects. They did not quantify the so-called catalytic effects, but just mentioned them. Even today, US studies do not quantify the catalytic effects. This changed around 2005 with studies in Germany and Switzerland (Forsyth et al., 2021). In Germany, well-known economists used this EIA concept to successfully influence decisions among others on the new Berlin airport (see Box 9.1). Catalytic effects take up the theme of connectivity and wider economic effects. The airport job machine is not only creating direct, indirect and induced jobs, but also leads to better connectivity making the airport region attractive for firms with even more jobs. The catalytic effect is very large. In the case of Berlin, it is said to be six times greater than the direct, indirect and induced effects. The 2015 study for ACI, mentioned earlier, only claimed catalytic effects that were 50% larger than the direct, indirect and induced effects. Connectivity and WEBs are serious issues of research as argued earlier, but they can also be misused to influence airport policy. The objective seems to influence policy for private interests.

Night curfews, noise and jobs

The idea of airports as job engines is also directed at environmental groups who question and oppose airport extensions. It can be applied to the setting of night curfews and noise. This was already foreseen by the USDOT paper from 1992.

Consider a recent example from the UK. According to a study by York Aviation (2021, p. 1) on behalf of airports and airlines, its study

> on the economic benefits of night flying is designed to address an evidential gap within the Department for Transport's existing framework for considering the economic impacts of night flights. The existing approach . . . does not consider a range of key economic benefits from night flying.

Department for Transport uses a CBA approach to evaluate policy. The York Aviation study proposes the following "key economic benefits from night flying" for 2019:

- direct impact: 24,200 jobs
- indirect and induced effects: 38,700 jobs
- catalytic impact: 213,200 jobs across the UK.

These are very large numbers which imply that the impacts and benefits from removing curfews on night flying (as preferred by airports and airlines) are very substantial. While the Department for Transport, which prefers to use a CBA approach, is unlikely to be convinced, they will look impressive to the general public. This makes a sober discussion of the benefits and costs of night curfews unlikely. Such command-and-control measures as night curfews are very often inefficient and there is a legitimate argument to be made that superior policies to limit noise are available, such as time-of-day noise surcharges or sophisticated noise budgets.

Box 9.1 Controversies in Airport Economics: What went wrong with Berlin Brandenburg International (BBI) airport?

BBI opened finally in 2020 after 13 years of delay. Its opening has allowed BBI to drop out of the news headlines, but important questions remain about what went wrong and what are the lessons? Mueller (2021) offers a detailed analysis. From the author's perspective, the failures and mistakes of BBI highlight the costs if policymakers do not pay enough attention to the economics of airports, as set out in this book. In 1991, it was forecasted that Berlin airport could triple passenger numbers by 2000. These forecasts were prepared by consultants using simple forecasting models, but they created high expectations. The planning process to identify the best airport location relied on much better forecasts and a mediation process with the stakeholders and the neighbours (see Chapter 2). But the political system took a different approach and selected a location influenced by lobbying and that may have given undue emphasis to the revenues from privatisation. This made local communities more alert and fuelled the environmental conflict (Chapter 8). If the approach to privatisation had emphasised airport competition and efficiency, this would have reduced the proceeds of the privatisation compared to the airport's value as a monopoly. So, competition from low-cost airports was blocked (Chapter 6). Moreover, the privatisation plan was abandoned due to legal conflicts with two bidders. It was believed that the state governments had the expertise to plan and build BBI at lower costs than private specialised project managers. Trust and commitment are key success factors for a relation-specific investment as the airport, the airlines and other stakeholders must cooperate to avoid opportunistic behaviour and realize the value of the investment. This is lacking.

BBI turned into a mega project and failed (Chapter 5). Managers and politicians were never really held to account even though the costs tripled. BBI has excessive fixed costs which are now sunk. Given that German airport regulation is based on a cost-plus approach, there is the danger that a large part of the inflated costs will be paid by the airlines, especially as the regulatory agency is not independent. As BBI was opened during the COVID crisis, it is too early to say whether or not the airport will charge for its output efficiently (Chapter 4) though one may doubt that an efficient charging regime will be chosen given the type of regulation and ownership that apply at BBI. The full economic costs of the failure of BBI are not really discussed in public and are far larger than the €3–5b cost overrun. Airlines and other stakeholders had to bear high costs of more than 10 years of delay. They will be careful to invest now in this high-cost airport as the lack of trust for investment with sunk cost characteristics. The approach taken with the BBI project lacked economic rationality and nowhere more so than in its reliance on an Economic Impact Assessment (EIA) approach to airport investment evaluation. The direct, indirect, induced and catalytic effects promised large economic gains of more than 50,000 jobs. This was the rationale for BBI. CBA was not used (Chapter 9) so the project lacked clarity about the expected overall welfare gain from BBI.

9.4 COVID-19 and airports

One of the largest shocks ever to strike the airport industry was the 2020–2022 COVID-19 pandemic. In response to the spread of the virus and in the absence of a vaccine, governments in a rather idiosyncratic fashion, took decisions to close normal air travel. This policy applied in particular from the end of the first quarter of 2020 to late 2021 on a worldwide basis (see ACI, 2021). The eventual impact on aviation remains to be fully seen. Very limited traffic, such as the distribution of medical supplies, continued. But airports found that at little notice, their revenues nearly ceased while part of their cost base was fixed, so that airports faced serious financial problems. This was averted only by the very large response of national fiscal policies which made extensive transfers to companies in the economy (generally) to allow them to wait out the pandemic crisis.

Public policy is normally directed towards goals such as efficiency (Chapters 4, 5, and 6) and environmental protection (Chapter 8). The COVID crisis was a reminder of the challenge of viability which, in the short run, requires a firm to have sufficient liquidity and in the long run, an ability to cover its costs. Even during the pandemic, airport assets were going to [survive] though not necessarily held by the owning entity.

In this part of the chapter, the two following issues are considered. For the main governance categories for airports, how did the pandemic affect these airports' charges? Second, when passenger traffic deviates substantially from the forecast, who should bear the demand risk—airports or their customers? Ideally, the entity which can bear the risks most cheaply should bear the risks.

The pandemic and airport charges

In 2020–2021, governments made substantial financial transfers to airports, in Europe particularly in the form of employment-support schemes and airports themselves borrowed very heavily (ACI, 2021). In effect, these measures allowed airports to survive the crisis, and most were in a position to postpone increasing charges. In the following, we discuss the likely direction of change of airport charges in the next few years, as conditions in the airport industry come closer to those of the pre-pandemic years (Forsyth et al., 2020).

As regards their governance arrangements, it is possible to group airports into the following four categories. Airports that are: price regulated; in public ownership; in competitive markets, or finally, not in competitive markets but unregulated. We consider these very briefly in turn and how their airport charges would respond to the pandemic (see Table 9.2).

Regulated airports: these are airports with market power and able to levy airlines (and ultimately passengers) with unduly high charges and are therefore often subject to some form of regulation. As described in Chapter 6, there are three principal formal regulatory methodologies. The COVID passenger demand collapse affected

Table 9.2 Summary of responses to demand shocks

Governance of airports	*Price tendency*
Rate of return regulation	Increase as average cost increases
Price-cap regulation	Cap is fixed and charges are not increased.
Light-handed regulation	Scope to increase charges
Public airports: less formally regulated	Scope for lower or constant unless full cost recovery is applied
Competitive airports	Decrease or constant charges but with risk of failure
Non-competitive non-regulated airports	Increase

Source: Authors' analysis

them in different ways. Under the rate-of-return (RoR) approach to airport regulation, the emphasis is on limiting returns rather than on controlling the level of charges paid. In the context of a collapse in passenger demand, for a given asset base, RoR regulation would produce a rise in airport charges in order to restore an airport's returns to the allowed rate. Those airports subject to a price-cap, on the other hand, faced a period of some years before the regulated charge would be reviewed and possibly reset. Normally, in order to protect the airport's incentive to find economies, the price-cap is not re-opened during the price-control period. However, in the context of a collapse in passenger demand, reopening the price-cap might be considered by a regulator, even though it would produce a (sharp) rise in airport charges, since a mechanical forecast of the ratio of (unchanged) costs to (reduced) traffic would yield much higher charges. In some cases, under price-caps, airlines have concluded long-term contracts with the airports, which would have the effect of protecting them from sharp price rises.

The third form of regulation is light-handed regulation (L-HR) which avoids formally setting or approving airport charges. Airports have the commercial freedom to decide prices (though they may be constrained by long-term contracts with airlines). The level and time trend of charges are then monitored. A final element of L-HR is that the public authorities reserve the right to introduce additional regulation should an airport show evidence of systematically using its market power to set unduly high charges. Arguably L-HR, under conditions of a collapse in airport passenger demand, would offer airlines the least protection from large price increases, at least in the short run. Over the longer term, the authorities might conclude that in the pandemic such airports exploited their market power that permitted the airports to protect themselves from the losses on the scale that would otherwise follow from the traffic demand collapse.

Turning to the other three airport governance categories, we again consider the pandemic's impact on airport charges. Many airports and especially regional airports are owned by governments or local authorities and are often considered not to require formal regulation, though some are regulated. There were a number of responses by such airports to the demand shock. As public bodies, some keep charges low, on occasion as a result of the policy of their government and in return for financial support. After a pause during the worst of the pandemic, others raised charges in order to cover costs.

The position of airports facing significant competition was altogether different. In this case, airport charges were constrained by competition in both the short and the longer term. The demand collapse threatened the financial viability of such airports and in particular their owners. As discussed in Chapter 3, airports have large, fixed costs, in particular debts used to finance fixed assets. Without public financial assistance, airports without significant revenues would have breached the terms of its loan agreements, provoking bankruptcy. Thus, under competition, competition required these airports to keep prices down, though at risk of bankruptcy of its owners, unless the competing airports were able to raise prices by formal or tacit agreement. The final set of airports are those that are non-competitive but also non-regulated airports. In this instance, neither competition nor regulation restrains price setting. A very large fall in demand could be offset at least partly by a large increase in charges, as long as it was profitable (revenue increasing) for the airport to do so.

To sum up, what impact is COVID expected to have on future airport charges? After the financial crisis of 2008 and the following years, airport charges were raised by many airports and by 2011 by most of them (Wiltshire, 2018). Future increases in airport charges are possible in the short to medium term. The scale of the traffic recovery will have a large bearing on the case for a price response. So too will public policy. The policy objective is to keep charges as low as is consistent with the long-term viability of airports subject to their meeting efficiency and environmental goals. Given that many governments provided financial aid to airports during the worst of the crisis, and that many other sectors of the economy suffered a large-scale loss of revenue and profits, governments should use the tools available—regulation, public ownership, policy statements—to limit any sharp increases in airport charges.

COVID and demand risk assignment

What are some of the other longer-term impacts of the COVID crisis on airports? One is that airports will be much less willing in future to bear the risk that passenger numbers fall far below forecasts. As long as traffic was increasing reasonably steadily, with only occasional and relatively modest slowdowns, there was a broad balance between the prospect of above-forecast and below-forecast traffic (and revenue) outturns. Over a medium-term horizon, it was reasonable to expect that revenues on average would be close to expectations. Under those conditions, airports seemed better able to bear the traffic risk. Airlines directly suffer financial distress in a traffic downturn and an increase in airport charges would be an additional negative impact to bear. Airport assets are long-lived so airports could, if necessary, postpone cost recovery to a future period.

The pandemic has changed such thinking. In future, airports will want to share the traffic risk with airlines. For example, modest traffic deviations (perhaps, plus/minus 10%) might mean airports would not seek a change in their charges but large traffic declines would lead airports to raise charges. For price-capped airports, formal traffic-sharing mechanisms are likely to form part of future price-caps. For airports that periodically negotiate charges with airline customers, more sharing of traffic risk will be sought by airports as part of future agreements. Unregulated airports with market power may publish charging schemes with explicit reference to deviations of the traffic outturn from the forecast.

As regards the welfare standard used in this book, which side of the industry should bear the risk? In terms of public policy, risk should be assigned to the party in the best position to manage that risk. Pre-COVID, as explained, this was considered to be airports. It is not so clear now. The speed and extent of the 2020 decline in demand meant that even a well-run airport would not have been able to adjust variable costs fast enough to avoid large losses. In addition, the scale of those losses makes it unclear whether these revenues could ever be collected in future. Certainly, the viewpoint that the airports possess steady revenue streams no longer seems to fully describe demand. The topic of demand risk is a subject under active discussion, and a consensus has yet to emerge. Traffic risk sharing would protect airport revenues (to some degree) but would also have some perverse effects, namely raising airport charges in an economic downturn. The best risk allocation policy in future may depend on the view taken as to whether airlines, facing higher airport costs, would be able, in turn, to protect their own revenues by passing on the cost increase to passengers by means of increased airline ticket prices. At present, this is one of a number of policy questions that have arisen from the pandemic and that continue to be investigated with reference to the welfare standard.

9.5 Conclusions

This chapter has examined two aspects of airports. We began with the impacts and benefits of airports and then turned to the effect on airports of the 2020–2022 pandemic.

There are a number of techniques available to assess airports, ranging from careful measurement of benefits to debatable estimates of airport impacts. The chapter reviewed these techniques in some detail, setting out their respective strengths and weaknesses. Measurements that estimate welfare effects, in other words, how much better off an airport makes the citizens of a country, which can be handled by CBA and some CGE models, were sharply distinguished from impacts on employment, GDP and other effects, which are best measured using CGE models. We are critical of the use of EIA models, for measuring benefits or impacts on jobs and GDP. Finally, the concept of an airport's wider economic benefits (WEBs), such as advantages arising from agglomeration and connectivity, is promising but yet to be explored fully.

Probably the greatest disturbance to the airport industry ever was caused was the COVID-19 global pandemic. The final part of the chapter therefore considered how, once the immediate crisis had passed, airports began to respond in the area of user charges. It is too early for conclusive research findings, but we argued that a given airport's response would vary according to ownership and the degree of competition faced. We expect near-monopoly airports to raise charges most and competitive airports least, with developments at regulated airports depending on the particular regime. What is certain is that in future airports will want to share the traffic risk with airlines, an approach that would make airport charges more volatile. The best approach to the sharing of the risks is yet to be determined.

References

ACI (2021) "2021 First-Half Update: European Airports Traffic and Financial Performance", available at www.aci-europe.org

Airports Commission (2014) *2. Economy: Wider Economic Impacts Assessments*, London, PwC, November

Airports Commission (2015) *Airports Commission Final Report*, London, Airports Commission, July

Burghouwt, G and R Redondi (2013) "Connectivity in Air Transport Networks: An Assessment of Models and Applications", *Journal of Transport Economics and Policy*, 47, 35–53

Forsyth, P (2021) "Assessing the Wider Economic Benefits of Air Transport", *Transport Policy*, 104, 11–18

Forsyth, P, C Guiomard and H-M Niemeier (2020) "Covid-19, the Collapse in Passenger Demand and Airport Charges", *Journal of Air Transport Management*, 89, 101932

Forsyth, P and H-M Niemeier (2021) "Economic Impact Analysis, Cost Benefit Analysis, and Computable General Equilibrium Modelling: Outline of Techniques and Where to Use Them", in A Graham, N Adler, O Betancourt, E Calderon, G Martini, H-M Niemeier and A Antunes (eds), *Air Transport and Regional Development Methodologies*, London, Routledge, 129–155

Forsyth P, H-M Niemeier and E Njoya (2021) "Economic Evaluation of Investments in Airports: Recent Developments", *Journal of Benefit-Cost Analysis*, 12, 85–121

Gillen, D, S Landau and G Gosling (2014) "Measuring the Relationship Airline Network Connectivity and Productivity", *Transportation Research Record*, 250, 66–75

Huderek-Glapska, S (2021) "The Application of an Input-Output Approach to Measuring the Impact of Air Transport on the Economy: A Critical Review", in A Graham, N Adler, O Betancourt, E Calderon, G Martini, H-M Niemeier and A Antunes (eds), *Air Transport and Regional Development Methodologies*, London, Routledge, 66–92

InterVISTAS (2006) *Measuring the Economic Rate of Return on Investment in Aviation*, Vancouver, InterVISTAS

InterVISTAS (2015) *Economic Impact of European Airports: A Critical Catalyst to Economic Growth*, Brussels, ACI Europe

Joint Study on Aviation Capacity in the Sydney Region (2012) *Report to Australian Government and N.S.W. Government*, Canberra and Sydney, Aviation Capacity in the Sydney Region

Jorge-Calderon, D (2021) *Aviation Investment Economic Appraisal for Airports, Air Traffic Management, Airlines and Aeronautics*, 2nd ed., London, Routledge

Mueller, J (2021) "A Case Study of the Politics of Airport Construction: The New Berlin Airport", in A Graham, N Adler, H-M Niemeier, O Betancourt, A Antunes, V Bilotkach, E Calderon and G Martini (eds), *Air Transport and Regional Development Policies*, London, Routledge, 240–267

Niemeier, H-M (2001) "On the Use and Abuse of Impact Analysis for Airports: A Critical View from the Perspective of Regional Policy", in W Pfaehler (ed), *Regional Input-Output Analysis*, Baden-Baden, Nomos, 201–220

United States of America Department of Transport, Federals Aviation Administration [USDOT] (1992) *Estimating the Regional Significance of Airports*, DOT/FAA/PP-92-6, Washington, DC, USDOT

Venables, A J (2007) "Evaluating Urban Transport Improvements: Cost-Benefit Analysis in the Presence of Agglomeration and Income Taxation", *Journal of Transport Economics and Policy*, 41, 173–188

Wiltshire, J (2018) "Airport Competition: Reality or Myth?", *Journal of Air Transport Management*, 67, 241–248

York Aviation (2021) "The Economic Impact of Night Flying in the UK", available at https://airlinesuk.org/wp-content/uploads/2021/08/The-Economic-Impact-of-Night-Flying-in-the-UK-2.pdf

York Consulting (1998) *The Economic Impact of Airports*, York, ACI Europe

10 Summary and conclusions

10.1 Introduction

A way of summarising this book is to think of it as making a contribution to four tasks. These are:

- Firstly, to documenting the key economic features of airports;
- Secondly, to showing how policies can be designed to achieve good performance of airports;
- Thirdly, to providing a brief assessment of key aspects of airport performance; and
- Fourthly, to recognising that reality obstructs good performance and to suggesting ways to improve performance in a politically realistic way.

The first aspect is "positive"—describing how things work. The second is "normative"—proposing policies to meet important objectives, such as keeping costs at a minimum for a given quality of service, keeping delays low, handling externalities such as noise well, and making decisions which recognise the wider economic benefits of airports. The third aspect is to assessing airport performance. The fourth might be described as "political economy"—dealing with the reality of various stakeholders with conflicting agendas vying for influence on policy.

Because of limited space, the book concentrates on the first three tasks and we do not analyse the political economy of airports specifically in much detail. Nevertheless, we do recognise how good performance and reality are married throughout the text of the book. In this summary, we attempt two things. Firstly, we set out a checklist of the big issues that should be addressed to foster good performance of airports. Secondly, give our impressions about how well these are handled in practice. In short:

What are the key aspects needing attention to get good performance from an airport; and

What is the reality—how well do airports perform?

DOI: 10.4324/9781003156901-13

10.2 What is needed for good airport performance?

Siting the airport well and linking it in with ground transport effectively

One of the first issues to consider concerns the siting of the airport—is an airport well sited?—an issue that was discussed in Chapter 2. For many airports now, the relevant question is whether to expand the airport on its current site, or to build a new airport, which may replace or complement an existing airport. Whichever is the case, there will be the question of how best to achieve ground access for passengers and cargo shippers—are roads adequate or will mass public transport be best?

Good, accurate forecasts of future demand

Good forecasts of demand are critical—to determine the need for additional capacity, to examine the options to allocate capacity such as pricing and slots, and to assess the need for new airports. Forecasting is discussed in Chapter 2. Good forecasts are broadly accurate forecasts which predict passengers and movements from key determinants while keeping other factors constant.

Good pricing at airports with adequate capacity

Airport pricing is discussed in Chapter 4, building on the discussion of costs in Chapter 3. For airports with ample capacity (and there are many, because investment invisibilities mean that airports are large), the problem is to make the best use of that capacity, while, usually, achieving cost recovery. For the most part, small to medium-sized airports achieve this using weight-based and, lately, passenger-based charges.

Allocating scarce capacity effectively at busy airports

Airport pricing has a different objective when the airport is busy and capacity scarce, as discussed in Chapter 4. Here the problem is less to cover costs than to allocate scarce capacity in a way that makes the best use of it. While pricing options—especially peak/off-peak charges—are feasible, they are not used extensively by airports. In most places, slot mechanisms are used, often in a price-regulated environment. This choice raises the question of which airlines get the slots, and whether slots are "owned" by those airlines; slot allocation often becomes a messy business. In most US airports, capacity is allocated by the willingness to suffer delays, which is a costly way of rationing scarce capacity.

Providing increased capacity and quality, but not before they are needed

Granted that airport capacity is often scarce, deciding whether additional capacity is worthwhile is a critical decision. There are several aspects to the airport investment decision. Some of these are dealt with in Chapter 5. For example, the investment decision is linked to ownership arrangements—often governments favour privatisation as a straightforward way to fund investments. The investment decision is also often linked to airport regulation, which is discussed in Chapter 6. Airport investments are often advocated as a means to wider economic benefits, going beyond those that passengers and shippers experience directly. This is discussed in Chapter 9.

Evaluating the need for regulation, and when needed, and implementing regulation which promotes efficiency

Airport regulation raises a host of issues well beyond the investment aspect. There is the basic question of whether, and how, to regulate an airport, and this is discussed in Chapter 6. Regulation has become controversial, since it affects the airport charges which airlines, and indirectly, passengers, pay. Some airports might be subject to competition and others are not, but those that are not, do not need to be regulated. If there is little or no competition, regulation may be warranted, and if so, the authorities need to choose between cost-based, incentive and light-handed regulation.

Monitoring productive and other aspects of performance

A core objective of designing different ownership structures, and regulatory structures, is to foster good performance from the airport—a matter which is discussed in Chapter 7. In earlier days, it was simply assumed that airports in public ownership would produce their outputs efficiently, at minimum cost, and also set their charges close to minimum cost. Reality has been quite different from this, so airport performance needs to be monitored and evaluated, to ensure that performance is good. In short, there is a need for benchmarking, which can be done by regulators, and increasingly, by the airports themselves.

Measuring and eliminating the environmental externalities of airport operation

The environmental performance of an airport is discussed in Chapter 8. For many years the key environmental aspect of airports concerned how noisy they were. Noise levels have been reduced over time due to less noisy aircraft. But since noise, particularly at night, is not priced effectively, noise levels are still too high. More recently, airports have become aware of their climate effects, as a result of their emissions of greenhouse gases. Fortunately, airports constitute a part of the air transport industry for which reducing emissions is relatively easy. It is easier for an airport to eliminate emissions on the ground than it is for airlines to reduce them in flight. This puts an obligation on airports to be in the forefront of emissions reduction.

Measuring and promoting the wider economic benefits of the airport

To conclude, we examine in Chapter 9 two different issues. Airport impacts and the "wider economic benefits" of airport development is a topic which has received considerable attention in recent years, and we explore what this means. Then we examine what the COVID-19 pandemic has meant for airports. Prompted by COVID-19 and other crises, resilience and flexibility are important aspects of airport performance.

10.3 How well does an airports perform?

To conclude this book, we look at the items on this checklist to see how well airports in practice conform to what economists would recommend. As we see, things do not always work as they should. This implies that there are plenty of ways to improve the economic performance of airports.

Siting the airport well and linking it in with ground transport effectively

As airports have been developed, there have often been problems with their location and with surface access. There have been several cases of airports not being well sited and we have previously referred to cases of airports that should not have been developed at all (Montreal's Mirabel airport and Spain's Don Quijote airport). The choice of airport sites involves balancing a wide range of conflicting objectives, so differing viewpoints are to be expected. This balancing should be carried out in the public planning process. The incentives offered by these processes differ greatly between countries. In Germany, misleading economic impact studies with unrealistic employment effects have play a key role, although decisions in the UK and Australia have been based on a cost benefit approach with more realistic estimations of effects. It is a widely shared view that planning processes are too long, but a greater concern is that they are dominated by special interests.

Good, accurate forecasts of future demand

Forecasting demand is a critical task. The science of good forecasting is well established, and it recognises the fact that there are many uncertainties in developing forecasts. But this is no excuse for the fact that, time and time again, forecasts are too optimistic, and sometimes wildly so. In this respect, airports are no different from other forms of transport infrastructure. Unrealistic expectations of the benefits of airports (see Chapter 9) and slack government processes lead to this result. In the end, systematically biased optimistic forecasts lead to costly airport expansions which come, at best too early, but in some cases which should have never been built at all.

Pricing and if needed subsidising of airports with large permanent over capacity

History matters—and this is also true for airports. In many countries, we find small regional airports with permanent excess capacity with such low levels of demand that they struggle to cover their operational costs. Many of these regional airports should have not been built at all, but now after they have been built the investment costs are sunk. Many of their operators struggle to manage them cost-efficiently, for example by requiring airport staff to carry out more than one role, if required. Subsidies are often given without incentives for efficiency. From a cost benefit view, WEBs, and other positive externalities (e.g., medical flights) might be a reason to keep them open, but very often regions would gain by closing airports and concentrating traffic on a single airport.

Good pricing of airports with adequate capacity

Airports with spare capacity are normally priced effectively, in the sense that they normally cover cost without much use of market power, and in a way that makes good use of capacity (by using weight-based or passenger-based pricing). This also lessens the welfare loss in cases where an airport's costs are too high.

Allocating scarce capacity of busy airports with scarce capacity effectively

The same cannot be said for pricing and capacity allocation of busy airports with scarce capacity. The stand-out example of this problem may be seen in the US, where many airports operate with chronic, and expensive, delays (even though solutions to this problem have been available for decades). Most countries have avoided the problems which beset US airports by the use of slots and, very occasionally, by pricing. Slots have their own drawbacks, including how to allocate them. Such problems were very evident during the fall in demand at the time of COVID-19, and also take the form of high profits gifted to airlines in possession of slots. Airlines strenuously opposed worthwhile extensions of capacity in order not to lose their slot rents.

Providing increased capacity and quality, but not before they are needed

Investment decisions in airports, both private sector and public, can involve careful evaluation of investment projects, the right regulatory incentives for investment, and an evaluation of major airport investments by government commissions. But there are several pressures which militate against good investment evaluation. These can include unrealistic estimates of the benefits of airport investments, the pressure to consider airports as prestige projects, and pressure for airlines to obstruct investments to safeguard airline rents.

Evaluating the need for regulation, and when needed, implementing regulation in a form that promotes efficiency

The arguments for regulation versus liberalisation depend on how competitive the airport market really is. The economies of scale and scope, and locational factors, tend to lead towards monopoly, but airports in the past have been located in many regions so that the catchment areas overlap. The strength of competition has to be assessed case by case, but this has only been done in Australia, Netherlands and in the UK. In terms of the interests of the stakeholders, airports and their industry associations will invariably prefer light-handed regulation, though airlines (and to an extent, their passengers and shippers), will seek tighter regulation. However, from an economics point of view, "light" versus "tight" is not clearly defined. The real issue is to set well-defined incentives for cost-efficient management, for good pricing of capacity and for increasing capacity at the right time.

Monitoring productivity and other aspects of performance

Benchmarking of airports performance, and especially benchmarking of productivity performance, has become extensive over the past two decades. What it shows is that performance varies widely across airports. This means that there are a lot of poor performers, and that there are big gains to be had if performance can be improved. To do so is not always easy, and will require careful reform of ownership structures, regulation and increased competition where possible. Privatisation very often leads to less competition as airports are sold in groups. Regulation then has to step in and needs to be carefully designed in terms of institutions and incentives.

Measuring and eliminating the environmental externalites of airport operation

Airports are well aware of the noise externalities they create, and they are now quite aware of the greenhouse gas emissions externalities they create. Pressures from governments and local communities are inducing them to lessen noise, along with local emissions. More could be achieved to lower the external costs of noise and of local emissions. The costs of greenhouse gas emissions are not concentrated locally but rather spread widely across the globe. As a result, there is mixed performance in terms of reducing emissions. In a number of cases, airports (following the lead from their industry associations) are making substantial efforts to reduce their emissions (often without much prompting by their governments). For others, there is not much action being taken.

Measuring and promoting the wider economic benefits of the airport

Currently, this is done rather badly. Either wider economic benefits are not included at all, or wider benefits are measured using questionable methods, leading to over-optimistic estimates of impacts and benefits. Occasionally, there have been some serious assessments (e.g., by the Airports Commission in the UK) but this area should be a priority for careful research.

10.4 Conclusions

The science of airport economics has been developed over the past fifty years, and answers to many of the problem and issues have been outlined. Others still remain to be resolved, such as the measurement of aviation's wider economic benefits, and these are being given attention as a field of research. There are also empirical questions which are still being investigated—how productive are particular airports, and what are the best measures of productivity? There are other ongoing debates, such as how competitive airport markets are, and which forms of regulation are most conducive to efficiency. That said, much of the science of airport economics has been well explored. The problem is that this science has often not been applied well. There are many aspects of poor airport performance which can be fixed. Essentially, this is a political economy problem. Conflicting objectives of diverse stakeholders and governments prevent airports from performing as well as they could.

Index

For Product Safety Concerns and Information please contact our EU
representative GPSR@taylorandfrancis.com
Taylor & Francis Verlag GmbH, Kaufingerstraße 24, 80331 München, Germany

www.ingramcontent.com/pod-product-compliance
Ingram Content Group UK Ltd.
Pitfield, Milton Keynes, MK11 3LW, UK
UKHW020006200926
475702UK00015B/2500
9780367742768